Big Bird and Beyond

BIG BIRD AND BEYOND

The New Media and the Markle Foundation

Lee D. Mitgang

FORDHAM UNIVERSITY PRESS
New York • 2000

Library of Congress Cataloging-in-Publication Data

Mitgang, Lee D., 1949–
Big Bird and beyong : the new media and the Markle Foundation / Lee D. Mitgang.—1st ed.
p. cm.
Includes bibliographical references and index.
ISBN 0-8232-2040-0—ISBN 0-8232-2041-9 (pbk.)
1. John and Mary R. Markle Foundation—History. 2. Mass media—Research—United States—History. I. John and Mary R. Markle Foundation. II. Title.
P87.M55 2000
384.55′06′573—dc21 00-027540

Printed in the United States of America
00 01 02 03 04 5 4 3 2 1
First Edition

For My Parents,
Herbert and Shirley Mitgang

CONTENTS

ACKNOWLEDGMENTS

Institutional histories are rightly held suspect—"advertisements for themselves," to borrow Norman Mailer's phrase. I was uncommonly lucky, then, that Lloyd Morrisett and the board of The Markle Foundation gave me unwavering cooperation, hundreds of hours of their time, complete access to confidential archives and records, along with generous financial support. Their comments and suggestions, always useful, were also lightly proffered. We all wanted the same thing: not a halo, but a readable, honest account of the foundation's work in its broader context. To the extent that this book fell short of that mark, the responsibility is entirely mine.

I thank Lloyd's successor, Zoë Baird, for honoring the spirit of independence that animated this project from the beginning.

I am indebted to the wise men and women who critiqued chapter drafts at different stages: Wally Neilsen, Bob Hochstein, Lloyd Morrisett, Edith C. Bjornson, and Ellen C. Lagemann. And to the two scholar-editors who conducted double-blind critiques of later versions at the behest of Dr. Lagemann, thank you both, whoever you are. At Fordham University Press, I cannot thank enough Saverio Procario, Anthony Chiffolo, and most especially my copyeditor, Terry Belanger, for believing in this book and for a painstaking job of editing.

The Markle Foundation staff helped me in ways large and small. Edith Bjornson's candor and unwavering friendship meant more than I can say. Amy Brisebois, assistant to the president, helped locate lost or elusive souls from the foundation's past. Karen D. Byers, the foundation's chief financial officer, patiently explained the legal and financial intricacies of Markle's program-related investments. Cathy Clark, program director, provided important insights about the foundation's recent high-tech ventures.

The staff at the Rockefeller Archives Center, in Pocantico Hills, New York, where most of the foundation's archives, grant files, and correspondence are housed, patiently guided me through boxcars of material and provided vital and speedy copying of thousands of pages of material. I am especially indebted to Dr. Darwin Stapleton, the center's director, for generously sharing his research on Courtney Smith, Markle's president-elect before Morrisett's presidency.

Numerous individuals agreed to discuss at length their dealings with The Markle Foundation in personal interviews or by telephone. Their names and affiliations are listed under Personal Sources in the Bibliography.

Finally, I cannot thank enough my wife, Gina; my daughter, Caroline; and my parents, Herbert and Shirley Mitgang, whose love, patience, and wise counsel guided me through this, and much more.

Introduction
The Neglected Field

IN THE SUMMER of 1969, a half million young people spent a rain-soaked weekend at a farm near Woodstock, New York, and declared, with defiance, a cultural revolution whose outer trappings were sex, drugs, and rock-and-roll. In the more mundane precincts of research laboratories, newsrooms, broadcast studios, and corporate backrooms, a less flamboyant revolution was also afoot—one that would, over the next three decades, change the way that billions of people wrote, read, learned, banked, shopped, voted, entertained themselves, and even thought.

That year, public television was barely two years old—cash starved and almost hopelessly disorganized. Yet, it was brimming with educational and cultural possibilities. Cable television was on the verge of challenging network broadcast's hegemony. Communications satellites would soon make it possible to defy distance and time zones, allowing home viewers to witness coronations, world cups, and wars in "real time." Computers—thousands of times faster and more powerful than any information tools ever created—were about to become as familiar in homes as toasters and washing machines. The regulated monopoly of telecommunications enjoyed by the American Telephone and Telegraph Company since 1910 would be dismantled in a few short years by such pesky competitors as MCI Communications and by antitrust action of the U.S. Justice Department.

"It would be hard to overstate the significance of the events of 1968 and 1969 in shaping the future of the communications sector and the course of public policy," Roger Noll of Stanford University and Monroe Price of the Benjamin Cardozo School of Law at Yeshiva University recently wrote. "Communications experts, whether in industry, government agencies, or universities and think tanks, realized that, all of a sudden, everything was up for grabs: who would offer what services to whom under what regulatory rules were no longer settled questions. Convergence with choice was just beginning and had created chaos that offered both threats and promises to everyone."[1]

At the same moment that Jimi Hendrix, Janis Joplin, and Country Joe MacDonald were playing discordant riffs at Woodstock, a gentler band of characters was preparing to burst to life on millions of television screens with a very different message. Elmo, Cookie Monster, the Count, and, gangling over them, Big Bird soon would be the inhabitants of a new show called *Sesame Street*. Premiering in November 1969, it would accomplish something never before attempted by commercial or public broadcast: use the might of the mass media to address, for millions of children, specific educational and literacy goals.

Joan Ganz Cooney is most often credited with the overnight success of *Sesame Street* and the Children's Television Workshop that produced it. No less important to their launch and their sustained success was a publicity-shy, scholarly, thirty-nine-year-old foundation executive, Lloyd N. Morrisett. For Morrisett, the birth of the workshop presaged the beginning of a twenty-eight-year philanthropic effort aimed at alerting the nation and the communications world to the limitless, yet tragically neglected, social, educational, and civic possibilities of the new media that were rapidly emerging in the late twentieth century. This book is about those emerging communications tools and the roles that Morrisett and The John and Mary R. Markle Foundation had in realizing their potential for the benefit of all citizens.

For The Markle Foundation, this mission was a wholesale break with its past, extraordinary for any foundation, much less one of such modest means. Starting with its establishment in 1927 by a Pennsylvania coal baron and his wife and through its first four decades, the foundation had been a supporter of academic medicine and research. By the late 1960s, the medical field was awash with federal and foundation money, and Markle's impact in that arena had paled nearly to insignificance. In 1969, the foundation turned to Morrisett, then a vice president at the Carnegie Corporation of New York, for new leadership and new direction.

Communications and mass media were then, and remain, neglected philanthropic fields. Although some foundations, particularly the Ford Foundation, had supported individual initiatives, few had devoted themselves heart, soul, and bankroll to the possible educational and civic uses of everyday mass communications media such as telephones, television, radio, films, newspapers, newscasts, books, and magazines.

During the next three decades, the unending challenge for Markle would be to identify where it belonged in an arena dominated by multibillion-dollar conglomerates and breakneck technological changes. With an annual budget of only a few million dollars, how could Markle help guide the public and the policymakers in making more informed, enlightened choices at a time of bewilderingly complex regulatory and economic realignment?

In taking on this often lonely philanthropic challenge, Morrisett would score a respectable number of notable and qualified successes—though none with the staying power or worldwide impact of the Children's Television Workshop and *Sesame Street*. Many other Markle initiatives fall under the heading of what foundations euphemistically call "learning experiences." Still other projects, in hindsight, might have been the result of naivete, hubris, or both. As with all philanthropic work, luck and timing often dictated results as much as money, hard work, sound management, or wisdom. And because so many of the projects described in this book are of such recent vintage, it seems wise to be cautious in judging what their significance has been or might eventually be.

From the beginning, four principles animated the many projects that Markle would pursue:

1. Access—opening the way for people of all backgrounds to use mass media and communications outlets to express their views and beliefs.
2. Equity—ensuring that all groups in society share the benefits of communications and information systems.
3. Content—guaranteeing that information reaches the public unhindered by censorship or unnecessary regulation.
4. Quality—encouraging the best, most wholesome content in mass media programming that enriches and educates as well as entertains.[2]

Within those broad aims, the foundation, under the presidency Lloyd Morrisett, sought to make its mark in a number of specific realms of communication.

Markle was among the nation's foremost funders of research on media, communications policy, and emerging information technologies.[3] Beginning in the 1970s, the foundation created a network of communications research centers at leading universities, including Harvard, University of California at Los Angeles (UCLA), Carnegie-Mellon, and Duke, and at think tanks such as Aspen Institute and RAND Corporation. The scores of scholars supported by Markle at these and other centers produced a library of more than a thousand books and articles on a wide range of topics, including the regulatory and economic aspects of cable television, the effects of television on children, the impact of the media on political participation, and the social and educational potential of multimedia technologies, the Internet, and electronic mail.

Markle also pumped millions of dollars into explorations of the social, political, and economic implications of the cornucopia of new communications technologies, starting with cable television in the 1970s and extending to computer-based tools years later. Well before the rest of the nation was paying serious attention to the issue, Markle spent $7 million in the early 1980s on projects aimed at exploring how computers could improve the lives of the elderly. It backed efforts by innovative software publishers to produce high-quality educational multimedia products considered too risky by traditional venture capitalists. In the mid-1990s, the foundation launched a multimillion dollar research and publicity campaign to promote "universal e-mail"—an idea that Markle believed would create powerful new avenues of communication to bring people and communities closer together.

Beyond its support of communications research, another neglected yet urgent priority beckoned Morrisett as he took office: the fairness, competence, and credibility of the news media.

If new technologies seemed to promise greatly expanded choices in the broadcast arena, the opposite was the case in the print world of 1969. For a variety of reasons, especially the rapid rise of television, the world of newspapers and of general interest magazines such as *Life* and *Look* was shrinking fast. Ownership of print media was becoming concentrated in fewer and fewer corporate hands. The competition that had enlivened the newspaper business for decades was giving way to the homogeneity of chain ownership and one-newspaper towns. The public's faith in the media had been badly shaken as Morrisett took office. Most immediately, the Nixon administration discovered political gold by assailing the media's alleged biases. By 1970, public opinion surveys were showing that fewer than one in five Americans approved of the press's performance.

For the next two decades, with widely differing degrees of success, Markle supported a variety of programs aimed at shoring up confidence in journalism by making the news media more responsible and responsive. The foundation assisted training programs for practicing reporters at universities, sustained organizations and individuals seeking to create more ethnic and gender diversity in the ranks of news gatherers, and created new outlets for objective media criticism. During the early 1970s, Markle rescued the *Columbia Journalism Review* from bankruptcy. It financed a well-received but short-lived public broadcast series of media criticism called *Behind the Lines*. A decade later, it spent millions of dollars to start *Channels of Communications*, a new magazine of objective television criticism, that aimed high but ultimately failed to survive. In defiance of the nation's most powerful newspapers and broadcasters, Markle helped to establish the National News Council, which, during its existence from 1973 to 1984, vainly sought to improve the media's performance and accountability by providing citizens a neutral forum for their complaints.

Throughout Morrisett's presidency, Markle also sought to explore how mass media might help reinvigorate modern democracy. In the post–Civil Rights era, Morrisett argued that the right to know had become as important as the right to vote. From the 1980s on, Markle spent more than $20 million on projects aimed at demonstrating how public and commercial television, newspapers, interactive cable and the Internet might be used to help overcome the voter apathy and cynicism that superficial, sound-bite journalism had helped to breed.

Even as the obstacles to easy success became more evident with each passing year, Morrisett never had any doubt that communications was an entirely appropriate and urgent mission for the small foundation that he lead. Recalling his earliest thoughts as president many years later, he wrote: "If, I said to myself, you believe in the long-term value of education, ways must be found to make greater educational use of the media, the greatest system of mass distribution of information ever invented."[4]

That Markle would have undertaken such a daring set of objectives starting in 1969 was as much kismet as conscious design. Morrisett was, in fact, an accidental president. Fourteen months before Morrisett assumed the presidency, Markle's board of directors had settled on Courtney Smith, president of Swarthmore College and a veteran member of Markle's board of directors, to lead the foundation. In January 1969, that initial choice was unexpectedly undone when Smith suffered a fatal heart attack while trying to quell student demonstrations at his previously sedate Quaker campus.

Barely five weeks after Smith's sudden death, Markle trustees turned to Morrisett, then a Carnegie Corporation vice president. It was natural for Markle's board to search within Carnegie's ranks for its next leader. Historically, the two foundations had strong ties. During the 1930s, Markle's board had turned to such Carnegie leaders as Frederick P. Keppel for guidance in establishing its philanthropic style and priorities. Markle's president from 1946 to 1969, John McFarlane Russell, had learned the ropes of philanthropy as an assistant to Keppel at Carnegie. Morrisett, at age thirty-nine, was already an established star at Carnegie. In March 1968, he and Cooney had made front-page headlines by announcing the cofounding of the Children's Television Workshop, creator of the trailblazing educational program, *Sesame Street*. The accessible, attractive Cooney quickly achieved world fame as the mother of educational children's television. The equally important role of Morrisett in ensuring *Sesame Street*'s success and survival never received recognition approaching Cooney's public acclaim.[5]

The thinking that went into *Sesame Street* and the Children's Television Workshop would form the template for much of Markle's work in the coming years. It demonstrated, to Morrisett's satisfaction at least, that television and the newer media that followed could be effectively harnessed to address educational, cultural, and civic goals with the right mix of money, talent, timing, and determination. Yet this stunning philanthropic accomplishment realized so early in Morrisett's career would prove tantalizingly difficult to duplicate in the years ahead.

Although mass communications had been relatively shortchanged by the philanthropic world, Markle was never entirely alone in its interest in the field. During the 1960s, the Ford Foundation spent more than $100 million to keep public television alive. Ford also provided essential early funding for the Children's Television Workshop, including a $5 million grant in 1973 that enabled it to expand. The Alfred P. Sloan Foundation formed a commission during the early 1970s to study the potential of cable television. Over the years, the Pew Charitable Trusts and the Annenberg Foundation have had programs aimed at improving the quality of journalism. The John D. and Catherine T. MacArthur Foundation and the smaller Benton Foundation have had a sustained interest in communications issues and public broadcasting. The Twentieth Century Fund was a partner with Markle during the 1970s in establishing the National News Council. The Carnegie Corporation sponsored a commission on educational television that led to the creation of the Corporation for Public Broadcasting. Prodded by Morrisett, Carnegie also provided a critical $1 million grant in 1968 that assured the successful launch of the Children's Television Workshop. More recently, foundations established and financed by the media and telecommunications industry, such as The Freedom Forum and USWest Foundation, have provided added support to projects aimed at exploring the educational possibilities of new communications technologies.

Nonetheless, from 1969 on, The Markle Foundation could lay claim to being among the few foundations with significant resources that concentrated solely on media matters and communication policy. If this claim was a source of institutional pride at Markle, it also led to a constant and largely unresolved frustration.

How, then, to explain this comparative neglect of mass communications by the nation's philanthropies? Communications differs crucially from many of the more heavily trafficked targets of foundation activity, such as health, education, the arts, community development, and social welfare. Technology, first of all, drives communications like few other fields. Many, if not most, of history's great communications epochs are delineated by the appearance of new technologies: papyrus in Egypt, the printing press during the Renaissance, the telephone during the late nineteenth century, radio during the first half of the twentieth century, and television following World War II.

The unprecedented onrush of technological advances in mass communications during the last third of the twentieth Century has made such neat historical delineations impossible. The frequency of epochal changes in the field of human communications has moved from millennia to megahertz. The last twenty years alone have witnessed the emergence not only of personal computers but also of cable TV, satellites, VCRs, fiberoptics, videodiscs, CD-ROMS, DVDs, and the Internet. Each technology is a revolution in its own right, yet all of them are interrelated. The energy and expertise needed to make sense of the bewildering fluidity and complexity of modern communications are enough to deter most foundations from plunging into the field as Markle did.

The highly technical nature of mass communications was only the first forbidding challenge for philanthropic action. Equally difficult has been the dominance of private enterprise and commercialism over public interest. Foundations, by their nature, depend on forging working partnerships with their grantees. Most often, they team up with other nonprofit organizations or foundations and with capable, uncompromised, public-spirited individuals to carry out their programs. These partners are plentiful in such fields as education or the arts. In the media world, any foundation must confront the near absence of potential public-interest partners. Particularly during the first years of his presidency, Morrisett and his staff at Markle had to create and nurture their own partners, often from scratch—or learn to do the job themselves.

As Morrisett observed early in his presidency:

> Among the great socializing, educational, and moral forces in society, mass communications is alone in being based on commercial profit-making, privately owned ventures. Closely related to the dominance of private enterprise is the relative absence of nonprofit, public interest activity within mass communications. This is a source of opportunity for the Markle Foundation as well as a problem in that there are few such organizations working effectively in the communications field to which the Foundation can make grants.[6]

For that matter, the very notion of public interest always had been a stepchild in American mass communications (in contrast, for instance, to state-owned systems such as the British Broadcasting Corporation). From the early days of radio, broadcasting had been regarded as a way to sell products and boost the image of its owners. During the 1920s, listeners tuned into *The Eveready Hour, Lucky Strike Orchestra, A&P Gypsies,* and *The Wrigley Review.*[7] The regulatory and legal battles fought many years later over the cross-ownership of newspapers and television stations in single markets or the regulation of cable television invariably have been decided more often by economic and political might than by considerations of public interest.

Another challenge facing any foundation entering the communications field has been the thicket of legal, regulatory, and constitutional complications. The frequent clashes between the First Amendment right to publish and the rights of fair trial and privacy are examples.[8] The regulatory and constitutional issues raised by emerging technologies, such as cable during the 1960s and 1970s and computers and cyberspace during the 1980s and 1990s, have demanded thoughtful, disinterested analysis. Yet, historically, the outcome of such debates has generally been determined not by dispassionate analysis but by the industry's hired guns, lobbyists, and compromised researchers. When Markle entered the field, there were few potential partners on university campuses, or elsewhere, with the expertise, public spiritedness, and lack of political or commercial bias to do the kind of objective policy analysis that Morrisett had in mind. Markle had to develop, almost from scratch, a kind of "farm system" for nurturing a communications brain trust, a difficult task for any foundation but especially so for a small one.

Finally, mass media, particularly broadcast, always have been regarded by their owners as principally vehicles of entertainment. The capacity of radio and television to educate, build community, or promote civic engagement, with only rare exceptions, has been an afterthought at best. Educational broadcasting has never occupied more than a tiny niche in a corporate culture driven by advertising dollars and audience share. "Television has, in fact, become pervasive, yet there remains a self-conscious attempt to ignore its importance," Morrisett would tell the author years later.

"What matters to the foundation is that denial causes us to pay little attention to the moral and educational uses of mass communications, uses that could clearly extend to conventional philanthropic concerns."[9]

If the inherent difficulties facing Markle in its newly chosen field were formidable, the national mood in the late 1960s nonetheless seemed to Morrisett a promising backdrop for tapping the social and educational potential of the mass media. Prosperity was America's presumed birthright, and President Lyndon B. Johnson's recently enacted Great Society and Civil Rights programs signaled a once-in-a-lifetime willingness by the federal government to use its power to extend well-being to the most historically neglected citizens. Indeed, *Sesame Street*, with its initial federal funding and its emphasis on lifting the fortunes of disadvantaged preschool youngsters, fit neatly with the activist tenor of the '60s.

Even as economic confidence was overflowing, however, the nation's moral, social, and cultural bearings were as uncertain as at any time since the Civil War. The optimism of the Civil Rights movement gave way to flames in scores of cities, including Newark and Detroit. Vietnam and its counterpoint, Woodstock, were creating discordant anthems.

The turbulence in the world at large was mirrored in the foundation community itself. Throughout the 1960s, Congress repeatedly challenged the customs, priorities, and tax privileges of nonprofit philanthropies. Congressman Wright Patman of Texas held four sets of hearings that produced 4,200 pages of testimony on the alleged "arrogance and contempt" of foundations. He accused them of "expert tax dodging." The Ford Foundation made an especially tempting target. During the 1960s, Ford provided travel and study grants to staff members of Senator Robert F. Kennedy of New York, while it supported desegregation efforts in Brooklyn and voter registration drives in Cleveland. Fairly or not, Ford became Exhibit A for those who charged that foundations had crossed the line into partisan behavior.

If some believed Patman's hearings could be dismissed as the work of a populist yahoo, foundations knew that they were in a more serious fight when hearings relating to the overhaul of the nation's tax laws opened in February 1969 before the House Ways and Means Committee. Suddenly, for foundations, it was all on the line: their tax-exempt status and their freedom from government interference with, or scrutiny of, their activities and priorities. As Morrisett prepared to assume Markle's presidency, front-page headlines were painting foundations as shadowy and unaccountable. Morrisett's boss at Carnegie, Alan Pifer, pointed out in testimony before the House committee that fewer than one in four major foundations published annual public reports of their activities (although most of the largest, such as Carnegie, did so).

In the end, the Tax Reform Act of 1969 imposed profound changes on the nonprofit world. Most significantly, the Act required a foundation to spend an annual sum equal to at least 5 percent of its assets, on average, for social purposes. Unquestionably, a decade of negative testimony and publicity also took its toll on the public image of foundations. In that climate, they had fresh reasons to be timid in undertaking projects that smacked of politics or undue controversy.

In April 1969, the Commission on Foundations and Private Philanthropy undertook a new study of foundations initiated by John D. Rockefeller III, partly in an attempt to blunt political attacks on their tax-exempt status and spending habits. Although generally defending the role of foundations, the study also documented several long-standing yet damning realities about foundation priorities. A mere 1 percent of the $1.6 billion spent by foundations in 1968 went to social science research.[10] Further, less than 0.10 percent of all foundation grants between 1966 and 1968 were regarded by foundations themselves as politically or socially controversial. Foundations, in other words, seemed habitually to be avoiding the very kinds of experimentation and risk that they, of all of society's great institutions, were ideally suited to pursue with the tax-exempt funds entrusted to their care.[11]

As Morrisett prepared to take charge of Markle in the summer of 1969, America's foundation community was under fire for a variety of reasons, including playing things too safe.[12] During the years that Morrisett would lead The Markle Foundation, few would accuse him of timidity. At the same time, many people, both inside and outside of Markle, would be puzzled by his reluctance to advance his causes more publicly.

A more cautious or conventional foundation executive might have concluded that promoting the ideals of access, quality, education, and public interest in the inimical world of mass communications was quixotic at best. Indeed, as this book demonstrates, many of Markle's projects over the next three decades would be thwarted by the vagaries of technology and economics, by public indifference to the issues that the foundation fought to elevate, and, not least, by the foundation's small size in an arena ruled by multibillion-dollar corporations. Still, with the premier of *Sesame Street* only weeks away as Morrisett boarded his commuter train from Westchester for his first day at Markle in September 1969, he was convinced that the small foundation might yet find ways to make its social mark in the neglected field of communications and the new media.

NOTES

1. Noll and Price, "Communications Policy," 11.
2. Lloyd N. Morrisett, *Collected Essays, 1969–1997* (reprint, New York: The Markle Foundation, 1998), 261.
3. Noll and Price, "Communications Policy," 4.
4. Morrisett, *Collected Essays*, 261.
5. Among many examples of this chronic oversight, an article in the "Education Life" supplement, *The New York Times*, 2 Nov. 1997, 28, repeated what has become the standard but incomplete portrayal of the origins of *Sesame Street*. It credited Cooney and Jim Henson, with no mention of Morrisett's equally critical role.
6. Lloyd N. Morrisett, "President's Review—1977" (transcript of speech delivered at board meeting of The Markle Foundation, Nov. 1977), 3, Markle Archive Collection.
7. Dominick, Sherman, and Copeland, *Broadcasting/Cable and Beyond:* 27.
8. Morrisett, Lloyd N., "The John and Mary R. Markle Foundation" (paper presented at Rockefeller Archive Center conference, 14 Oct. 1979), 8–9.
9. Morrisett, interview, 2 July 1997.
10. *Foundations, Private Giving and Public Policy*, 1.
11. Ibid., 83.
12. Twenty-eight years later, Morrisett still agreed with that commission finding. When the Peterson Commission report was issued, he spent $2,500 out of his discretionary funds to help distribute the report in book form.

Big Bird and Beyond

1

Enter Sesame

THE MAJORITY of U.S. foundations, particularly smaller ones, are, from the start, perpetually shackled to missions imposed by their charters and their founding families. Some 70 percent of independent foundations concentrate their giving on local causes, according to data collected by The Foundation Center, as do virtually all publicly sponsored "community" foundations established to aid specific communities or regions. Similarly, the majority of company-sponsored foundations tend to concentrate their activities in fields related to the business interests of their founding corporations. The Robert Wood Johnson Foundation, for example, centers its grants on health and health education, arenas closely corresponding to the products of Johnson & Johnson.

From the beginning, The John and Mary R. Markle Foundation was different. It was among the minority of philanthropies, such as the Ford Foundation, whose original charters were so broadly worded that they could pursue almost any priority they wished and change course dramatically when the time seemed right. At Markle, the moment for a radical shift in mission arrived in September 1969, when Lloyd N. Morrisett assumed the presidency and decided, with the board's blessing, to change the foundation's focus from medicine to mass communications.

John and Mary Robinson Markle left only vague guidelines on how to spend their fortune. When the foundation was established in 1927 with an initial $3 million bequest, John Markle stipulated only that the foundation should strive "to promote the advancement and diffusion of knowledge among the people of the United States to promote the general good of mankind."[1] Indeed, a two-word phrase appearing years later in the 1969 annual report captured its founders' liberal spirit that proved, in many ways, as valuable a legacy as the millions that Markle and his wife bequeathed: "Born Free."

During its history, the foundation has had five presidents, beginning with John Markle through Zoë Baird, Morrisett's successor in 1998. Each had considerable latitude to put his or her stamp on the foundation's activities. More than any of his predecessors, however, Morrisett used that freedom to shape an entirely new mission.

Beyond Markle's liberal charter, the foundation's tradition of flexibility can be traced to a policy borrowed from the Carnegie Corporation of having a lay board of directors rather than specialists. No doctors were ever on Markle's board when it supported academic medicine. Similarly, no one directly from the media or communications industry would ever serve on the board during Morrisett's term. As Morrisett would later put it, The Markle Foundation's ability to change course and to make independent judgments about programs to be pursued has been regarded by other foundations with something approaching awe.

The tenor of the foundation's earliest years was set by its first leader, John Markle himself.

Markle, the son of an anthracite coal operator, was born in 1858 and grew up in Hazelton, Pennsylvania. At the age of twenty-one, he took over his father's firm, G. B. Markle & Co. As a businessman, Markle displayed the ethics of his time: paternalism toward his workforce through the operation of company towns, stores, and medical facilities, a determination to gain as much control as possible over anything affecting his profits, from coal extraction to transportation to finance, and a loathing of the emerging labor movement that threatened to alter the economic system that had nurtured his rise to wealth and power.

In 1884, Markle married Mary Robinson and thereby gained important connections to the Morgan railroad and finance interests. Mary Markle's stepfather was a partner at J. P. Morgan. One of her brothers was a partner at the banking firm of Drexel, Morgan and Co.[2] After Markle's death in 1933, J. P. Morgan, Jr., would lead The Markle Foundation as its second president, and the foundation's board would include Morgan associates throughout the three decades prior to Morrisett's presidency.

As head of the nation's largest independent coal company, Markle took pride in his ability to talk face to face with his workers and persuade them with the force of words rather than the thuggery of private antilabor police. Still, he would have nothing to do with unions. In 1902, he went to the White House to plead, unsuccessfully, with President Theodore Roosevelt to call out the National Guard to squelch a coal strike.[3] Discouraged by the apparent end of his paternalistic methods of dealing with miners, Markle gradually withdrew from active management of the coal business. In 1902, he and his wife moved to New York City and began giving away wealth as zealously as they had acquired it.

By 1926, Markle had sold his business interests to members of his family for a reputed $8.5 million. Having no heirs, he and his wife took the advice of lawyers and friends at Drexel, Morgan Bank and created their foundation. An Associated Press dispatch, dated February 4, 1927, announcing the establishment of the foundation, quoted Markle:

> . . . [E]very dollar that you have in excess of the cost of living is evidence of your success in the commercial world as much as your diploma from a college is evidence that you have passed the curriculum. With these funds in your possession, you become trustee for your fellow man and should so use these funds.[4]

Until his death in 1933 at age seventy-four, Markle ran the foundation largely as a private charity with no unifying theme to his giving. He donated more than $1 million to his alma mater, Lafayette College, $250,000 to a pension fund for ministers, and $500,000 to the Salvation Army for a women's shelter.[5] Beneficiaries also included thirty individuals, needy persons or former employees, whom Markle deemed worthy of a helping hand. Several survivors mentioned in Markle's will were still receiving regular checks from the foundation in the 1990s.

Among the more famous examples of Markle's grandiloquent style of giving concerned the McAuley Water Street Mission, a shelter in New York for "hoboes." The mission needed $100,000 to build the shelter. At a dinner, Markle announced his intention to give them the entire amount, but the mission's trustees balked at his generosity. Apparently, they wanted to make more new friends for the mission by allowing for smaller contributors. But Markle reportedly wouldn't have anyone crimping his philanthropic impulses: "I won't give a cent under $100,000," he replied. Whereupon the mission solved the problem in classic philanthropic style: it added $40,000 more to its fund-raising goal.[6]

Though never quite in the same league as John D. Rockefeller or Andrew Carnegie in social standing, wealth, or the ruthlessness with which he acquired it, Markle exhibited the outer trappings of the turn-of-the-century industrialist. He wore a thick mustache and goatee and enjoyed Cuban cigars. His oft-stated intention to use his "excess wealth" to benefit the less fortunate could hardly be confused with a personal vow of poverty. The Fifth Avenue mansion inhabited by the Markles was the subject of differing descriptions. A commissioned biography, *John Markle: Representative American*, published in 1929, portrays it as merely a comfortable two-story flat, albeit filled with expensive baubles and artwork. Press accounts, apocryphal or not, gave a different picture—describing the Markle compound as having twenty-four rooms, three kitchens, four elevators, and twenty-six telephones. Finding such quarters too confining for themselves (the Markles had no children) and their seventeen servants, they reportedly built seven more rooms on the roof.[7]

After Markle's death on July 10, 1933—his wife had died six years earlier—their estate endowed the foundation with $15 million.[8] Because of their paternalistic charitable impulses, the manner in which they accumulated their fortune, and the religious underpinnings of their motives, the Markles were very much a product of a time when antitrust regulations, the union movement, and the income tax were bringing the Gilded Age to a close.

J. P. Morgan, Jr., assumed Markle's presidency after its founder's death. Archie Woods, a director and vice president since 1931, became treasurer in 1933. For the next eleven years until a car accident claimed his life, Woods directed the foundation's day-to-day operations. He and the other directors decided that the foundation should move from being the idiosyncratic charity operated by its founder to more targeted goals.

For guidance, they turned to Frederick P. Keppel, the venerable president of the Carnegie Corporation. No record exists of the advice that Keppel gave Morgan and the rest of the Markle board. It is likely that he encouraged the foundation to narrow its focus and pursue activities of pressing public interest that had few sources of financial support.[9] In December 1935, after a year-long review of its options, the board settled on the first coherent mission at Markle: providing grants-in-aid for individuals engaged in research in the medical and physical sciences. At the time, they were logical philanthropic targets because individual researchers received little of the outside funding from government or other sources that would eventually become available decades later. Under the leadership of Woods and the Morgan-dominated board, the Markle Foundation gave approximately $5 million in grants-in-aid to researchers. Such grants would remain the foundation's dominant activity until 1946.[10]

THE MARKLE SCHOLARS-IN-MEDICINE PROGRAM

By the end of World War II, spending on medical research by government, business, and large philanthropies was on the rise and dwarfed the funds that Markle was able to distribute. Once again, the time seemed right for the foundation board to reconsider its program. It turned to a prominent Carnegie figure, John McFarlane Russell. Under his leadership, the foundation entered its third era, which lasted until 1969.

Russell was born in 1903, the son of James Earl Russell, dean of Teachers College, Columbia University.[11] As a young man, John had traveled widely with his father and assisted him in surveying educational methods in Australia, New Zealand, and Africa for the Carnegie Corporation. Eventually, the younger Russell joined Carnegie and spent ten years as an assistant to its president, Frederick Keppel. In 1940, he was an assistant to James B. Conant, president of Harvard University. Following two years in the army, Russell was named secretary of the Army and Navy Committee on Welfare and Recreation. In 1946, the Markle Foundation appointed him its first executive director and conferred the title of president in 1960.

The board asked Russell to devise a new program within the field of medical research, but he knew little about that philanthropic domain when he first took office. After touring medical schools during his first two years as president, Russell concluded that a special area of need was keeping young, promising medical scientists from straying into higher-paying private practice or full-time research. Young medical faculty members, at the time, earned an average of just $4,000 and served on a year-to-year basis. Although fellowships for promising medical educators existed, they were often highly specialized—for example, to perform cancer or polio research.[12]

Russell hit upon the idea of establishing a fellowship program. The schools would nominate candidates, the foundation would choose from among them, and fellows would each receive the then handsome sum of $5,000 per year for five years—later increased to $6,000—on top of their university salaries. Schools, for their part, would be required to support the young faculty members over the longer term and provide the foundation with annual reports on their activities.[13] Medical school deans immediately hailed the idea, and the Markle Scholars-in-Medicine Program was born in 1948. During the next twenty-two years, 506 scholars—nearly all men—from ninety U.S. and Canadian medical schools received a total of $16 million in Markle support.

The Markle Scholars Program quickly gained a loyal following at the nation's medical schools. For the young scholars, the honor was deeply flattering. The money was good, there were virtually no strings on how it could be spent, and a national camaraderie soon developed among the scholars that proved valuable throughout their careers. Each year, the foundation hosted, at its own expense, a gathering of the scholars and their wives at vacation spots throughout North America and the Caribbean. For junior faculty members, who spent most of their time closeted in research laboratories and clinics, the Markle meetings were a rare, welcome chance to blow off steam and hear speakers discuss social issues. The 1968 annual meeting, for example, held at the Beach Club Hotel in Naples, Florida, discussed "The City: Chaos or Community?"[14]

Years later, Dr. Andrew Wallace, a 1965–1970 scholar, who went on to become dean of Dartmouth University Medical School, recalled those years as a once-in-a-lifetime opportunity for establishing intellectual and social connections beyond his field of cardiology. "When I got my Markle award at age thirty,"

Wallace said, "my salary at Duke was about $12,000, and the Markle award was $5,000 a year for five years. I was allowed to use the money any way I wanted to further my professional development. The fact that your institution selected you came as an enormous vote of confidence. So it was extremely flattering and motivating."[15]

Still, as might be expected in such a competitive process, the Markle program generated a certain amount of envy. Some in the medical community accused it of elitism. Myths grew up about how candidates were accepted or rejected by the selection committees. As was noted in a board-sponsored review of the program:

> . . . [T]here is a widespread belief that the Markle candidate must be personable, is handicapped if he is in preclinical science, must not be too eccentric, must be able to communicate his ideas freely and under various and trying circumstances, is picked to some degree by the "pillow talk" of committee members' wives, comes from a school approved by John Russell, and must be able to hold his liquor like a gentleman. . . .
>
> . . . [W]hile there may be some elements of truth in this mythology, it is far from the whole truth.[16]

By the end of its first decade of operation, more fundamental questions were emerging about the program's usefulness. The economics of academic medicine had brightened considerably since the Markle Scholars Program began. Academic salaries were rising, and extensive federal support for medical research was available from the newly formed National Institutes of Health (NIH) and the National Science Foundation. By 1959, all Markle Scholars in the United States were receiving support from NIH.[17] During the early 1960s, Markle board members felt that a fresh look at the foundation's priorities was again in order.

The board hired Donald B. Straus, president of the Health Insurance Plan of Greater New York, to conduct the review. His 171-page report, submitted in September 1962, provided fuel for both supporters and skeptics. To the program's loyalists, the key finding was that the program still had merit and should be continued. On the other hand, a survey of the scholars found that 78 percent would have remained in academic medicine without the

Markle grant. The Straus report also determined that unsuccessful candidates for scholarships were advancing about as well as winners in salary and rank—thus seemingly undercutting a central contention by the foundation that its scholars were doing better than losers.[18]

In short, the Straus report concluded that the Markle Scholars Program still had a powerful following and conferred prestige and lifelong professional connections on its awardees, but its actual value to both scholars and society as a whole was increasingly questionable. The other reality was that Russell, the embodiment of the Markle Scholars Program, was nearing retirement.

The Straus report gave the Markle Scholars Program only a temporary reprieve. As Russell prepared to relinquish the presidency in 1968, supporters persisted in hoping that the program would survive the transition. By the late 1960s, however, the changing economic tides of academic medicine and Russell's impending departure as Markle's president had thrown wide open the question of the foundation's future direction.

Into this vacuum stepped Courtney Smith.

Smith had been elected to the Markle board in 1953 shortly before he assumed the presidency of Swarthmore College. A native of Iowa, Smith had graduated from Harvard in 1938 with a specialty in seventeenth-century English. He spent 1938 and 1939 as a Rhodes Scholar, then returned to Harvard where he was a teaching fellow and English tutor until 1944.[19]

In what he called a "revelatory experience," Smith became a race relations officer with the U.S. Navy in Pensacola, Florida. Already a New Deal Democrat, he encountered for the first time the literary and intellectual contributions of black authors such as Richard Wright. When he accepted a teaching appointment at Princeton University after the war, he took the then-audacious step of incorporating those writers into his English literature courses.[20] Those bold, early steps at Princeton on behalf of African American intellectual thought would make all the more ironic his death two decades later in the midst of a campus conflict centering on the issue of race.

Princeton housed the Rhodes Scholar program during the 1940s and 1950s, and Smith was soon administering it. In 1952, he took charge of Princeton's Woodrow Wilson Fellowship and, a year later, was named American secretary of the Rhodes Scholar program.[21] By age thirty-five, he was a nationally recognized authority on academic fellowship programs. In October 1953, when he assumed the presidency of Swarthmore, he took the Rhodes Scholar program with him from Princeton to his new campus.

Smith's rise to prominence in academic circles and his expertise in administering fellowships caught the attention of Markle's trustees just as they and Russell were launching the new Scholars-in-Medicine Program. They invited Smith to help structure their program.[22] His work impressed them enough that they named him a Markle trustee in 1953. By 1966, he was chosen by fellow board members to chair the Committee on Future Plans that would decide the fate of the scholars program and the future direction of the foundation.

Smith's committee deliberated for two years. Although distracted by numerous civic commitments in Philadelphia and the growing stresses of his college presidency, Smith soon dominated the committee.[23] Its members included Markle's board chairman, Stuart W. Cragin, vice president, Morgan Guaranty Trust; Jarvis Cromwell, director emeritus, Dan River Mills, Inc.; Walter H. Page, president, Morgan Guaranty Trust; and William M. Rees, chairman and president, The Chubb Corporation.[24]

In 1967, the committee wrote to forty-seven prominent Americans in various fields and asked each to share "what disturbs them in America today and how a small private foundation might contribute to solutions." The list included David Rockefeller, chairman, Chase Manhattan Bank; statesman Ralph Bunche; artist Alexander Calder; lawyers Lloyd Garrison and Bethuel Webster; leading journalists John B. Oakes, James Reston, and Walter Lippmann; and foundation leaders Clark Kerr, head of the Carnegie Commission on Higher Education, and Alan Pifer, president of the Carnegie Corporation of New York.[25]

Only a handful of those replies survive. Kermit Gordon, president of The Brookings Institution, said that the scholars program no longer served a useful purpose. Dr. Colin MacLeod of The Commonwealth Fund favored reorienting the program to create better linkages between medicine and social science. Robert Ebert, a Markle Scholar and dean of the Harvard Medical School, thought that the foundation should stay in medicine but concentrate on the establishment of training programs in the social sciences for physicians—an idea seconded by Pifer.[26]

The committee also sent letters to fifty Markle Scholars and asked them what ought to become of the program. To no one's surprise, the majority of the scholars wanted their cherished program continued, although some questioned if it could, or should, survive without Russell's leadership. According to the committee's surviving notes, there was strong sentiment that, whether or not the scholars program lasted, Markle should at least continue to concentrate on academic medicine in some form.[27]

During its two-year existence, the futures committee considered at least a dozen possible missions for Markle, from innovations in medical education and paramedical programs to academic law and education in religion.[28] By mid-1968, the list apparently had been narrowed to three possibilities: pollution, higher education governance, and community and urban medicine with emphasis on the problems of minority communities.[29]

Judging from surviving documents, Smith might have been leaning toward focusing Markle's future attention on improving higher education governance and leadership. Specifically, he might have been thinking about an expanded scholarship program aimed at enticing promising young academics into university administration. Considering his own mounting stresses as a college president, such thoughts would have been understandable. Certainly, mass communications never occurred to Smith as a possibility for Markle.

As the futures committee deliberated, Russell announced his retirement as Markle's president. Almost immediately, in July 1968, trustees named Smith to succeed Russell as president. As a stormy academic year was about to begin at Swarthmore, Smith had turned himself into a lame-duck college president.

The prospect of leaving academia for the more sedate presidency of a small foundation in New York City must have been appealing to Smith. The strains of college leadership had taken their toll. Indeed, the best explanation for Smith's quick acceptance of the presidency of a modest-sized foundation—seemingly a lateral career move for a nationally prominent college president still in his prime—was that it offered a graceful exit from Swarthmore. Besides, he had grown to love New York and looked forward to prowling its streets and shopping at Brooks Brothers for his favorite suits.[30] He and his wife had already picked out an apartment in Manhattan.

As the 1968–69 academic year opened, Swarthmore's faculty were questioning Smith's sometimes autocratic governing style. Students were demonstrating for increased enrollment of blacks, and they knew that Smith sympathized with their cause. Throughout his presidency, he had championed student rights and intellectual freedom—defending, for example, the right of a student group to invite Gus Hall, general secretary of the U.S. Communist Party, to their campus.[31] Still, the campus reached a crisis point on December 23, 1968, when students presented Smith with a set of "nonnegotiable demands" and threatened to do "whatever is necessary" unless Smith publicly accepted those demands. He refused and admonished students to change their "demands" into proposals.[32] As the impasse continued, students occupied the admissions office in January 1969.

"We have lost something precious at Swarthmore," he wearily told students and faculty three days before his death, "the feeling that force and disruptiveness are just not our way."[33]

Exactly where Smith would have led the Markle Foundation will never be known. The Scholars-in-Medicine Program, if it survived at all, probably would not have remained the sole preoccupation of the foundation. If Smith had settled such questions in his own mind, he never revealed his answers to anyone.[34]

THE MAN FROM *SESAME STREET*

At the moment that Courtney Smith's death threw Markle's plans for transition into turmoil, Lloyd Morrisett was also eager for change. James Perkins, his close friend at Carnegie, had assumed Cornell University's presidency in 1963. Morrisett's early foundation mentor, John Gardner, had left Carnegie in 1965 for a cabinet post in the Johnson Administration. Alan Pifer became Carnegie's president, and Morrisett was named vice president. Morrisett respected Pifer, but the two were never close personally. He briefly flirted with the idea of rejoining Perkins at Cornell as academic vice president.[35] By 1968, Morrisett was consumed with creating the Children's Television Workshop and was feeling increasingly hemmed in by the administrative burdens of his Carnegie vice presidency.

Why Morrisett rose so quickly to the top of Markle's list of presidential candidates in the wake of Smith's death is a matter of speculation. Gardner suggested to the author that John Russell had probably tapped his contacts on Carnegie's board for possible candidates: "Lloyd, when he was offered the job, was unquestionably one of the stars at Carnegie and it would have been a natural thing for Markle's board to have sought him out."[36]

Morrisett offered a similar speculation. "My memory is that I got a call from [Markle board chairman] Stuart Cragin, and he invited me to have lunch. Why did I get that call? There was a strong historical connection between Markle and Carnegie. John Russell, because of his past connections with Carnegie, might have suggested that they try there. Another possibility is that Stuart Cragin had social connections with people on the Carnegie board."[37]

Whatever the precise circumstances, Cragin and fellow Markle board member William Rees decided to invite Morrisett to lunch in early February 1969 at the private downtown Manhattan dining room of Morgan Guaranty Trust to discuss the foundation's presidency. Morrisett quickly made it plain that his interests lay in the media, not in medicine. It wasn't that he lacked respect for Markle's prize accomplishments in medicine. The Markle Scholars Program had been a model for several other fellowships, including the White House Fellows Program. Many scholars had gone on to prominence in academic medicine and other fields. The record would later show that 3 university presidents, 7 vice presidents, 2 vice chancellors, 1 provost, 11 deans, 14 associate deans, and 134 department chairs had been Markle Scholars.[38] Dr. James Comer, a Markle Scholar in 1969, would gain national prominence as a school reformer and child advocate.

Still, Morrisett's blunt declaration of independence from the Markle Scholars Program did not faze Rees or Cragin. Other members of the Markle board, particularly the older ones with sentimental ties to the medical mission, were baffled by Morrisett's interests in mass communications. Even after he took office, some of them remained dumbfounded by the national acclaim for his prize creation, the Children's Television Workshop. Nonetheless, even the doubters at Markle soon recognized the logic of a small foundation in the nation's media capital taking on the neglected field of mass communications. And Morrisett seemed to be the person who just might pull it off.

Recalled James Pitney, a Markle board member from 1965 to 1975: "We picked the man, and we felt that we had to give the man the opportunity to see if his program was going to work, even though there was a feeling of bewilderment about the program, or how much it could contribute in the future."[39]

As Rees related to the author: "Lloyd impressed us mightily. He struck us as a very bright fellow who wasn't wishy-washy. He had very definite ideas."[40]

On February 25, 1969, only days after their Wall Street lunch with Morrisett, Russell and Cragin sent wires to the rest of the Markle board announcing that Morrisett had agreed to be the foundation's fourth president.

A native of Oklahoma City, Morrisett was born on November 2, 1929, the son of Jessie Watson Morrisett and Lloyd Newton Morrisett, a high school principal who had spent his early years teaching in a one-room schoolhouse. The elder Morrisett disliked his middle name, never used it, and passed on only his middle initial to his son. Both parents were liberal southern Democrats. His mother, especially, had revered President Franklin D. Roosevelt. Neither parent, however, was a political activist or an ideologue, nor was Morrisett himself. Yet, years later, in 1973, he would find his name on President Richard Nixon's infamous "enemy's list" consisting of people believed to be that administration's bitterest ideological foes—an honor that Morrisett took perverse pride in but was never able to explain satisfactorily.[41]

In 1933, when Lloyd was four years old, the family moved to New York to escape the brunt of the Dust Bowl and the Depression. His father earned a Ph.D. at Columbia Teachers College and became an assistant superintendent of schools in Yonkers.[42]

The frustrations that his father experienced as a school administrator left lasting impressions on the younger Morrisett. He inherited a lifelong interest in education and learning but also a wariness about public education's capacity to act decisively or to try new approaches. Years later at Markle, Morrisett remained passionate about understanding and promoting learning, but he was never tempted, as a number of other foundation executives were, to be a "school reformer."

"My dad left Yonkers in 1940, and one reason was he thought schools were too political," Morrisett recalled. "Fifty years later, the New York [State Board of] Regents took over the Yonkers schools because they were too political. Nothing had changed in fifty years! That's just an example of the inertia that's built into public education."[43]

Dinner conversation in the Morrisett household frequently centered on school matters, and Lloyd grew up assuming that he would follow his father into academic life. In 1941, the Morrisetts moved to California, where his father taught educational administration at the University of California at Los Angeles (UCLA). Morrisett attended Oberlin College, graduated with a philosophy degree in 1951, and developed a lifelong attachment to that rural Ohio campus.[44] Finding psychology more to his liking, he did graduate work at UCLA for two years in that field. He caught the eye of a rising young professor, Irving Maltzman, who asked Morrisett to be his research assistant and then gave him a golden opportunity to boost his academic standing by coauthoring nearly a dozen scholarly papers.[45]

Beginning in 1953, Morrisett spent three years at Yale University and earned a doctorate in experimental psychology. There he met Professor Carl I. Hovland, a leading psychologist who founded the Yale Communications and Attitude Change program and whose pioneering work in the study of communications and learning would be called "the largest single contribution [to the field of social communication] any man has made."[46] In later years, Morrisett would credit that apprenticeship with sparking his interest in communications.[47]

In 1956, Morrisett landed a teaching job in psychology at the University of California at Berkeley's school of education. During his two years there, the seeds of a lifelong fascination with computers were sown when he met Ed Feigenbaum and Julian Feldman, two brilliant young assistant professors who had studied with Herbert Simon, one of the century's pioneers in the field of computers and human learning.

By this time, however, Morrisett was having his doubts about academic life. The career he had taken for granted since boyhood lacked mystery and excitement, and he was unimpressed by the seriousness of his students. Searching for direction, Morrisett joined the Social Science Research Council in New York as a staff member from 1958–59. At the council, he became friends with Simon, Allen Newell, and George Miller, professor of psychiatry at Princeton University, all world leaders in the study of how computers might simulate patterns of human thinking. Newell, a faculty member of what was then the Carnegie Institute of Technology (later Carnegie-Mellon University) was credited with laying much of the groundwork for the emerging field of cognitive psychology, which became Morrisett's lifelong scholarly passion.

It was during his brief stay at the council that he first encountered the Carnegie Corporation. At a conference hosted at the council, he met a Carnegie staff member, Fred Jackson, who was immediately impressed by Morrisett and his links to some of the best minds in social science. Jackson mentioned Morrisett to Carnegie's president, John Gardner, and a lunch was arranged. Gardner and Morrisett discovered that they had much in common. They talked about psychology, new developments in learning, and the scientific understanding of creativity. Gardner invited Morrisett to join Carnegie as his executive assistant. Morrisett accepted and began a ten-year stay at Carnegie.[48]

"I knew literally nothing about foundations," Morrisett recalled, "but I was fascinated. I liked the atmosphere of the organization; I liked John and his approach to what they were doing. He was a psychologist, and that gave me some affinity to him."[49]

Morrisett's first years at Carnegie were happy ones. Gardner was president and the warm, garrulous James Perkins was vice president. Morrisett developed a specialty in early education and became engaged in projects concerning human creativity. For five years, he was a member of Carnegie's Committee on Assessing the Progress of Education, chaired by Ralph Tyler and, later, George Brian.[50] The committee's work paved the way for the congressionally mandated National Assessment of Educational Progress, which, during the 1990s, remained the most highly regarded national testing program in math, science, reading, and language skills.

Morrisett also became interested in overcoming the disadvantages of poor and minority students before they enter school. He was especially struck that foundation projects, even those pursued by such large foundations as Carnegie, rarely reached more than a few hundred students. He began to wonder: What could a foundation do to have an impact on the lives of not just hundreds but millions of preschool children?

As such questions increasingly preoccupied him, Morrisett took the advice of an old California friend, Julian Ganz, and struck up a new acquaintance with Ganz's cousin, Joan Ganz Cooney. At the time, she was a young producer at New York's public television station, WNDT Channel 13. She and Morrisett soon became friends and occasional lunch companions.[51]

The story of the so-called "dinner party" in February 1966 at Cooney's Gramercy Park apartment, where the idea of the Children's Television Workshop was first hatched, is well known in television circles. Along with two or three other couples, Morrisett and his wife Mary were at Cooney's apartment to celebrate her first Emmy award for a public TV documentary on poverty. The Morrisetts had two young daughters, and the talk soon turned to children's television.

Recalling the dinner conversation years later, Morrisett said that he asked Cooney, "Do you think television can be used to teach young children?"

"I don't know," Cooney replied, "but I'd like to talk about it."[52]

Shortly afterward, Morrisett invited Cooney to prepare a report for Carnegie on the possibilities of children's television. The result was a groundbreaking study titled "The Potential Uses of Television in Pre-School Education." What Cooney imagined in her report was revolutionary—a children's series as entertaining as anything on the air and capable of teaching solid, measurable educational skills in language and math.

Armed with that report, Morrisett began to pursue his many contacts in foundation, government, and educational circles. Most important, he approached his friend, Harold ("Doc") Howe, then U.S. Commissioner of Education. Howe, it turned out, was quite keen on government programs for disadvantaged youngsters and agreed to put up $4 million, roughly half the start-up money needed for the Children's Television Workshop (CTW). Within Carnegie, Morrisett overcame resistance to projects in television and secured another $1 million, one of the largest commitments by the foundation during the decade. Howe then convinced the Ford Foundation to reverse an early turndown of the CTW project. Altogether, Morrisett's and Howe's efforts reaped a nearly miraculous $8 million for this gamble that defied conventional media wisdom. Had Morrisett been any less effective in lining up financial support, Cooney's report likely would have become just another long-forgotten foundation idea.

The political atmosphere was nearly perfect for attracting those funds. The spirit of President Lyndon B. Johnson's Great Society and the Civil Rights era was still alive in Washington. As Morrisett told the author, "There was a lot of attention being paid to the educational gap suffered by minority, poor, educationally deprived children, who were pretty typically three months, six months behind their peers. In Lyndon Johnson's call for the Great Society, and in the moral ardor which he projected, I think that there was a lot more conviction than there is today in the belief that education was vital for the youngest children. And when *Sesame Street* appeared, here was a relatively easy way to get it on a large scale."[53]

On March 21, 1968, the Children's Television Workshop was announced at a press conference in the Waldorf Astoria Hotel. The news made page one in the next day's *New York Times*.

The group that went on to create *Sesame Street* in a rented public television studio on West 55th Street in Manhattan was surely among the most eclectic assortments of talent ever assembled. Besides Cooney and Morrisett, there was Jim Henson, a hip puppeteer whose creations had thus far appeared mainly in commercials and on the Ed Sullivan Show. A team of veteran children's television scriptwriters and producers worked alongside a group of learning experts, enlisted by Morrisett, including Gerald Lesser from Harvard and Edward Palmer of the Oregon State Division of Higher Education.

On November 10, 1969, *Sesame Street* premiered on public television. Morrisett, by then at The Markle Foundation, and

Cooney watched the show along with its other creators in a suite at the Essex House overlooking Central Park. Turning to Cooney, Morrisett quietly said, "Joan, we did it."[54]

Even with a hit on their hands, *Sesame Street*'s unprecedented mix of serious education, fun, and stylish production was greeted skeptically by some broadcasters and educators. Subsequent critiques worried, for example, that the heavy use of quick-flashing animation to teach the alphabet and numbers might undermine the attention spans of young children for traditional schoolwork. Nonetheless, the show was instantly embraced by children and parents. In its first season, *Sesame Street* reached more than half of the nation's 12 million three-to-five-year-olds.[55] Eventually, the program would be broadcast in seventy languages and seen in 140 countries. In a relatively bold stroke for television in 1969, many of the show's performers were black, Hispanic, and Asian. Morrisett was particularly pleased that repeated studies after its premier and during subsequent years demonstrated that the program did what it was designed to do: educate as well as entertain.

Sesame Street's success was never equaled or approached—a tribute to the program but also a foreboding of the difficulties encountered by Morrisett during his years at Markle in repeated attempts to insinuate public interest goals into the commercially driven culture of broadcasting.

What made the inner man from *Sesame Street* tick remained mysterious even to those who knew him best. Morrisett's old friend from Carnegie, James Perkins, could only summon up monosyllabic descriptions—"clear-headed," "serious," "intelligent," "quiet," "buttoned-up." Cooney said that Morrisett's style "is cerebral, intuitive, and very precise. He's very persuasive. But as long as I've known him, I've never been clear what drove him."[56]

"We had the very best of professional relationships," said Forrest Chisman, Morrisett's first program officer at Markle. "But I never knew him well at all. Professionally, he really backed his people. He set very high personal standards and within those confines it was the best job I ever had. From the start, we took it for granted that any foundation that didn't fail sometimes wasn't doing its job. But I had to make an appointment to see him, even though my office was twenty feet away."[57]

Several traits repeatedly colored Morrisett's actions as a foundation president. He was not fearful of risk. That alone made him a standout in the foundation community. As long-time public broadcasting leader, James Day wrote of his friend many years later: Morrisett "has a gambler's impulse to place his bets—but not until the odds have been carefully weighed."[58]

He was also a social scientist to the bone, a true believer in the power of research to suggest workable solutions to vexing social problems. Repeatedly, researchers and scholars turned down for funding by other foundations found a more sympathetic and sophisticated ear at Markle. Morrisett's abiding faith in the power of social science to diagnose and address society's ills led him to spend millions of dollars in fostering some of the most important thinking ever done in the field of communications—and also to misspend millions on what some might describe as flights of academic fancy.

He could be outwardly formal and even curt. He admitted his own difficulties in establishing close personal relations before his arrival at Markle: "That was one of my immediate problems and still is, really," he said in an oral history of the Carnegie Corporation two years before assuming Markle's presidency. "I found that in meeting new people I seldom took the time to establish easy relationships. I always wanted to start talking of the business at hand, and this is not the best way to deal with people, as a foundation officer."[59]

Still, he sought to establish an unpretentious tone at the foundation. He was always "Lloyd," generally forgoing the academic affectation of "Dr." Morrisett. His piercing blue eyes occasionally lit up to reveal a puckish sense of humor. His outward all-business style belied a deep loyalty and even sentimentality for people with whom The Markle Foundation dealt over the years. Indeed, his aversion to conflict sometimes led him to stay with projects and people longer than prudence alone would have dictated. A key part of the foundation's style of forming close partnerships with beneficiaries was its ironclad rule, under Morrisett, of never funding any project or person without a personal visit.

Morrisett's faith in young, bright, and relatively untried people also became part of the foundation's leitmotif. Throughout his career, he preferred to hire and work with "natural athletes," as longtime board member D. Ronald Daniel characterized them. A number of the youthful program staff attained leadership positions in education and philanthropy. Hannah Bartlett, Morrisett's assistant from 1969 to 1972, went on to a long career as a program director and consultant at the Cleveland Foundation. Chisman, executive assistant at Markle from 1970 to 1975, became director of the Southport Institute for Policy Analysis in Washington. Kandace Laass, a program officer from 1974 to 1976, was later director of membership, programs, and services at the U.S. Chamber of Commerce. Kendra O'Donnell, program officer from 1977 to 1979, became headmaster of Phillips Exeter Academy. Jean Firstenberg, program officer from 1976 to 1979, became director and chief executive officer of the American Film Institute. Mary C. Milton, program officer from 1979 to 1985, formed her own company, M2 Interactive Corporation. Deborah Wadsworth, program officer from 1980 to 1984, was named executive director of the Public Agenda Foundation. Larry Slesinger, a program officer from 1985 to 1988, went on to be a vice president of the National Center for Non-Profit Boards in Washington. Jocelyn Hidi, at Markle from 1989 to 1992, became a partner in a successful international importing business in Toronto, Canada.

Morrisett, himself an early bloomer, had been plucked from academic life at age twenty-nine by Carnegie's John Gardner. "Judgment matures very early in people who have judgment," Gardner told the author, in describing the young Morrisett whom he first met. "They have that compass needle, and the capacity to make decisions. And Lloyd had that, along with the capacity to say no."[60]

Morrisett was especially ahead of his time in his professional dealings with women. During his presidency, more than 80 percent of Markle's senior program and financial officers were female. Given his aversion to ideology in general, however, it's probable that Morrisett was more gender-blind than feminist. Morrisett's selection of Cooney to prepare the Carnegie study that led to the Children's Television Workshop was only the first such gamble that paid off. Among his earliest large grants was one to Peggy Charren, the unknown suburban Boston housewife whose fledgling grassroots organization, Action for Children's

Television, became one of Markle's most enduring successes. An early set of grants went to Red Burns, a young female film instructor at New York University, who became an important innovative force in channeling communications technology to community and social goals.

"He was a fabulous mentor, very deliberate in his teaching, at a time when there weren't a lot of astute, empathetic men mentoring hot-shot young women," said program officer O'Donnell. "I will never forget my job interview with Lloyd. He looked at my resume and immediately figured out all the embarrassing things about it. I was a single mother. I had to get a job. I'd had to balance these things and get my Ph.D. All of which was agonizing to me because I had not done the traditional things. But then he looked up at me and said, 'My God, you must have guts. You must be so persistent!' It was one of these transforming comments. And I said, yes, I guess that's what it means."[61]

Morrisett's relationship with his own board, in comparison with other foundations, was also somewhat unusual. What the board might have lacked in programmatic expertise—given the lay status of its members—was made up for in flexibility, lack of bias, openness to new ideas, and a broad base of knowledge in other fields beyond communications. Morrisett often turned to board members for broad strategic and financial advice and kept them closely informed over private lunches. Still, when it came to setting priorities or specific grants, the board invariably deferred to Morrisett and his staff's recommendations.

"It's the only foundation board I've ever sat on, and that includes five or six, in which members of the board play zero role in grant-making other than formal approval of the recommendations by the staff," said Joel L. Fleishman, a board member since 1976 and its chairman from 1988 to 1993. "In most foundations about which I have personal knowledge, members of the board play at least some role in advocating particular proposals to the staff. Markle is at the other end of the scale on that. On the whole time I've been on the board, we've never turned down a recommendation of the staff."[62]

As Morrisett explained it, the reason that board members at Markle virtually never vetoed a project was not because they were expected to be rubber stamps or raise no questions. Morrisett believed strongly that he owed prospective grantees a certain loyalty and allegiance. Once they had gone through the time and expense to prepare proposals and be vetted by Markle's staff, "you can't really do that in good faith unless you expect to be backed up at the board level. You can't ask to get a dean's approval, to make travel arrangements, and do all these things that rearrange a person's life. There's a strong moral commitment. The board can ask a lot of questions, and indicate doubts. But ordinarily these are details, rather than in-principle disagreements."[63]

Another trait that marked Morrisett's dealings was his lack of outward emotion under fire. Once he made a decision, he stuck by it, a helpful attribute in a position that required him to deal with occasional grant seekers who had outsized egos. Early in his presidency, he had a memorable encounter with Lester Markel, for four decades the absolute monarch of the Sunday New York Times until his retirement in the late 1960s. In 1971, Markel approached Morrisett for several grants for projects concerning public television. Insulted by what he saw as the desultory pace of Markle's approval process, he wrote Morrisett a bristling letter:

"I have had dealings with other foundations but my experience with you is unique. Maybe my career does not justify better treatment, but I am sure a number of other people would disagree with you. Therefore, I say frankly, if this is the modus operandi of the Markle Foundation, there is something radically wrong at 50 Rockefeller Plaza [then Markle's headquarters]."[64]

Morrisett responded to Markel's fire with frost: "I think there has been a regrettable misunderstanding about our attitude toward you personally and about the way in which we normally consider proposals," he wrote. Markle, he explained, considered some one thousand requests for grants per year, and each deserved "the fullest review possible."

"I regret any inconvenience our procedures may have caused you," he concluded.[65]

Lester Markel did not get his grant.

One of the more enigmatic traits of Morrisett's presidency was the low profile that he kept for himself and his foundation. He gave few speeches and only occasionally wrote op-ed or journal articles. The best record of his evolving beliefs can be found in his yearly essays appearing at the beginning of the foundation's annual reports since 1969—hardly the most flamboyant venue for broadcasting his views. The many people who benefited from Markle's support over the years, including Charren, Cooney, and Harvard Professor of Psychology Howard Gardner, piled up press notices and collected awards and honors. Morrisett, their frequent partner and patron, and the foundation that he led rarely sought or received publicity.

Part of the explanation was Morrisett's shy temperament, but another part was his stated belief that Markle would be freer to experiment and take risks by avoiding the spotlight. "I've always thought," Morrisett told the author, "that it was very advantageous not to be among the first ten foundations in size. They get more publicity, and not to be on that list has been very useful because you don't get the same kind of criticism and scrutiny. You're more able to push the envelope, if you will, of what foundations can do."[66]

The failure by Markle and Morrisett to develop an effective public relations strategy was frequently debated within Markle. "I was all for raising our profile and Lloyd's profile, but Lloyd just could not have been less interested," Chisman said. "My point was that we didn't have a lot of money and we could accomplish a lot of what we wanted through greater visibility. He agreed, but he just wouldn't do it. Part of it may have been philosophical, part of it is that it just wasn't his style."[67]

Although clearly enjoying his role as a foundation leader, Morrisett sometimes reflected on its difficulties: "Not everyone is cut out to be a foundation officer. The job of a foundation officer is a lonely one in some respects. It's lonely in the respect that you are in a position to have some say over whether another person receives money or not. And this creates, for some people, a certain invidious character in human relationships."[68]

Pressed to summarize what drove him throughout his career, Morrisett pointed to research on human motivation by a fellow psychologist, David C. McClelland, who taught at Harvard and Boston Universities. McClelland theorized that three basic human needs affected individual and organizational behavior: the need for achievement (figuring out how to do something better or more efficiently); the need for affiliation (maintaining warm and friendly relationships); and the need for power (the desire to control others or influence their behavior). "After reading [McClelland's] work," Morrisett said, "I identified myself as high on achievement motivation and relatively low on both others."[69]

On March 5, 1969, the board of trustees publicly announced Morrisett's presidency, and the news appeared the next day in two brief paragraphs on page twenty-six of The New York Times. Over lunch at the Algonquin Hotel a day later, Russell, the outgoing president, assured his young successor of his "complete freedom" to take the foundation in the new directions he planned. Morrisett indicated that his next weeks would be busy, but that he intended to turn to serious planning for the transition in July and August.[70]

Morrisett would often recall the old joke by a Carnegie colleague upon learning of his acceptance of a foundation presidency: "Congratulations. You've just had your last bad meal, and your last sincere compliment."

A NEW MISSION

By settling on Morrisett, Markle's board had effectively sealed the fate of the Scholars-in-Medicine Program. Most of the medical scholars knew little about Markle's new president, or *Sesame Street*, or the communications field. Board Chairman Cragin and Russell took steps to smooth the transition. They mailed letters in June 1969 to hundreds of friends of The Markle Foundation to clarify that they, not Morrisett, had decided to end the scholars program and they hoped that "the friendships and associations growing out of the program" would continue after the presidential transition.[71]

Russell's letter was particularly gracious:

> Because termination (of the Scholars program) before long is obvious and because it seems so unfair to ask a new president who has not been personally involved to close out my program, I have asked the Directors to allow me the privilege of ending it during my tenure. . . .
>
> This letter is to let you know that no further Scholar appoint-

> ments will be made. I am pleased that this is so because Lloyd now will have the same freedom to establish a new program that I had when I was first appointed in 1946. . . .
>
> I am sure that each of you will, after full consideration, support my stand and, more importantly, support Lloyd Morrisett as he works toward a new Markle future.[72]

On September 2, 1969, as New Yorkers braced for a final, post–Labor Day blast of 90-degree heat, Morrisett boarded the 7:40 A.M. southbound train from his suburban Irvington home in Westchester for his first day as president. When he arrived at what were then Markle's headquarters, 522 Fifth Avenue, he was greeted by a staff inherited from his predecessor: Dan Martin, Russell's assistant; Virginia Dunlap, the foundation secretary; and several office aides. All were capable and likable, but they were strangers to Morrisett and had no particular interest in advancing his plans. Instantly, he felt lonely.

The president's office reflected his predecessor's style, not his. The narrow room was dominated by a long conference table that had doubled as Russell's private desk. Totally unsuitable, Morrisett thought. Within weeks, at the October 22 board meeting, Morrisett obtained permission to move the foundation to more capacious quarters on the ninth floor of 50 Rockefeller Plaza, two floors above the New York headquarters of the world's largest news-gathering organization, the Associated Press, where it would remain until 1987.[73]

At his first board meeting, Morrisett outlined his early ideas for the foundation's new mission. Henceforth, he said, Markle would be concerned with:

> (1) the effectiveness with which mass media provide individuals in our society with the information and education they need;
> (2) the ability of professionals within the mass media to achieve their most worthwhile professional aspirations, considering particularly the effectiveness of the education of professionals, organizations that support their performance, and the structure and regulatory problems of the mass media; and
> (3) the effects of mass media and communications on society and how these effects are likely to change in the coming years with the rapid implementation of even more advanced technology.[74]

Several weeks later, Morrisett expanded on those goals in a letter to Winston O. Franklin of the Charles F. Kettering Foundation. His objective, he wrote, was:

> . . . to strengthen the educational uses of the mass media and communications technology. It is based on the knowledge that the communications media—television, radio, newspapers, magazines, books and films—are playing an ever greater part in society. Much of this is due to the educating effects of the media and the ways in which they provide information, shape attitudes and opinions, and influence our view of ourselves and the world. Through grants for research and studies, educational programs, and special projects, the Foundation will attempt to foster a better understanding of the media themselves and to improve their educational services.[75]

That fall, Morrisett began assembling new staff. Hungry for a familiar face, he hired Hannah Bartlett, a thirty-one-year-old administrative assistant at Carnegie who had worked with Morrisett on educational testing projects, and who was imbued, as he was, with the Carnegie ethos of philanthropy.

His second hire was Forrest Chisman, a twenty-six-year-old political scientist from the University of Toronto, with an Oxford University pedigree and a flair for diplomacy that would prove valuable during Morrisett's first trying years. During his job interview at one of Morrisett's favorite lunch spots, the Coffee House Club in Manhattan, he struck an immediate chord by mentioning his familiarity with Morrisett's revered Yale psychology mentor, Carl Hovland. Enticed by the novelty of the job and the then-handsome $15,000 salary, Chisman accepted the offer.[76]

Much as Morrisett and his young staff would have liked to turn full throttle to their new mission, they first had to confront some unfinished and not altogether pleasant business: ending the Scholars-in-Medicine Program, which had been in existence for twenty-two years. The challenge was to end it without open warfare with the Markle Scholars and the medical establishment that had grown so fond of its largesse.

The Markle board had agreed not to name any new scholars after 1968. Still, some five hundred scholars and alumni were alive and in positions of prominence in top universities. If wooed and won, they might be valuable allies, but, if alienated, they could be thorns in Morrisett's side. And there were definite inklings that many of the scholars neither understood nor welcomed Morrisett's future plans.

As Chisman later characterized it, Morrisett decided to "kill the program with kindness"—ending it with finality while quelling any resentments and perhaps, in time, building friendships with the scholars themselves. As costly in time, energy, and money as that would prove, it was better than the alternatives. An unceremonious end would have been viewed as antagonistic. Keeping the program alive in the highly unlikely event that some other foundation or organization would assume its costs would have been unconscionably wasteful.

Still, such "kindness" came at a price. In its waning years, the Scholars-in-Medicine Program cost more than $1.5 million—money, as a consequence, denied Markle's new mission. The foundation was obliged to make annual $6,000 payments to each of the 125 most recently named scholars. The payments would not end until 1974, the fifth year of the last class of 25 scholars. During fiscal year 1969–70, payouts to the scholars totaled $612,000, compared with $461,000 for projects in communications.[77] An additional $936,000 was distributed to the scholars through 1974.

The ending of the Markle Scholars Program also cost precious staff time. As a peace gesture, Morrisett decided to continue Russell's custom of making personal visits to scholars at their medical schools. In doing so, he hoped to get to know the scholars individually and explain the foundation's new mission, but this meant weeks on the road during his first year in office.

Morrisett also decided to continue the lavish rite of annual scholars meetings. Under Russell's presidency, the meetings had been held in such vacation havens as Aspen, Lake Placid, Jasper National Park in Alberta, and Yosemite. Expenses were always paid for the scholars and their spouses. Guest speakers, along with entertainment and dinner dances, were customarily featured. In 1969, the meeting at the Williamsburg Lodge in Virginia cost nearly $50,000.

The meetings hosted by Morrisett rivaled his predecessor's in opulence: Harrison Hot Springs, British Columbia, in 1970; Dorado Beach Hotel, Puerto Rico, in 1971; Castle Harbour, Bermuda, in 1972; Hotel Del Coronado, San Diego, in 1973; and The Homestead, Hot Springs, Virginia, in 1974. More than three hundred scholars and spouses attended the final meeting, all expenses paid, at a cost of $56,511.[78]

In an adroit move, Morrisett encouraged the scholars to form their own committee to explore whether their program could survive on its own or with outside backing from the Association of American Medical Colleges or some other foundation. The committee, chaired by Dr. Alexander M. Schmidt, former head of the U.S. Food and Drug Administration, met several times during 1969 and 1970 and concluded that there was little point in dragging out the inevitable end. In effect, Morrisett had placed the scholars in the position of signing their program's death warrant.

Such steps, however, did not spare Morrisett some of the most uncomfortable moments of his presidency. The first occurred just a month after Morrisett assumed office, at 8 p.m., October 1, as he was being introduced for the first time to the 321 scholars and spouses at their annual meeting after dinner in the Virginia Room at the Williamsburg Lodge. Ironically, the theme of the annual meeting was "Problems in Communications," an accurate if unintended characterization of what followed at the meeting itself. Some of the scholars seemed determined to give the new president a chilly greeting. Morrisett would later call that first meeting "very difficult."

"Many, the majority, thought it was incredible that the foundation would turn away from the program that they loved. There were attempted insurgencies, groups that said they would get together and talk to the board and tell them that this wasn't the thing to do, and to get the Scholar program to be continued. Nothing ever came of that, though I suspect some of the board members were talked to. That was a very difficult time as far as I was concerned," Morrisett said.[79]

In fact, for the new president, it was two days of almost nonstop abuse, and the resentments still festered a year later when the scholars met at Harrison Hot Springs in October 1970. This time, Morrisett brought along his *Sesame Street* colleague and friend from his Yale graduate school days, Gerald Lesser, to help explain the foundation's new mission to the scholars. As he and Morrisett showed video segments of *Sesame Street* to the doctors, "there was almost a revolution," Lesser recalled. "*Sesame Street* was a pretty substantial distance from anything those doctors understood. They almost tossed us across the Canadian border."[80]

Whatever emotions he felt, Morrisett held his fire. The scholars were a valuable source of long-term expertise and prestige well worth mollifying. (Indeed, twenty-eight years later when Morrisett was preparing to retire, the foundation even agreed to host a reunion of the scholars and their wives at a resort hotel in Phoenix, Arizona, at a cost of $250,000, to commemorate the fiftieth anniversary of the start of the Markle Scholars Program.) Still, it was clear in those early years that Morrisett and Lesser were trying to describe a communications revolution to a largely uncomprehending and unsympathetic audience.

Eventually, the raw feelings faded and the new mission was accepted. In the background, John Russell proved a firm ally. Until Russell's death in March 1986 at age eighty-three, he and Morrisett corresponded regularly. Russell's notes were always extravagant in praising Morrisett's initiatives.

The friendly overtures to the scholars eventually paid off. The combination of Morrisett's diplomacy and the foundation's growing track record in the communications field gained him allies among the scholars. As Morrisett shifted the foundation's focus to communications, he decided to draw upon Markle's pool of medical expertise. Several of his first projects blended the foundation's accumulated knowledge in medicine with its newer interests in the media. These, in turn, helped coax the scholars into the fold of the foundation's new mission.

In September 1969, Morrisett met with a Markle Scholar, Dr. Richard Bergland, professor of neurosurgery at Pennsylvania State University, about the possibility of making television videotapes for use in medical instruction. The result, six months later, was a $340,000 grant to the Society of Neurosurgeons Research Foundation, Inc., to develop tapes demonstrating neurosurgical operations in 1970. There were some two thousand neurosurgeons in the United States at the time, many practicing in remote areas with little access to the latest techniques. The idea was to produce and distribute about twenty films demonstrating advanced or unusual neurosurgical methods. The audiovisual kits were favorably reviewed in 1973 in the New England Journal of Medicine. Thereafter, television became an integral part of almost every neurosurgery training program in the United States.

Other attempts by Markle to marry medicine and the media were not as smooth. In 1972, the foundation sought to begin a television series to carry health information for young adults and their parents. Though aimed at an adult audience, Morrisett turned to the Children's Television Workshop to produce it. The resulting twenty-six-week prime time series, called *Feeling Good*, premiered in the fall of 1974 on 240 Public Broadcasting Service (PBS) stations, with $7 million in funding from Markle, the Robert Wood Johnson Foundation, the Corporation for Public Broadcasting, and a range of corporate backers. The programs used the *Sesame Street* formula of catchy songs, animated cartoons, and mock commercials to convey serious educational content. Radio humorists Bob Elliot and Ray Gould were recruited to write songs for the series. Joan Cooney described it as "the most ambitious attempt yet to use television on a regular basis to convey health information."[81] Still, reviewers and adult audiences never responded warmly to the *Sesame Street*–style production antics.

Another early effort to produce health-related television programming also misfired but for different reasons. In 1972, Markle provided $350,000 to the University of California–San Francisco Medical School to produce a year's worth of three-minute health education features for use on commercial television newscasts. The target audiences would be the poor, minority groups, the elderly, working parents, and youth.[82]

As Morrisett would quickly discover, the idea of offering educational programming during precious evening hours challenged the core economics of commercial broadcasters. One unknown was whether television stations would want the health spots in the first place. An even tougher question was whether stations would be willing to pay for the spots once the start-up money from Markle was exhausted.

The health spots, titled "Vital Signs," were well produced and provided health advice on a range of everyday subjects from hypertension, chronic fatigue syndrome, aching backs, and cancer to what should be in medicine chests. They featured informed reporters and even a former Miss America, Nancy Fleming. During 1973, when they were offered at no cost, local television stations eagerly snapped them up. Sixty-three local stations from New Orleans to Oklahoma City to Paducah, Kentucky, ran the health programs, which reached an estimated 44 million viewers.[83]

The project demonstrated that television newscasts were an excellent medium for providing educational content. Yet, by mid-1974, the series collapsed. Not a single television station ran the spots once the programs were no longer offered free. The point was painfully clear: even the best public service or educational programming never would be self-sustaining because it challenged broadcasters to fill airtime with programming that would cost them money, rather than with revenue-producing commercials. And Markle, with its limited resources, was in no position to pump funds endlessly into such television production projects to keep them alive.

"That," Morrisett told the author years later, "was a very interesting economic lesson about the television world for us."[84] It was a lesson that would repeat itself in Markle's ventures in the future.

NOTES

1. Susan Kastan, "John Markle: 1858–1933" (biography prepared for The Markle Foundation's World Wide Web site), 25 Mar. 1997, 5.
2. Susan Kastan, "Mary R. Markle: 1860–1927" (biography prepared for The Markle Foundation's World Wide Web site), 25 Mar. 1997, 1.
3. Kastan, "John Markle," 4.
4. The Associated Press, "His Wealth to Mankind: John Markle Is Carrying His Life Code into Effect," *The New York Times*, 4 Feb. 1927.
5. "John Markle, Philanthropist, Coal Man, Dies," *The New York Times*, 11 July 1933.
6. Ibid.
7. Ibid.
8. Lloyd N. Morrisett, "The History of the Markle Foundation," in *The John and Mary R. Markle Foundation: Information* (foundation pamphlet), 1985, 5.

9. Lloyd N. Morrisett, "The John and Mary R. Markle Foundation" (paper prepared for a conference at the Rockefeller Archive Center), 14 Oct. 1979, 2.
10. Strickland and Strickland, *Markle Scholars*, 6.
11. Ibid., 11.
12. Ibid., 12–14.
13. Ibid., 16.
14. Markle Board of Directors, minutes of meeting, 21 June 1968, 2.
15. Wallace, interview, 22 July 1997.
16. Donald B. Straus, "Report to the Directors of The John and Mary Markle Foundation on the Program of Scholars in Medical Science," Sept. 1962, 30.
17. Strickland and Strickland, *Markle Scholars*, 43.
18. "The John and Mary R. Markle Foundation, Annual Report, 1954–55," 9.
19. The Markle Foundation, news release announcing Courtney Smith's designation as president, 17 July 1968, 1.
20. Stapleton, interview, 7 July 1997. (Dr. Darwin H. Stapleton, a Markle Scholar, and his wife, Donna H. Stapleton, are preparing a biography of Courtney Smith).
21. Ibid.
22. Ibid.
23. Ibid.
24. Committee on Future Plans, minutes, 31 Mar. 1967.
25. Courtney Smith, memorandum to Stuart Cragin, Jarvis Cromwell, Walter Page, and William Rees, 27 Mar 1967.
26. Committee on Future Plans, minutes, 29 June 1967.
27. Courtney Smith, "Report from Committee on Future Plans," memorandum to Board of Directors, The Markle Foundation, n.d., 1–2.
28. Ibid., 2–5.
29. Committee on Future Plans, minutes, 20 June 1968, 2.
30. Stapleton, interview, 7 July 1997.
31. Walton, *Swarthmore College*, 74.
32. Stapleton, interview, 7 July 1997.
33. Courtney Smith, "Statement to Faculty and Students," 13 Jan. 1969; text reprinted in *The Phoenix*, Swarthmore College student newspaper, 14 Jan. 1969.
34. Rees, interviews, 1 and 8 July 1997.
35. Perkins, interview, 27 June 1997.
36. Gardner, interview, 15 May 1998.
37. Morrisett, interview, 2 July 1997.
38. Strickland and Strickland, Markle Scholars, 75–81.

39. Pitney, interview, 21 Oct. 1997.

40. Rees, interview, 1 July 1997.

41. The appearance of Morrisett's name on Nixon's enemies list remained an unsolved curiosity years later. As reported in *The New York Times*, 28 June 1973, his name appeared under the heading "academics," and he was described as a "professor and associate director, Education Program, University of California." Although both he and his father had taught in California during their careers, the description would seem to fit more closely his namesake father. Still, Morrisett always assumed that the authors of Nixon's list had intended to include him, rather than his father, and had simply mixed up their credentials. As Morrisett explained to the author: "Actually, I could see no reason whatsoever that my father, a professor of education, would be on the list. In my case, foundation people might have been suspect, I was associated vaguely with public broadcasting, and foundations were being attacked as liberal institutions that had overstepped their legal mandates. As a result, I have always thought that I was the rightful heir to the title. In retrospect, I believe that some parts of the Nixon administration were so inept that my inclusion could have been a mistake. It was, to say the least, weird."

42. Morrisett, interview, 16 July 1997.

43. Ibid.

44. Morrisett served on Oberlin's board of directors, 1972–88, and was board chairman, 1975–81.

45. Morrisett, interview, 2 July 1997.

46. Shepard, *Carl Ivor Hovland*, 246.

47. Lloyd N. Morrisett, "Standing on the Shoulders of Giants" (address, 1997 Markle Foundation annual dinner), 20 Apr. 1997, 11.

48. Morrisett, interview, 2 July 1997.

49. Ibid.

50. Lloyd N. Morrisett, "A National Assessment of Educational Progress," (address, National Association of Manufacturers Education Committee Spring Meeting, Washington, D.C., 2 Apr. 1969), 7.

51. Lloyd N. Morrisett, interview by Robert Davidson, in *Children's Television Workshop: The Early Years* (transcript of oral history, part of a collection of oral histories published by Children's Television Workshop on the 25th anniversary of CTW), March 1993, 32.

52. Lloyd N. Morrisett, reconstruction of conversation with Cooney, in ibid, 33.

53. Morrisett, interview, 16 July 1997.

54. Joan Ganz Cooney, interview by Davidson, in *Children's Television Workshop: The Early Years* (transcript), 19.

55. Lloyd N. Morrisett, "*Sesame Street* May Be Path for Other Technologies in Teaching," *The New York Times*, op-ed, 11 Jan. 1971.

56. Cooney, interview, 9 Sept. 1997.
57. Chisman, interview, 8 July 1997.
58. Day, *Vanishing Vision*, 167.
59. Carnegie Corporation Project, Lloyd N. Morrisett, interview by Isabel Grossner, 19 July, 1967, 46.
60. Gardner, interview, 15 May 1998.
61. O'Donnell, interview, 19 Nov. 1997.
62. Fleishman, interview, 13 Oct. 1997.
63. Markle staff meeting, September 1988 (taped transcript).
64. Lester Markel, letter to Lloyd N. Morrisett, 29 Feb. 1972.
65. Lloyd N. Morrisett, letter to Lester Markel, 17 Mar. 1972.
66. Morrisett, interview, 16 July 1997.
67. Chisman, interview, 8 July 1997.
68. Carnegie Corporation Project, interview of Morrisett by Grossner, 32.
69. Morrisett, interview, 29 June 1998.
70. John Russell, conversation with Lloyd N. Morrisett, 6 Mar. 1969 (written record).
71. Stuart W. Cragin, letter, "To the Friends of the Foundation" announcing the change in Markle's mission, 19 June 1969.
72. John M. Russell, letter (reprinted in "The John and Mary R. Markle Foundation, Annual Report, 1968–1969,)" 5–6.
73. Board of Directors, The Markle Foundation, minutes of meeting, 22 Oct. 1969, 3. According to longtime Foundation Secretary Dolores Miller, the foundation was headquartered at 50 Rockefeller Plaza until June 1987 when it moved to its offices at 75 Rockefeller Plaza. The foundation moved its headquarters in 2000 to 10 Rockefeller Plaza.
74. Ibid.
75. Lloyd N. Morrisett, letter to Winston O. Franklin, Staff Consultant, Charles F. Kettering Foundation, 25 Nov. 1969.
76. Chisman stayed at Markle until 1975 and eventually became director the Southport Institute for Policy Analysis in Washington, D.C.
77. "The John and Mary R. Markle Foundation, Annual Report, 1969–1970," Report of the Treasurer, 69, 73.
78. "The John and Mary R. Markle Foundation, Annual Report, 1973–1974," Report of the Treasurer, 72.
79. Morrisett, interview, 2 July 1997.
80. Lesser, interview, 14 July 1997.
81. Children's Television Workshop, news release announcing prime-time health series, 13 Nov. 1973.
82. Lloyd N. Morrisett, interview with faculty and administration members at University of California–San Francisco, 12 Oct. 1972 (written record).

83. Leona M. Butler, "The Demonstration of a New Approach to the Use of Commercial Television in Health Education for the General Public" (report prepared for The Markle Foundation), 1 Nov. 1973, 9–10.

84. Morrisett, interview, 16 July 1997.

2

Beyond Big Bird: Markle and Children's Television

THE MORRISETTS were early risers in the 1960s. The older daughter, Sarah Elizabeth, was often awake by 7 A.M. and, like many children, headed from bed straight to the television set. Morrisett sometimes looked on as she sat in front of the screen, transfixed by nothing more than station test patterns and commercials. Television, he decided, must have something mighty powerful about it if it could so mesmerize young viewers. If this medium, present in 96 percent of American living rooms, was so devastatingly effective at selling cola, candy, and Barbie dolls, Morrisett wondered, could its power also be harnessed to solve the nation's most vexing educational problems?

As Morrisett was beginning his presidency at Markle, however, the concept of using television as a teacher was by no means universally accepted. It was, and remains thirty years later, alien to the ethos of commercial network programmers or advertisers and, for that matter, of many educators. Cy Schneider, a veteran advertising executive whose work dates from *The Mickey Mouse Club* and who later helped found the cable TV network Nickelodeon, served up the cold truth about how network programmers view children: "Television is not there to instruct kids. Kids don't want to be instructed. They go to school for that. They expect to be entertained by television, but that isn't television's responsibility, either. Television's real responsibility is to corral an audience to watch commercials, because without the commercial it doesn't exist, except public television."[1]

Even on public television, Morrisett's ideas about purposeful educational programming for young children were novel in the 1960s. "Educational television," as public television was commonly called in its early years, was still just a gangling teen in a growth spurt but with little money to fill out its frame with quality programming.

The first educational television station was established in 1953. By 1966, there were 114 educational television stations around the country—a disunited agglomeration licensed most often to states, local governments, and universities.[2] Twenty-four-hour programming was unheard of. The broadcast day of the flagship public station WNET Channel 13 in New York was six hours long, from 5:30 P.M. to 11:30 P.M. State and local governments carried much of the operating costs of those stations, but, through the mid-1960s, the Ford Foundation provided $120 million to keep educational television alive.[3]

A large share of programming came from National Educational Television (NET), with which nearly all educational stations were affiliated. During the 1960s, $6 million of NET's $8 million annual budget came from Ford.[4] NET produced no programming on its own, but it procured and distributed five hours of public affairs and cultural programming each week, much of it from the British Broadcasting Corporation. It provided a meager two and a half hours a week of children's programming.[5]

By the late '60s, only 12.5 percent of U.S. households watched any educational television during an average week.[6] Those who did were overwhelmingly older and highly educated, and much of the programming catered to them. A study of two of the largest educational stations, WQED in Pittsburgh and WGBH in Boston, found that, in March 1966, fewer than 5 percent of viewers were students.[7]

What was called "educational TV" in the 1960s, then, was predominantly adult education. Almost nothing of value for children existed before Morrisett and Cooney developed *Sesame Street.*

In 1967, when Morrisett was vice president of the Carnegie Corporation, the Carnegie Commission on Educational Television proposed that a federally chartered, nonprofit, and nongovernmental "Corporation for Public Television" be formed to "receive and disburse governmental and private funds in order to extend and improve public television programming."[8] That year, Congress approved and President Johnson signed the Public Broadcasting Act. That led, in 1968, to the uneasy partnership between the Corporation for Public Broadcasting, whose purpose was to funnel money into station development and programming, and the Public Broadcasting Service, which was supposed to manage the loose confederation of local public stations.

As Markle prepared to turn its attention to mass communications, the corporation was hardly America's answer to the world-renowned BBC. So feeble and underfunded was it that a *New York Times* editorial dismissed it as "a butterfly without wings."[9] Certainly, its ability to draw audiences was no match for the high-gloss programming offered by the commercial networks.

Beyond the weakness of public broadcasting in its early days, there was an even larger reality militating against genuine educational programming. Throughout its history, the broadcast media, and most especially television, existed to gather the largest possible audiences and deliver them to advertisers. Programming decisions by networks were usually composed of equal parts of conformity and cowardice. They were certainly not routinely driven by any notion of serving the specific needs of the young, the old, or any other special group. Only a few months before Morrisett assumed Markle's presidency, in fact, commercial television glaringly demonstrated its devotion to homogeneity by canceling CBS's *Smothers Brothers Comedy Hour.* Despite high ratings and loyal following, the show's mildly acidic political humor proved too pungent for the network to handle.

Children, especially, were under the spell of television no matter how time wasting or silly the offerings. According to estimates, preschool children were averaging as much as fifty hours per week of television viewing, more hours than any other age group.[10] What they watched was less than worthless. In 1969, children could fill every waking hour with *Bozo the Clown*, *The Munsters*, *F-Troop*, *The Three Stooges*, *The Beverly Hillbillies*, *Batman*, *Abbott and Costello*, cartoons, and still more cartoons. Virtually alone in this "vast wasteland"—as former Federal Communications Commission (FCC) Chairman Newton N. Minow enduringly branded TV in his 1961 speech to broadcasters—were the commendable *Mister Rogers' Neighborhood* on public television, the gentle puppets on NBC's *The Shari Lewis Show,* and CBS's *Captain Kangaroo.* Beyond these programs, not a single redeeming children's show appeared on commercial television during the prime after-school, predinner hours between 4:30 and 6:30 P.M.

Even worse, children's entertainment often featured violence or racial and gender stereotyping. One minute of every five in children's programming was devoted to commercials, twice as many as on the typical prime-time adult show. Overwhelmingly, the products peddled were sugar-laden vitamins or cereals, fast-food burgers, candy, and soft drinks.

Minow's "wasteland speech" threw a temporary scare into the three commercial networks. They responded by offering a half-hearted assortment of "quality" children's programming with names such as *Exploring* and *1,2,3 Go* to ward off further scrutiny or regulation. But those shows, whatever their educational value, were generally not entertaining or produced well enough to compete with other commercial offerings.

How could it be, Morrisett wondered, that so little time, money, or research was being devoted to this endless neglect of broadcasting's potential by government, academia, and, especially, foundations?

SUPPORTING THE WORKSHOP

Because Morrisett was one of the founding parents of the Children's Television Workshop and its board chairman for twenty-eight years, his contribution to the workshop was both clear-cut and sustained. As president of The Markle Foundation, however, his relationship with the workshop was more sporadic and indirect, and he dealt mainly with the support of research that helped verify the educational and social value of *Sesame Street* and other programs.

In October 1969, not surprisingly, the first major grant of Morrisett's presidency, $250,000, went to CTW. Indeed, Morrisett had made the grant a virtual condition for his accepting the foundation's presidency. For the foundation, the grant was a virtually risk-free way to announce its presence in the mass communications world. Besides, Morrisett relished the thought of seeing the name of The Markle Foundation, as a major funder, roll across the TV screen every time *Sesame Street* aired. "Getting credit on the air was very useful to Markle," he explained, "because it announced that we were in this field, that we were an important player."[11]

"Preschoolers view more television than anyone else, and society has a special obligation to see that they are well-served," Morrisett said at the time. "The Children's Television Workshop is a vital new attempt to combine education and entertainment in a way that will help prepare children for first grade."[12]

Despite this initial grant and others that followed, Morrisett's personal role at the workshop over the years was far greater than anything that The Markle Foundation itself did. He became chairman of CTW in March 1970 when it was incorporated as a nonprofit organization. He was, in fact, quite busy with the workshop during his first months as Markle's president. Following the premier of *Sesame Street,* Morrisett took an active hand in developing *Electric Company,* which aired in October 1971, ran for six seasons, and was the first regular series to attempt to teach reading to elementary school youngsters who were having difficulty with that skill.

As the workshop's chairman, his main goals were to keep CTW true to its root mission of education, to ensure its financial independence, and to stay abreast of new technologies that might serve as effective teaching tools. Over the years, he was credited with encouraging CTW to undertake a variety of ventures that freed it from reliance on government and foundation support. Some of these undertakings involved cable television, interactive computers, and the opening of new theme parks.

There was also an obvious synergy between the workshop's activities and the emerging mass communications mission at Markle. Throughout Morrisett's presidency, but especially during the 1970s, the two organizations shared ideas, collaborated on projects, and provided each other with talented individuals. CTW personalities, including Joan Cooney, Gerald Lesser, and Franz Allina, participated in or advised numerous Markle projects. Lesser, for example, received a research grant from Markle in 1970 to study how television captures the interests of children and another grant later on to study how effectively *Sesame Street* was achieving its educational objectives. Allina contributed to Markle's cable television projects during the 1970s. Cooney served on the National News Council, Markle's unsuccessful initiative during the 1970s to make the news media more publicly accountable.

One of the early dilemmas faced by the workshop was how to ensure that *Sesame Street* was reaching children from disadvantaged backgrounds who most needed help with school readiness and literacy. An early Markle-financed initiative, called Sesame Mothers, sought to address that problem. In April 1970, the Institute for Educational Development, a nonprofit research and development corporation, proposed an experiment to recruit volunteer inner-city mothers in Chicago and Los Angeles to act as community leaders and to invite five or ten children to watch *Sesame Street* in each of their homes and to work with instructional materials.[13] The project, which cost Markle $169,000 and lasted through mid-1971, succeeded in attracting scores of mothers and hundreds of children in both cities. The project foundered after a year, however, having failed to achieve its larger goal of spawning a nationally televised "pre–Head Start" program. Such ambitions were clearly beyond the resources of Markle, Morrisett would later tell the institute's president, Sidney Marland.[14] Besides, by then, the obvious source of continued funding, the U.S. Office of Education, was far less politically inclined to sink millions of research dollars into a Great Society–style project such as Sesame Mothers.

Sesame Street's production quality, popularity, and accomplishments as an educational vehicle would remain unrivalled for the next thirty years. Expensive as it was, it put to rest any doubts that television could combine humor, surprise, and lack of preachiness while addressing specific and urgent educational goals. Thanks in part to extensive research financed by Markle, it became, by far, the most studied and analyzed television program in history. The conclusions were consistent: children who watched excellent educational programs such as *Sesame Street* tended to do better academically, not just in the early years but right through high school.

STUDYING CHILDREN'S TELEVISION

In dollar terms, Markle's support for research on strengthening the quality and content of children's television was fairly modest, possibly a reflection of Morrisett's growing puzzlement about how to translate theory into widespread practice. During Morrisett's presidency, the foundation awarded a total of $2.9 million for fifty-six such grants. The period of heaviest concentration was between 1969 and 1980, when children's welfare was still high on federal and foundation agendas. The research topics ranged from the straightforward to the esoteric, but the four principles that were the watchwords of Morrisett's entire presidency—equity, access, quality, and content—set the tone for those explorations.

Markle funded a 1972 study at the University of Pennsylvania's Annenberg School of Communications to examine ways to free children's programming from the bondage of commercial advertising. A 1973 paper examined how persons of color were treated on network children's television. That same year, William H. Melody of the Annenberg School produced a widely publicized critique of commercials on children's television, "Children's Television: The Economics of Exploitation."

Faculty at the University of Wisconsin's Mass Communications Research Center produced an analysis of adolescent television use. A study by two University of Minnesota researchers examined what sorts of lessons children were learning about family and personal conflicts on such network programs as *All in the Family*, *Happy Days*, and *The Waltons*. In 1977, Markle funded a report examining the feasibility of creating a "National Endowment for Children's Broadcasting" to supply needed financing for quality programming. Ten years later, in 1987, Peggy Charren, president of Action for Children's Television, coauthored a Markle-backed study, "TV News & Children," with Carol Hulsizer.

One of the more intriguing projects was an attempt in the mid-1970s to study the effects of television on children in Micronesia and South Africa, among the last remaining places on earth where entire populations of children were still growing up without TV. The idea originated with the Micronesian Congress, which was alarmed by the creeping influence of modern media on their relatively violence-free culture. There had been frightening local rumors of rapes after films depicting violence or sexual assaults were shown on the remote islands. The prospect of television's arrival left this isolated culture deeply uneasy.[15]

The Micronesian Congress approached Paul Ekman, a professor of medical psychology at the University of California–San Francisco with strong research credentials. He had helped write the Surgeon General's 1972 report on television violence. He also had a career research award from the National Institute of Mental Health and had been doing pioneering work on the subject of human emotions and nonverbal behavior. In 1972, Ekman approached Markle for a grant to support the Micronesian project and a similar effort in South Africa.

The prospect of taking advantage of this last opportunity in human history to study the effects of television on children growing up in a virtually TV-free society, though clearly risky, was electrifying at Markle. In 1973, the foundation granted Ekman $112,000 for the studies, with additional funding from the National Institute of Mental Health. What followed, however, was a classic case of how bad luck and politics could combine to undo a seemingly well-conceived social scientific scheme.

The design of the experiment seemed straightforward enough. In Micronesia, English-speaking high school students of the Marshall Islands would be exposed to several hours per week of American television programs either with "pro-social" constructive behavior—such as Mister Rogers—or more antisocial, aggressive behavior. The students then would be observed in their playgrounds to see how, if at all, television had changed their behavior.[16]

As Ekman would later describe it, the issue of parental consent was the project's downfall. Students in the Pacific Islands often came from homes that were hundreds, even thousands, of miles away. It was therefore nearly impossible to gain parental consent for them to take part in the project. Instead, Ekman received a broad agreement from the Micronesian government to do the work and to obtain the cooperation of village elders under whose jurisdiction each high school fell.[17]

That wasn't enough to satisfy Ekman's own university. Like others throughout the United States, the University of California had established a "committee on human subjects" to ensure that faculty conducting experiments that involved minors followed rigorous procedures for parental consent. Thirteen months went by as Ekman quarreled with his university over the lack of such formal consent. Finally, the committee agreed to let the project go forward if it got a letter of consent directly from the Micronesian Congress. Incensed by this seeming intrusion into its sovereign decision making by an American university, the congress coldly refused.[18]

The final blow came shortly afterward. Commercial television arrived in Micronesia in 1975, thus rendering the experiment meaningless.

Ekman fared no better in South Africa. The project was to be similarly conducted among black South Africans, except that local researchers, rather than foreigners, would do the field work. The experiment, in fact, proceeded smoothly. But the South African government would never permit release of the data—probably because they feared, Ekman assumed, that the results might be racially sensitive.

For Ekman, the project was a disappointment and a waste of two years, though he recalled years later that Markle and Morrisett remained patient and understanding throughout. After his discouraging experiences, Ekman vowed never again to do research on television.[19]

"I've always preferred to do high-risk research. That's how you find out something interesting," Ekman said. "But it's much harder to do that now. Maybe Markle would still fund it. But this kind of work would never be supported now, at least not by the federal government."[20]

A more successful example of Markle's research was the work done on children's television at Harvard's Graduate School of Education during the 1970s. Howard Gardner, a renowned developmental psychologist and the founder of "Project Zero," which studied how children learn by using the arts, produced a considerable body of work on how children first encounter and understand television. From 1976 to 1979, Gardner and his codirector, Laurene K. Meringoff, used Markle funds for a project called "Children—Stories—Media," which produced a series of studies on the viewing habits and levels of understanding of preschool children. How well, for example, do children separate fact from fantasy in television? How do they correlate the traits of cartoon superheroes to the behavior of real people? Do children end up wishing they were television characters with unrealistic attributes, or do they respond to more true-to-life characters on television? How well do young children distinguish between commercial messages and regular programming? Gardner stated:

> Probably the most striking general outcome of this series of studies is a documentation of the extreme rapidity of the children's learning about television, and the broad range of information and viewing skills acquired.
>
> Although they receive little direct tutelage from their parents, and although many facets of television turn out to be quite complex, even covert, these children have by school age already made most important distinctions concerning the nature of various special programming features (e.g., commercials, previews, and channels), and various of the relationships between television fare and everyday life."[21]

Gardner's work also went to the heart of Markle's concerns about television-as-teacher. Do children really connect what they learn on television to their own lives? Here, the findings were murkier: "It is . . . unclear," Gardner wrote, "to what extent the children actually invoke the knowledge they have accumulated during their normal viewing of television, as opposed to simply producing it upon an experimenter's request."[22]

Gerald Lesser, Morrisett's old friend and Children's Television Workshop colleague, was another productive source of research at Harvard during that period. In 1972, the foundation granted Lesser $72,000 to start the Center for Research in Children's Television. Continuing to function until the late 1980s, the Harvard-based center produced some twenty major research publications. During its early years, it served as a research arm for CTW. The idea, Lesser wrote in his grant proposal, was that Harvard faculty would benefit from contact with the workshop and its expertise in children's programming. Harvard, for its part, would provide basic research on children's television that CTW was not in a position to conduct.[23]

One of the more intriguing products of Harvard's research dealt with children's eye movements. As Lesser later recalled, CTW and Morrisett were deeply engrossed at the time in producing *Electric Company.* "No one had a real good idea how to teach reading over television," Lesser said. "It almost sounded like an oxymoron, since TV and reading were thought to be alien."

He realized that "you have to know precisely what you need to do to get kids to pay attention to print on the television screen."[24] Simply put, where on the television screen should the print appear so that children are most likely to read it?

Lesser set up a laboratory to study children's eye movements as they watched television. "We found out that kids' eyes roam the periphery of the screen. They don't stay fixed on the center."[25] As *Electric Company* was being developed during the early 1970s, the Harvard researchers met frequently with the workshop's producers and their findings on eye movements were directly applied to the television programs.

FOUR LADIES FROM BOSTON: ACTION FOR CHILDREN'S TELEVISION

The Markle Foundation, as distinct from its president, might claim only incidental credit for nurturing *Sesame Street* and the Children's Television Workshop. The foundation could take far more credit, however, for bringing to life another of broadcasting's most important and enduring maverick voices: Action for Children's Television, a grassroots group founded in January 1968 by Peggy Charren and three other suburban Boston working mothers.

The "four ladies from Boston," as they became known at Markle, became favorites of Morrisett's. Between 1971 and 1991, Action for Children's Television (ACT) would receive more frequent and sustained support from Markle than any other person or organization in the children's television field. As with the gregarious Joan Cooney, Charren was a perfect foil for the publicity-shy Morrisett. For more than two decades, no one in America was more visible or effective in making children's programming a priority in Congress and on front pages.

Charren had grown up with two driving passions, a love of

books and an equally strong devotion to the First Amendment. "I grew up with McCarthyism," she recalled. "I had an uncle who was kicked out of Hollywood, a screenwriter. That's a central factor of who I am."[26]

After a youthful stint of running the film department at New York's WPIX television station in 1949, Charren married, moved to New England, and started a book fair business. She might have done that forever if not for the conflicting demands imposed by the birth of her first daughter. As time passed, she wondered what she might do with herself that would be of broader significance. Her thoughts turned to television—was there some way she could get book-based programming on the air?

"I thought it would lead kids back to books," Charren said. "And that's how I got started with ACT, to see if I could help make children's television as diverse and delightful as a good children's library. I thought the whole thing would take two or three years. I thought the television market would expand to accommodate book programs. How about that for naivete?"[27]

In 1968, Charren began gathering fellow Newton mothers in her living room to talk about television violence and what they might do to get more and better children's shows on the air. She studied the Federal Communications Commission (FCC) and the regulatory laws affecting television licensing. Before long, however, the group shrank to the nucleus of the four women who would eventually found ACT. In addition to Charren, they included Evelyn Sarson, a British native and a journalist; Lillian Ambrosino, a Harvard-educated teacher and educational radio producer; and Judith Chalfen, who also worked in commercial and educational programming.

From 1968 to 1970, the four working mothers kept their infant organization alive with their own money and the $3 annual dues received from about 240 ACT members. With Charren's natural gift for publicity, respect for factual research, and a guerrilla style of public protest that appealed to newspaper columnists and others, ACT was making an impact far out of proportion to its tiny size and budget. Early on, for example, its members did something no one else had bothered to do. They counted the minutes of commercial and product promotion time on various children's programs, including the well-regarded *Romper Room*, which presented itself as a wholesome, televised "school" for children under age five.

"What we found," Charren and the other mothers wrote at the time, "surprised even us. The teacher sold products, encouraged the children to join her in presenting the commercials or in using the products sold in some way. Virtually all the toys and materials used on the programs had some association with the Romper Room name. And the whole program, in effect, was a commercial for Romper Room products."[28]

The ACT mothers presented their findings before two Senate hearings. In February 1970, they gained further respect for providing a well-reasoned brief to the FCC that proposed an outright ban on selling by hosts on children's television.

In October 1970, the ACT mothers made fresh headlines by taking to the streets of Boston to protest a local television station that had cut the hour-long *Captain Kangaroo* in half to make room for the popular but inane *Bozo the Clown*. They gathered 2,500 signatures on petitions to restore *Captain Kangaroo* and organized a picket of the TV station that included children carrying balloons. With local news cameras running, the station did itself no particular good by denying the use of its bathrooms by the picketing children. A couple of months later, the station caved in and restored *Captain Kangaroo* to its full hour.

Even before ACT had any money from outside sources, Charren and her small group were challenging national network brass to meet their demands for better children's programs. In 1968, they wrote to the heads of all three networks and asked to meet with them. CBS was the only one that agreed.

The meeting went poorly at first. Charren and her companions found themselves seated with a small group of polite but mildly condescending middle managers. Losing patience, Charren demanded to see Michael Dann, the head of CBS network programming. To her surprise, the executives agreed to hunt him down. When he arrived, Charren grinned and played her winning card: "Mike, how are you?" she said. "I go bird-watching with your wife on Martha's Vineyard."[29]

From that moment, Charren recalled, the tone of the meeting changed from amused condescension to respect. She asked Dann why CBS, with all its middle managers and vice presidents, had no one in charge of children's programming. Dann commented that it was an interesting point. "A week later," Charren said, "they appointed one. It was just window dressing, but we had actually done something."[30]

Despite its early successes, it was clear by 1970 that ACT could not survive without substantial outside funding. Then, Charren learned that the man who had sired *Sesame Street* had taken over the Markle Foundation, but it would take a year and several meetings for Morrisett to warm to either Charren or ACT.

In their grant proposal to Morrisett in January 1970, Charren and her partners wrote:

> Success would not only hopefully lead to the improvement of television via a new attitude toward children. It might restore some measure of faith in established institutions. These are days of despair, of turning to new and extreme answers for old problems. In calling a lucrative industry's attention to its social responsibility, we are no different than those who would end the pollution of our atmosphere, and by so doing save us all. . . .
>
> Will you help?[31]

Help came, but not quickly. Morrisett agreed to meet Charren, Ambrosino, and Sarson for the first time in March 1970. They came away encouraged but empty-handed. Six months passed. Hearing no further word from Markle, they wrote again in August to tell Morrisett that time was running out for ACT. "We are in genuine trouble," they said. "We have letters from fourteen foundations declining to give us funds while congratulating us on our splendid work."[32]

Even that plea did not produce much at first. Morrisett granted ACT $6,700, enough to pay a few office bills, out of his discretionary funds. Another meeting at Markle was arranged, this time with Morrisett's assistant, Hannah Bartlett, in January 1971.

Bartlett's assessment of ACT's grant request was glowing: "The 'ladies from Boston' proved quite attractive, articulate, and self-assured [far from the pushy, Women's Lib type]," she wrote Morrisett in her record of the meeting. "They have seen their organization become nationally known and the demand for information and services too much for them to handle as things stand. Therefore, they visualize their proposed . . . office becoming the headquarters of a national organization."[33]

On March 18, 1971, word finally came that Markle's board had approved a grant of $164,500. Over the next two decades, Markle would award ACT nine grants totaling $833,340—nine grants from a foundation that seldom gave any person or organization more than one or two.

"It was a miracle. It was mind-boggling," Charren said years later. "What always impressed me was Markle's reaction to ACT. If you give money where there's no track record, like us, that's a very tough grant to make. That first grant set us up as a force to be reckoned with."[34]

During the next twenty years, ACT and Charren would appear countless times in the headlines and before Congress, the Federal Trade Commission, and the FCC on behalf of children's television. Also, through its prodigious membership drives and with the help of the Carnegie Corporation and the Ford Foundation, ACT gained financial independence from Markle.

In May 1971, ACT asked parents to unplug their television sets for a single day and do other things with their children. In November 1971, ACT petitioned the Federal Trade Commission to ban vitamin ads on children's programming. A consent order in 1976 effectively ended such ads. In 1972, ACT representatives testified at the hearings held by Senator John Pastore, chairman of the Senate Communications Subcommittee, on television violence. Emphasizing that the reason for violence on TV was that it sells, the ACT members urged that children's television be freed from the pressures of commercialism. That same year, *Romper Room*'s hostesses stopped doing commercials. In 1974, ACT hosted an International Festival of Children's Television in Washington, D.C. It established an ACT Achievement in Children's Television award to commend people committed to producing quality material for young audiences.

During the Reagan years in the 1980s, ACT conducted signature campaigns to counteract efforts by the "Moral Majority" to censor television programming, and it waged a successful court battle to block the FCC from eliminating its policies dealing with the overcommercialization of children's television. ACT also began to focus on newer media, such as home video, and decried their use to plug toys and other commercial products, and it attacked expensive "900" telephone numbers designed to lure children to talk to their favorite cartoon characters or television heroes. In 1989, ACT campaigned unsuccessfully against Whittle Communications' plans to introduce commercial television into elementary and secondary schools.

ACT's crowning moment came at midnight, October 17, 1990, when the Children's Television Act, which limited the amount of commercials permitted in children's programming, became law. The Act further required that commercial broadcasters attend to the educational and information needs of children and required the FCC to ensure compliance. It was a cautious first step by Congress to rescue children from the wasteland.

In 1992, twenty-four years after its founding in Charren's living room, ACT went out of existence. Charren remained active in children's advocacy and still eagerly answered the many telephone calls from reporters, legislators, and others whenever the subject of children's TV came up.

ACT must be judged as one of Markle's most durable and effective accomplishments. It combined the energy and political savvy of four ladies from Boston and a foundation willing to back what seemed to be, at first, a very long shot after other funders had balked. As Charren said years later: "Without Markle, there would have been no Action for Children's Television."[35]

"THE OTHER SIDE WON"

"Signs are mounting," Morrisett wrote optimistically in his first presidential essay in 1970, "that the importance of television for children will not continue to be ignored in the future as much as it has been in the past."[36]

Time did not vindicate that early optimism.

Thanks in considerable measure to Morrisett's work as CTW's board chairman, *Sesame Street* in 1998 was completing its third decade as a worldwide institution. Thanks to research grants from Markle, the benefits of what Morrisett called "purposive" educational television—programs such as *Sesame Street* or *Electric Company* designed with deliberate teaching and learning goals in mind—have been convincingly documented. Sustained by Markle funds, Peggy Charren and ACT helped to raise the nation's consciousness about the effects of television violence and commercialism on children. And, as will be described in chapter 4, the coming of cable television increased the quantity, if not necessarily the quality, of children's programming. All of this took place, at least in part, because of the national dialogue on children's programming that Markle and those it supported helped to promote.

In 1995, Charren's efforts on behalf of better children's television earned her the Presidential Medal of Freedom. In 1990, Joan Cooney was inducted into the Academy of Television Arts and Sciences' Hall of Fame. Characteristically, the role of Morrisett and Markle in improving children's programming remained known mainly to the cognescenti of the broadcast and research communities.

Nothing that Markle or anyone else did, however, altered the harsh truth that educational programming remained alien to the profit-making and commercial imperatives of broadcasting. The crop of children's shows that appeared on cable was more plentiful and generally more benign than the shows that Morrisett's two daughters had known when they were growing up in the 1960s. Still, relatively little programming emerged that fostered learning in the deliberate way that *Sesame Street* had done. Like the welfare-bashing politicians of the 1980s who tried to pass off ketchup as a legitimate vegetable, networks in 1997 were passing off *Weird Al* and programs about National Basketball Association stars as "educational programming."[37]

Children's television gradually faded as a Markle priority during the 1980s and 1990s. "I became convinced," said Morrisett, "that television is frozen in an economic structure that makes it almost impossible to have significant change. It's not that the people in television are venal, it's not that they're not public spirited. It's that given the structure of television, practically speaking they can't make decisions other than the kinds that they make. So coming to that conviction after a lot of work, it just seemed to me there was really no reasonable way that we could have much of an impact."[38]

Still, the intriguing possibilities of television-as-teacher were never entirely out of Morrisett's thoughts. Four of his first dozen presidential essays were devoted to the need for better children's programming. As late as 1995, Markle was still funding occasional studies on children's television. Researchers at the University of Kansas and the University of Massachusetts, for example, documented that children who watched the most educational television, such as *Sesame Street*, did better academically, not only in elementary school but through high school as well.

By 1981, Morrisett conceded that "the optimism of my first essay (concerning children's television) has not been justified. . . . The public agenda has shifted. The problems of children once so compelling have been displaced by other pressing concerns. Increasing amounts of federal funds are no longer being directed toward new educational efforts. The flow of money that funded an advance in children's television has stopped. In addition, the current popular philosophy of deregulation has killed any hope that the FCC will mandate programming to serve children. Almost none of the forces that supported growth in quality television for children in 1969 remain strong."[39]

In 1983, as various government and foundation commissions made headlines decrying the "rising tide of mediocrity" of American education, Morrisett again dedicated his annual essay to children's television—this time, calling television "America's Neglected Teacher."[40]

Morrisett wrote:

> It is ironical that on the one hand we bemoan the quality of education in the United States while ignoring a teacher that is in the homes of 98 percent of all Americans.
>
> Like it or not, television has become a vital and integral part of the cultural and intellectual life of almost every child. . . . Researchers have been studying television and children for over twenty years and have produced more than three thousand scientific reports on its use and impact . . . but we have made remarkably limited application of what we have learned.[41]

Beyond question, Markle-financed advocates, such as Peggy Charren, and the body of research that the foundation supported at Harvard and elsewhere strengthened the case for the value of educational programming. In the end, however, if wide-scale improvement in children's television were truly possible, Morrisett no longer had much faith that any foundation, much less a small one, could effectively accomplish it in the post–Great Society climate.

"The bulk of children's television," Newton Minow told the author, "is financed largely on the air by toy manufacturers who see kids as a market rather than as children."[42]

Or, as Morrisett's Children's Television Workshop colleague Franz Allina glumly put it, "The other side won."[43]

NOTES

1. Quoted in Kisseloff, *The Box*, 463–4.
2. Carnegie Commission, *Public Television*, 239.
3. Ibid., 27.
4. Ibid.
5. Ibid., 23.
6. Ibid., 251.
7. Ibid., 254.
8. Ibid., 5.
9. *The New York Times*, 19 July 1968, editorial.
10. Lloyd N. Morrisett, "The Age of Television and the Television Age," (President's Essay in "The John and Mary R. Markle Foundation, Annual Report, 1969–70"), 5.
11. Morrisett, interview, 16 July 1997.
12. The Markle Foundation, press release announcing a $250,000 grant to the Children's Television Workshop, 6 Nov. 1969.
13. Institute for Educational Development, "Proposal to The Children's Television Workshop," 14 Apr 1970, 9–10.
14. Lloyd N. Morrisett, letter to Sidney Marland, 21 Oct. 1971.
15. Ekman, interview, 3 Sept. 1997.
16. Paul Ekman, "An Experimental Study in South Africa of the Effect of Aggressive and Prosocial Television Programming on the Social Behavior of Children" (proposal to The Markle Foundation), 1973.
17. Ekman, interview, 3 Sept. 1997.
18. Ibid.
19. Ibid.
20. Ibid.
21. Howard Gardner and Laurene K. Meringoff, "Fourth Annual Report to The Markle Foundation, December 1980: Children—Stories—Media," 3.
22. Ibid.
23. Lesser, interview, 28 Aug. 1997.
24. Ibid.

25. Ibid.

26. Charren, interview, 23 July 1997.

27. Ibid.

28. Peggy Charren, Evelyn Sarson, Lillian Ambrosino, Judith Chalfen, and Joanne Spiro, proposal to The Markle Foundation with request for funding, January 1970, 2–3.

29. Charren, interview, 23 July 1997.

30. Ibid.

31. Charren, Sarson, Ambrosino, Chalfen, and Spiro, proposal, 7–8.

32. Lillian Ambrosino, Judith Chalfen, Evelyn Sarson, and Peggy Charren, letter to Lloyd N. Morrisett, 1 Aug. 1970, 2.

33. Hannah Bartlett, Peggy Charren, Judith Chalfen, and Carol Liebman, record of interview at The Markle Foundation, 19 Jan. 1971.

34. Charren, interview, 23 July 1997.

35. Ibid.

36. Morrisett, "Age of Television," 7.

37. Lawrie Mifflin, "Can You Spell 'Compliance,' Boys and Girls?" *The New York Times*, 11 Sept. 1997, C13.

38. Morrisett, interview, 16 July 1997.

39. Lloyd N. Morrisett, "Paying for Children" (President's Essay in "The John and Mary R. Markle Foundation, Annual Report, 1980–1981"), 7–8.

40. Morrisett, "Television: America's Neglected Teacher" (President's Essay in "The John and Mary R. Markle Foundation, Annual Report, 1982–1983"), 7.

41. Ibid., 9.

42. Minow, interview, 18 Sept. 1997.

43. Allina, interview, 17 Sept. 1997.

3

The Diffusion of Knowledge

As Markle was entering the communications field in 1969, media worlds were set to collide.

Cheap and nearly universal access to new troves of entertainment, cultural, and educational programming and instantaneous two-way communication were just around the corner in workplaces and living rooms—all of this resulting from the convergence of an unprecedented flood of new technologies: computer microchips, cable television, satellites, fiber optics, and microwaves. Those same tools, however, were rapidly blurring historic boundaries that had long kept the peace among corporate titans and had prevented commercial warfare within and among the information industries.

As one of the century's leading social scientific thinkers and a longtime Markle grant recipient, Ithiel de Sola Pool of the Massachusetts Institute of Technology (MIT), observed at the time, vast systems of communications that had grown up in ways that were distinct yet generally complementary—the telephone system, the postal system, newspapers, and broadcasting—were headed on a collision course.[1] Entire industries feared for their profitability or, in some cases, their survival. The resulting clashes would by no means be confined to the world of the media. Every sector of economic life that relied on information—from Wall Street to the defense establishment to America's classrooms—was about to confront inevitable and possibly painful realignments as a result of this onrush of new communications technologies.

As the presumptive referees of these struggles between old and emerging corporate warriors, federal and state regulators and lawmakers were in the hot seat. They, after all, were supposed to be the guardians of the public interest, with primary responsibility for establishing a sense of rationality, if not actual fair play, in these corporate conflicts. Yet, in 1969, the Federal Communications Commission found itself operating within a framework of a thirty-five–year-old statute that was, as University of Michigan communications expert Charles Shipan recently characterized it, "nearing senior citizen status."[2]

The 1934 Communications Act was drafted at a time when the monopoly of AT&T in telecommunications was universally assumed and radio was the only widespread broadcast medium. By the late 1960s, with radio seemingly in the shadows, the cable industry bracing to do battle with the established TV networks, and AT&T's hold in telecommunications no longer a given, it was clear that the rules of the communications game, both inside and outside Washington, were going to be rewritten. The questions were: by whom and for whose benefit? If Washington lobbyists alone dictated the rules as new industries elbowed into the information field and older ones scrambled to adjust, any notion of the public good almost surely would be left in the dust. The challenge for Markle, as Morrisett saw it, was to help provide a much-needed rational and ethical basis for those policy debates.

As he prepared to steer The Markle Foundation into this gathering storm, Morrisett's outlook was, if anything, guardedly optimistic. Fresh from his success with *Sesame Street*, he believed that new technologies such as cable television might multiply educational programming many times over, open the airwaves to civic education and discourse, and bring live concerts and other artistic programming into living rooms.

Faced with an environment dominated by corporate might and regulatory confusion, Morrisett, the inveterate social scientist, felt that a small foundation might do at least some good by helping to fill the research void in the communications field. A once-in-a-lifetime opportunity could be lost, he feared, unless leaders of government and industry had in hand solid, dispassionate evidence with which to weigh the educational, civic, and cultural benefits of communications along with profitability. Yet, few communications experts on college campuses, at think tanks, or in government were doing the work needed to make sense of this fast-changing, complicated world. "Policy making on every level," Morrisett observed at the time, "is . . . hampered by the lack of systematic, objective, and independent studies of policy alternatives and their implications."[3]

During the next twenty-eight years, Markle became a leading bulwark of research in communications policy. The immediate problem was that, unlike more heavily trafficked philanthropic areas such as education, health, and social service, there were hardly any nonprofit organizations or unaligned experts to whom Markle could turn to carry out grant projects or to help keep the foundation's thinking fresh. Without such centers of communications research at university campuses or think tanks, the foundation would find itself sending its ideas into a void.

To be sure, research in communications had been taking place at some leading campuses. Much of the best work was being done not by communications specialists but by psychologists and other scholars outside traditional communications departments. Beginning in the early 1970s, Markle decided to help establish durable campus-based centers devoted entirely to the study of communications policy. It spent nearly $3 million during the 1970s to establish and support six such communications policy centers. Three centers concentrated almost entirely on producing research: The RAND Corporation's Communications Policy Program, MIT's Research Program on Communications Policy, and Harvard University's Program on Information Technologies and Public Policy. Two other centers produced research and also concentrated on the training of future communications policy specialists: the Center for the Study of Communications Policy at Duke University and the Communications Law Program at the University of California at Los Angeles, the nation's first program preparing young attorneys for public advocacy and legal scholarship in the communications field. Finally, Markle became a principal source of funding for The Aspen Institute's Program on Communications and Society. Aspen became the foundation's favorite forum for refining its program ideas and making contacts in government, industry, and academia.

Years later, in 1989, the foundation added a further means of supporting and honoring its most favored researchers and drawing on their expertise in a more sustained way. It designated three Markle Fellows who would receive annual funds to support their own activities while adding their wisdom to the foundation's programs. Three individuals earned that distinction: Washington policy activist and communications expert Henry Geller, space scientist Bruce Murray, and communications law scholar Monroe Price.

During Morrisett's first years as president, four topics dominated Markle's research focus: cable television, children's programming, politics and the media, and the characteristics and qualifications of the journalism profession. In those early years, however, the foundation's research portfolio always included numerous samplings from a range of communications topics in Markle's search for program priorities that helped spawn major policy initiatives not pursued until years later. During the 1970s, a study by Sidney Kraus of Cleveland State University on presidential debates and research at the University of Wisconsin helped break ground on how the media affects political activity and voting patterns—major preoccupations at Markle during the 1980s and 1990s. In 1975, Pomona College sociologist Monica Morris examined how television might better serve various needs of the elderly, an age group that would become a major foundation preoccupation a decade later. Grants in 1974 and 1976 to University of Pennsylvania researchers on special-interests television audiences helped fuel Morrisett's eventual interest in developing a system of ratings that was more audience sensitive than the Neilsens.

In retrospect, Morrisett's support for research and research centers might seem, on balance, more reactive and opportunistic than premeditated. At RAND, Duke, Aspen, Harvard, MIT, and UCLA, plans for conducting communications research were, in fact, already afoot before Markle arrived on the scene. In each case, Markle stepped in with critical start-up or support money where virtually no other foundations had shown any interest.

The issues explored in the research supported by Markle were not airy abstractions. Most often, they had implications for entire industries and profound consequences for citizens and communities. For example, should cable television be freed from its regulatory shackles to grow uninhibited? Should cable franchisers be required to provide certain community or educational services as a condition for their growth? How essential was increased minority representation in the media? Should television stations be required to provide free airtime to all sides of a political argument or be compelled to offer closed captioning for the deaf as a condition for keeping their broadcast licenses?

In a time of fierce conflict among media titans, merely raising such issues, much less hazarding solutions, was more than almost any other institution was attempting.

THE RAND CONNECTION

The Markle Foundation's first major effort to create a research and policy center was at The RAND Corporation. Founded as an independent entity in 1948, RAND's public image had been tethered mainly to defense research. By the early 1960s, the Santa Monica, California, think tank was exploring ways to diversify its interests. An opportunity presented itself in 1962 with a contract from the National Aeronautics and Space Administration to study the commercial uses of satellites, including their communications potential. Leading that venture was Leland L. Johnson, a Yale-educated economist. Previously, Johnson had caught the attention of Washington lawmakers and telecommunications industry leaders with an analysis of the likely effects of satellite technology on telephone rates. In 1969, after a brief sojourn in government as a communications adviser to President Lyndon B. Johnson, he returned to RAND, where he set about building a communications research program. Leland Johnson assembled a stellar team at RAND that included physicist Walter Baer and economist Rolla Edward Park. By the early 1970s, Henry Geller, who was wrapping up nearly a decade as the FCC's general counsel, had joined the team.

What RAND lacked was start-up money to establish its research effort. Johnson telephoned Morrisett for support in September 1969. The conversations led to Markle's largest early grant: a three-year, $500,000 grant that, together with support from the Ford Foundation and the National Science Foundation, gave the RAND program its needed liftoff. Markle went on to provide RAND with nearly $1 million through 1976.

Not just the size of the grants, but the near-absence of any strings, made them distinctive and welcome at RAND. Researchers were left free to roam the range of communications issues.

They churned out scores of reports on cross-ownership of newspapers and television stations, copyright law, the role of telecommunications in urban libraries, and even an assessment of the work of the Children's Television Workshop.[4] By far, the largest volume of work concerned cable television (see chapter 4).

The relationship between RAND and Markle soon became a cornerstone of Morrisett's presidency. As previously noted, Morrisett served on RAND's board from 1973 on and as its chairman from 1985 to 1995. RAND housed some of the nation's premier communications economists, and Markle turned to them repeatedly throughout Morrisett's presidency. In the 1980s, Johnson and Stanley Besen produced reports for Markle on international telephone rates and telecommunications policy. During that same decade, RAND conducted a novel experiment that produced early evidence that elderly people were both willing and able to use computers to better their lives. In the 1990s, RAND researchers produced landmark work on the feasibility of making electronic mail universally available.

The quality of the work at RAND was consistently high. Nonetheless, Markle's institutional goal of establishing a permanent, self-sustaining research program on communications policy at RAND was never fully realized. As Morrisett said years later: "Our grants were supposed to be the kernel of a program that would be on the order of $2 million a year. They would be able to aggregate other funds to the program to make it that way. It never happened. The RAND research was very good, and widely used. But RAND could never get it to the critical stage to sustain it as a program."[5]

CAMPUS CONNECTIONS: M.I.T. AND HARVARD RESEARCH CENTERS

Markle provided start-up support for two campus-based research centers during the early 1970s—each located at a world-class university and led by acclaimed social scientists.

The Research Program on Communications Policy at MIT was founded in 1973 by Ithiel de Sola Pool, one of the century's most prolific and iconoclastic social scientists. Markle supplied seven grants totaling nearly $500,000 between 1973 and 1980, with additional support coming from the National Science Foundation and other federal agencies. Drawing on the expertise of MIT's departments of electronic engineering, political science, economics, and management, Pool's program was well positioned during its eleven-year existence to delve into the political, social, and economic questions raised by emerging technologies.

Previous work by Pool included the impact of computers on privacy, the effects of television on children, and the potential of cable television to bring about greater citizen participation. His award-winning 1963 publication, *American Business and Public Policy*, had created a new social scientific model for understanding the behavior of politicians, lobbyists, and business people. Pool's 1973 work, *The Handbook of Communication*, became a standard college text. As his colleague, Lloyd S. Etheredge, noted years later after his death, Pool wrote, coauthored, or edited two dozen books and several hundred articles and had "seldom repeated himself."[6]

Pool's projects were theoretical but with a strong practical bent. In 1975, for example, Pool's program produced a study of the feasibility of transmitting live performances from Lincoln Center for the Performing Arts via pay television. The research, conducted with a $76,700 Markle grant, aimed to show how pay television might shore up the then shaky finances of Lincoln Center and give audiences around the country unprecedented access to cultural events in the bargain. The report concluded that pay television might work, as long as 3 to 4 percent of cable subscribers, or roughly 100,000 subscribers at the time, were willing to pay $10 per month for a total of forty to fifty-two offerings per year.[7] The system ultimately designed for Lincoln Center broadcasts used UHF with pay cable, as well as corporately sponsored live broadcasts on public television.

Pool's center conducted biweekly seminars for prominent people in the field and developed in-service training programs for FCC staff. It published scores of reports on topics that included federal cable regulations, satellite broadcasting, violence in Japanese television, social impacts of the telephone, and an especially visionary project that anticipated, by nearly two decades, the coming of electronic mail on an international scale.

Pool died in 1984 at age sixty-six, a brilliant, enigmatic figure who had become an admired adviser to Morrisett on a range of Markle projects. The son of a rabbi of Portuguese descent, Pool never wrote a word in his many volumes about Judaism or Israel. A Trotskyite in his youth, he later conducted psychological research for the military during the Vietnam War that made him a target of antiwar activists on campus.[8] Even after being diagnosed with fatal cancer in 1980, he completed three books and more than forty journal articles. For years after Pool's death, the relationship with Pool and MIT evoked deep frustration in Morrisett. Both he and Pool had wanted to establish a new model of communications study at MIT that would teach a new generation of scholars, journalists, and others to consider emerging technologies in relation to existing ones and in their historic and cultural context. MIT simply was not ready to support such a program despite Pool's brilliance and prestige.

In 1999, Pool's and Morrisett's vision was finally realized. David Thorburn, director of the MIT Communications Forum and the Markle-supported Media in Transition Project, told the author that he had succeeded in starting up a Comparative Media Studies Program for undergraduate and graduate students, whose structure owed directly to the years of thinking and support by Pool and Morrisett. As much as any Markle project, the delayed results of the MIT grants speak volumes about the hazards of making hasty judgments regarding the impact of foundation support.

At Harvard, Markle had quicker results in establishing an enduring research center. In 1973, the Center for Information Policy Research was established with a $60,220 planning grant from Markle. Its leader for the next 25 years was Anthony G. Oettinger, a professor of linguistics and applied mathematics, whose massive resume included more than 50 publications on communications technology and policy. His 1969 book, *Run, Computer, Run: The Mythology of Educational Innovation,* accurately foretold that computers would not automatically improve education. A refugee from wartime Germany, Oettinger was a brilliant figure at Harvard who jealously guarded his center's independence. The methods Oettinger used in running his center were shaped in part by sour experiences with the nation's science and technology establishment. From 1967 to 1972, he had chaired the newly formed Computer Science and Engineering Board at the National Academy of Science (NAS), whose charter was to study the policy implications of new technologies. He came to regard the NAS as a stultifying bureaucracy whose research findings were tailored to please whichever government agency financed it. After his fledgling committee was scrapped in 1972, he decided to establish a more independent research center at Harvard. "What clicked in my mind," Oettinger said years later, "was that if the idea was to shed light on how computers and technology would affect national policy, who the hell needed the 'prestigious NAS,' when I could use my base here as a tenured professor at Harvard?"[9]

The immediate need in 1972 was start-up money to hire staff and set program priorities. For that, he turned to Markle. "My first impression of The Markle Foundation was that I felt comfortable for the first time. Most foundation executives are greeters. Lloyd was the first decent, intelligent, and open-minded foundation executive I had ever met," Oettinger said. "The Markle money was enormously influential as leverage. If I hadn't had that, I wouldn't have got started."[10]

What Oettinger offered during the next twenty-five years was not readily available elsewhere to corporate and government leaders: a place to turn for objective information to help them chart their way through a communications world of fast-changing forces and unpredictable trends. The scope of Oettinger's research was, in his own words "uncommonly broad," and included the international arena; information property, privacy and security; strategic and tactical uses of information; financial services; media; literacy and education; and the postal service.[11] Like Morrisett, Oettinger was convinced that the traditional divisions between different sectors of the information field were fast becoming obsolete.

To Oettinger, the keys to his center's longevity and effectiveness were nonpartisanship and independence—no consulting or corporate board memberships, no drafting of legislation predicting the future, or making policy recommendations. Most important, he wanted to maintain a diverse set of financial backers and clientele so that no single source could harm the center's independence by threatening to withdraw its support.

Nonetheless, Oettinger's center was not an immediate hit with potential funders. Through 1973, Markle was the center's financial lifeline. Oettinger's pleas for support were turned down by scores of corporate, foundation, and government donors. According to Oettinger, one bemused leader in the motion picture industry told him, "I understand what you're after, but the last thing we need in this industry is truth."[12]

The fortunes of the Harvard center began to turn in the mid-1970s as a series of fast-breaking events in the information industry created a demand for the kind of comprehensive, unbiased research that Oettinger offered. The first rumblings of antitrust actions against AT&T suddenly called for an impartial look at the inner workings of the telecommunications industry. The more forward-looking newspaper executives recognized that the electronic revolution was about to transform the way they operated. The cable television industry was experiencing growing pains and continuing regulatory battles over its place in the broadcast firmament.

The breakthrough came in 1974 when Oettinger offered his services to Robert Lilley, then chairman of AT&T. As the conversation went on, Lilley suddenly came alive: "You must be aware," he told Oettinger, "that over the years, we've had every leading economist in the United States on our payroll at one time or another. Nobody ever believes what they say because we paid for it. But what you are proposing is different. If you write something in our favor, it might be believed because we were only one of many funders. If you write something against us, we can ignore it because, again, we didn't fully pay for it."[13]

Thus, in 1974, AT&T became the center's first major corporate supporter. By 1976 the center had assembled fifty backers, including the Arthur D. Little Foundation, Encyclopedia Britannica, the Federal Reserve of Boston, General Electric, International Business Machines, Nippon Electric, Southern Railway System, and Zenith Radio Corporation.[14] By then, the center had also completed fifty projects and had developed working relationships with the White House Office of Telecommunications Policy, the Senate Foreign Relations Committee, the communications subcommittees of both houses of Congress, and other agencies.[15]

Over the years, the center's work appealed most to the avant-garde of communications—those who cared more about future trends than quarterly profit swings. William MacGowan, chairman of MCI, was one such fan of the Harvard center. "Essentially," Oettinger said, "the folks who support us think that on the whole it's better if there's some enlightenment out there, that their cause would be helped in a more knowledgeable environment. Those who play things more close to their chest don't want us. We are at best foolish and worst, dangerous."[16]

Morrisett counted the Harvard center as one of the foundation's more enduring communications research successes. By the late 1990s, the center had produced some six hundred publications. The titles suggest their scope and breadth: *U.S. Communications Policy: A Survey and Database of Executive Orders and Congressional Acts over 24 Years*; *Mapping the Information Business*; *Shifting Boundaries in the Information Marketplace*; *The Foreign Exchange Market: A Descriptive Study*; *Post-Cold War Secrecy Policy*; and *Freelance Writings in the High-Tech Age: A Conflict of Interests*.[17]

AT&T's Lilley called the center's work "a distinguished contribution not only to the world of research . . . but to all of us whose life is caught in the business of communication."[18] Robert G. Marbut, former president of Harte-Hanks Newspapers, said: "We have been looking for years to find some source external to our own industry that is looking objectively and with perspective at the entire information industry. Yours is the only one that I have seen. . . ."[19]

For its investment of $200,000 between 1972 and 1979, Markle had seeded an enduring, nonpartisan communications research center on the nation's most prestigious university campus. Beyond his scholarly attainments, Oettinger stood out in Markle's history as that rare bird: a talented researcher who was also an entrepreneur willing to do the sales work to keep his center alive and independent over the long haul.

MEDIA CONNECTIONS: PUBLIC POLICY STUDIES AT DUKE UNIVERSITY

In 1965, while Morrisett was still at the Carnegie Corporation, he administered a small research grant to a young Yale law instructor, Joel Fleishman, who was writing his dissertation on the international enforcement of individual rights. When Fleishman found that he could not complete the work, he did something unusual in the annals of foundations—he returned the grant. The gesture impressed Morrisett and marked the beginning of a warm colleagueship that lasted for three decades. An early result was the financing by Markle of a new center of communications research and public policy that Fleishman had been organizing at Duke University. The project was a pet of Duke's president, Terry Sanford, who wanted a place on campus devoted to the interdisciplinary study of policy making. He recruited Fleishman, a native North Carolinian who had recently completed a Ford Foundation study on public management education, to develop the concept.

By 1971, Fleishman had drafted a plan for a new Institute of Policy Sciences and Public Affairs with features designed to ensure its durability in the university setting. First, it would be a full-fledged, degree-offering program. Second, Duke's policy institute would be just that—an institute rather than a separate school or department cut off intellectually from other academic or professional disciplines. Third, it would contain three distinct centers, each sponsoring multidisciplinary study and research: health, criminal justice, and communications policy.[20]

The program began modestly in 1972 with a small internship program and a few undergraduate courses. Fleishman contacted Morrisett for help in putting the communications policy center on sound footing. In June 1973, Markle obliged with a $300,000 grant and, over the next decade, provided more than $1 million in support. Fleishman's goals, closely aligned with Morrisett's, were to conduct interdisciplinary research on the social rather than technical aspects of communications, especially in areas that point to larger policy issues.

"The goal," Fleishman told the author, "was to educate future people in communications, law and other fields. We thought it was important for well-educated undergraduates to know something about the media at a time when it was taking on a greater measure of importance in society. There weren't any undergraduate programs in the country focusing on communications policy and exploring issues created by relationships between politics and the media, the media and social behavior, the media and learning.

So we were really looking to provide an opportunity for students to learn about these fields, whatever their professional goals. And we thought there would be a sizable number who would go into journalism, or politics, or law. That basically came true."[21]

Over the next two decades, scholars at Duke's center conducted an array of media and communications research. In 1976, Markle provided $30,000 to Duke political scientist James David Barber to analyze how print and electronic media shape public opinion about presidential candidates by using the 1976 campaign between Jimmy Carter and Gerald Ford as a model. Shortly thereafter, Barber became the center's director and substantially increased the program's research output.

A hallmark at the center was its Duke Fellows program, which brought practicing journalists and academics together each year on campus. In 1979, Markle granted $450,000 to help finance the program. From the 1970s through the 1990s, the center hosted more than five hundred Duke Fellows from leading publications, including *The Washington Post*, *The New York Times*, Time, Inc., and Knight-Ridder, Inc. The fellows included such leading journalists and thinkers as Ben H. Bagdikian, Hugh Sidey, David Broder, and Douglass Cater. The center also attracted an equally distinguished lineup of instructors. Gene Patterson came from *The Washington Post* in January 1972 to teach undergraduates, and veteran NBC newscaster Sander Vanocur served as the program's first director. By the 1990s, the Duke fellowship program reached around the globe and drew journalists from Canada, Japan, China, Germany, France, Poland, Latin America, the former Yugoslavia, Austria, Africa, and the former Soviet bloc nations.

Duke entered into an additional collaboration with Markle in 1979. Henry Geller, one of Washington's most knowledgeable communications lawyers and public interest advocates, was leaving government after many years. Morrisett badly wanted to set him up in Washington as an independent voice—a kind of "communications" Ralph Nader—but an academic base was needed to relieve Geller of the administrative burden of operating a policy center. Markle established and funded the Washington Center for Public Policy Research, which Geller would operate independently, but, under the arrangement, Duke would administer the

Markle grants to the center. In exchange, Geller would teach courses at Duke's communications center.

"I jumped at the opportunity," Fleishman recalled years later. "I always wanted to increase the number of courses taught by reputable people in the field, and the opportunity to have Henry Geller teach at Duke was terrific for us."[22]

By the 1990s, the Duke Institute of Policy Sciences and Public Affairs was taking fresh leaps in growth and prestige. In 1991, it received an unrestricted $3 million gift from the DeWitt Wallace–Reader's Digest Fund and another $3 million to fund three endowed professorships. Political columnist David Broder occupied one of the endowed chairs. Ellen Mickiewicz, a top international expert who had helped form the Carter Center's Commission on Radio and Television Policy at Emory University, became the James R. Shepley Professor of Public Policy Studies. In 1994, she became director of the Duke communications program. A year later, Pulitzer Prize columnist William Raspberry taught at the center, as did journalist and presidential adviser David Gergen.

Duke's institute, perhaps as much as any research center supported by Markle, had the necessary ingredients for longevity in the campus setting. It had the power to confer degrees on students and tenure on faculty, and it maintained strong ties to other schools and departments on campus. Also, it was perceived on campus as homegrown—the creation of the university's own president, rather than an outside foundation leader. In 1992, the original Institute of Policy Sciences and Public Affairs had been renamed the Terry Sanford Institute of Public Policy. That same year, the Center for the Study of Communications Policy was renamed the DeWitt Wallace Center for Communications and Journalism. When the Sanford Institute moved into plush new, $15 million headquarters in December 1994, its central corridor was named Fleishman Commons. Fleishman served on the Markle Foundation's board of directors from 1976 through 1997 and was Markle's board chairman from 1988 to 1993.

THE LEGAL CONNECTION: COMMUNICATIONS LAW AT UCLA

Another research and policy void that Morrisett sought to address early in his presidency was communications law. Public-interest lawyers specializing in that field were scarce in the early 1970s. A few law schools offered scattered courses in communications law, but none offered the subject as a full-scale specialty.[23] Young, well-schooled public advocates were needed as a counterweight to the corporate legal departments and lobbyists who were calling the shots in the Washington policy circles. At the grassroots level, public-interest lawyers with the expertise to take legal action on behalf of individuals and groups wronged or neglected by the media were also needed.

In 1970, Monroe Price at UCLA's law school was already an established communications expert. He had recently served as deputy director of the Alfred P. Sloan Foundation's Commission on Cable Communications. Prior to approaching Markle for funding, Price had started an internship program that sent small numbers of law students to the FCC and elsewhere to get a taste of communications policy. Price wanted to expand his program, and he was especially eager to attract minority students because so many conflicts in communications concerned underrepresented people and communities.[24]

In May 1971, Price presented Morrisett with a nine-page proposal for a program of "intensive training" in research and first-hand job experience for about ten law students a year. The internship and research would focus on four needs: (1) minority access to the media, (2) children's television, (3) cable television in East Los Angeles, and (4) improved delivery of public broadcast signals. "The combination of the clinical internship and the public interest research at the law school is designed to produce a small but expert group of public interest communications lawyers," Price wrote.[25]

UCLA was particularly well placed to support a communications program. Los Angeles abounded with media experts, and the university had many communications-related courses in several disciplines. The law dean, Murray L. Schwartz, supported Price's goals and assured Markle program officer Forrest P. Chisman that he would absorb the new program if it could be successfully launched.[26] Morrisett worried at first that a grant supporting a public advocacy program might be mistaken for political ax grinding by his foundation. In 1972, however, he agreed to supply a two-year, $144,000 grant that allowed the program to begin full-swing that autumn.

Especially during its early years, the program gained a reputation as ultraliberal. Its first director, Geoffrey Cowan, was a thirty-year-old *Village Voice* columnist and legal activist who had argued cases for an environmentalist group, Friends of the Earth, and had written articles about the role of lawyers in the civil rights movement. Under Cowan's leadership, the UCLA program produced research and advocacy that quickly caught the local media's attention.

During the program's first year alone, UCLA students took on more than forty cases.[27] They convinced the *Los Angeles Times* to carry a page of news each day in Spanish. They pressed for more jobs for women in television programming and helped to file a brief to block an FCC license renewal to a San Diego station that failed to hire more women. One of the law students, Peter Lopez, helped force local broadcasters into giving free airtime under the FCC's fairness doctrine to United Farm Workers leader Cesar Chavez so that he could rebut an agricultural labor relations ballot measure that would have harmed or destroyed his union.

UCLA lawyers negotiated with local broadcasters to air messages urging residents to drive less and promoting mass transportation.[28] In a letter to the National Broadcasting Company (NBC), they protested a Gulf Oil Company advertisement that they alleged was one-sided on the issue of oil imports. NBC disputed that interpretation but agreed not to broadcast the ad again.[29]

In November 1972, the UCLA law students, working with attorneys in San Francisco and Washington, persuaded two large cable companies who wanted to merge to lease at least one channel at $1 per year to local organizations in every community in which they operated. Press accounts described it as the first time that citizens groups had negotiated successfully with a national cable company. The merger was eventually blocked by a Justice Department suit, but both cable companies said that they would still honor the agreement brokered by the UCLA students.[30]

None of this endeared the UCLA center to media executives who did not enjoy being lectured by upstart law students on what was or was not in the public interest. Cowan's students broke the final straw when a group of them conducted a survey on how well Los Angeles broadcasters were complying with FCC regulations. Not content with mere number crunching, the students went public, to the annoyance of area TV stations.

Richard W. Jencks, a vice president of CBS, wondered if the UCLA Communications Law Center was producing "zealots rather than scholars" whose activities were creating the legal pretext for intrusive, anti-First Amendment government regulation of broadcasters.

"I fear," Jencks wrote Cowan, "that once your students accept the idea that government power can be beneficent in 'improving' the electronic media, they may fail utterly to bear in mind the small print on the label which tells about the possible unfortunate side effects arising from misuse or over-use of the remedy."[31]

As Morrisett later put it, some broadcasters clearly regarded UCLA's communications program as a breeding ground for future enemies. "When you've got a program like the UCLA communications program which is developing public interest lawyers, it would be fairly natural for (media executives) to say that this program is going to feed these organizations which are causing all this mischief."[32]

Markle's funding ended in 1977, but the UCLA program lasted through 1990 and trained fifty to seventy students each year. The program kept afloat by convincing the university to increase its support; by attracting corporate contributions from AT&T, ABC, and a number of cable companies; and by reaching a deal with the Federal Communications Bar Association to publish its thrice-yearly *Federal Communications Law Journal*.[33] Eventually, the loss of the publishing rights to the communications law journal and internal leadership battles led to the program's demise.

The seeds of communications policy law also took modest root on a few other campuses. Angela Campbell, editor-in-chief of the communications law journal while a student at UCLA, established a clinical communications law program at Georgetown University. Monroe Price went on to establish a communications law program at the Cardozo School at Yeshiva University and, as noted earlier, was named a Markle scholar.

CONNECTING TO SOCIETY: THE ASPEN INSTITUTE

Of all the centers that Markle helped create during the 1970s, none received more money or developed a closer relationship with the foundation than the Aspen Institute's Program on Communications and Society. During nearly three decades, the foundation would provide Aspen more than $2.1 million, including $400,000 to help establish its communications program in 1971. Aspen produced considerable research, but its claim to fame was always as a safe, sedate harbor for government, industry, and academic leaders to discuss a range of policy issues. It became a kind of foundation for foundations—a place for the leaders and staff of Markle and other foundations to sound out ideas and broaden their contacts.

The founder of Aspen's communications program was Joseph E. Slater, who became Aspen's president in 1969, the same year that Morrisett assumed Markle's leadership. Slater had had a varied career as an oil economist and international affairs specialist at the Ford Foundation. He developed an interest in the connections between communications, education and foreign affairs. In 1967, he had helped launch the International Broadcast Institute based in Rome and London.[34]

The need for a calm setting to discuss communications policy was obvious during the late 1960s, as the Nixon White House was busily roiling the waters for the news media and public television and as the broadcast industry was nervously poised for cable television's expected growth. In October 1970, Slater assembled a group of prominent acquaintances in the communications field to discuss how Aspen might help in shaping the looming policy debates. The gathering included Edward Barrett, dean of Columbia University's School of Journalism, and Sig Mickelson, a former CBS executive who was then with *Encyclopedia Brittanica.* Also attending was Douglass Cater, a forty-seven-year-old Washington journalist and former adviser to President Johnson, who had recently helped shepherd the Public Broadcasting Act through Congress.[35]

Cater told Slater and the other participants that there was an urgent need for an institution that could explore the humanistic dimensions of communications policy. Slater invited Cater to draft a proposal.[36] The resulting "Design for a Communications Media Institute," underwritten by small grants from the Ford, Benton and Markle Foundations, was completed in the spring of 1971. The mission that Cater proposed for Aspen was extravagant:

> "The time is propitious for a non-governmental institution dedicated to serving the public interest in matters relating to the communications media. While initial emphasis might be on critical issues relating to telecommunications and technological change, this institution should include within its mandate all the media. It should view the media as a whole—newspapers, radio, television, cable, magazines, books, films. It would address immediate and specific issues by which communications policy is shaped. But at the same time, it should engage in broader and longer range analysis in order to anticipate the future public interest.[37]

Cater had consulted more than one hundred representatives from journalism, government, and other interested parties in drafting his plans for the center. In the process, he built a cadre of future contacts and support. Nonetheless, his proposal met with almost instant opposition. Over lunch with Cater at the Century Club in Manhattan on April 16, 1971, Slater, Morrisett, and other foundation and media leaders shot down the blueprint as too broad to be manageable.[38] What finally doomed the Cater plan was the reluctance of the Ford Foundation to fund it, coupled with suspicions among media executives about any self-appointed group that might poke around in their affairs.

The Cater plan might have been dead, but Slater clung to his idea for a communications center at Aspen. Discussions of a scaled-down version of Cater's proposal resumed that summer among Slater, Cater, Mickelson, Barrett, Elie Abel (who succeeded Barrett as dean of the Columbia University School of Journalism), Morrisett, and William Benton, head of the Benton Foundation. They agreed upon a leaner Program on Communications and Society that would concentrate on four areas: government and the media; television and social behavior; public broadcasting; and cable and the new technology.[39]

From there, things moved quickly. By October 1971, the

Aspen program had a full roster of proposed research plans and seminars in its four policy areas.[40] Cater was named to lead the new program, and, by the fall of 1971, he had assembled a blue-ribbon advisory panel that gave the center instant credibility.[41] In December, Markle provided $400,000 in start-up grants spread over four years: $267,000 to Aspen for conferences and workshops and $133,000 to the Academy for Educational Development to serve as Aspen's research arm. The Benton Foundation provided another $160,000.

Aspen, Morrisett said, ". . . represents a major attempt to bring together men [sic], ideas and institutions to pioneer in the communications field, to identify the main communications issues confronting society, to help define policies to support the public interest and to develop effective programs to implement these policies."[42]

Cater's first focus was the U.S. Surgeon General's 1972 report on television and violence, "Television and Growing Up: The Impact of Televised Violence," a document so blandly worded that *The New York Times* mistook it as a clean bill of health for TV and misleadingly headlined its story, "TV Violence Held Unharmful to Youth."[43] A month after the Surgeon General's report was issued, Cater and Stephen Strickland produced an analysis that praised it for establishing a causal link between television violence and actual youth violence but criticized it for permitting a "unilateral industry veto" over the committee that produced it.[44]

Turning in 1972 and 1973 to the financing and improvement of public television, the Aspen program sponsored a study of the economics of public broadcasting by Stanford University professors Wilbur Schramm and Lyle Nelson. The report provided a basis for the system's long-term funding.

Aspen sought early on to provide a refuge for reasoned dialogue between government regulators and media industry executives on various points of chronic friction: FCC rule making, tax policy, postal rates, antitrust, copyright, secrecy, and subpoena powers.[45] A meeting of such media and government leaders in August 1972 helped establish Aspen's reputation as an island of quiet productivity by building a consensus around a list of concrete proposals for improving news coverage in Washington. Among other actions, the group suggested redeploying the Washington press corps so that fewer were covering the White House and more were assigned to cover Congress and relatively neglected executive agencies.

The conference also considered how a proposed National News Council might function. Several of the group's ideas were eventually adopted when the ill-fated council came into being with joint financing by Markle and the Twentieth Century Fund in 1973. (See chapter 5 for details of the council's history.)

Markle funded an Aspen "Workshop on Uses of the Cable" in 1973, led by Walter Baer of RAND and Richard Adler, a former Oberlin College English professor. The project raised, for the first time, a crucial yet neglected set of questions concerning how cable television might promote continuing education and gain wider audiences for the performing arts and cultural programming. It also explored how to spread cable's benefits to those who could not afford to pay. The workshop broached the fascinating question of how to make a "humanistic claim" on cable television by tapping into the community of scholars and artists who cared about the cultural significance of broadcasting.[46]

The early years of the Aspen-Markle relationship reached a high point in 1975 when Cater opened a Washington office to connect Aspen's discussions to the policy deliberations at the FCC and in Congress. Forrest Chisman, Morrisett's assistant since 1970, left Markle to head the new office. Henry Geller, who was finding that his zest for zealous legal action did not mesh well with the more genteel customs at RAND, signed on with Aspen's Washington office.

With Geller's help, the Aspen program had one of its most visible triumphs. On the eve of the 1976 presidential election, Geller decided to press the FCC to clear away the regulatory obstacles to televised presidential debates, which had not taken place since the Kennedy-Nixon campaign in 1960. A strict reading of the 1934 Communications Act seemed to demand that any such debates would require equal time for the many fringe candidates for president, effectively killing their prospects. Only once, in 1960, did the FCC temporarily waive the requirement and only then because John F. Kennedy and Richard M. Nixon, the two major presidential rivals, wanted the debates for their own political reasons. Thereafter, a succession of presidential contestants decided that it was not to their political advantage to press for similar rules.

Geller felt that public interest, not political expediency, ought to settle the debate question. In a petition filed with the FCC, Aspen's Washington office argued that because the equal time provisions exempted "on-the-spot news events," that exemption ought to extend to presidential debates as well. Thanks in part to that successful petition, the first televised debates in sixteen years took place in 1976 between President Gerald Ford and candidate Jimmy Carter.[47]

In later years, the relationship between Markle and Aspen grew even closer. Markle financed more than twenty-five Aspen Forums as the foundation's attention shifted away from traditional media during the 1980s and 1990s. When the foundation turned to such matters as the future of electronic publishing, using computers to improve the lives of the elderly, and the educational potential of multimedia software, Aspen gatherings were critical events for educating Markle's staff and helping them meet the most creative people.

The Aspen-Markle connection strengthened further under the leadership of Charles Firestone, head of the UCLA Communications Law Center during its final years, who became director of Aspen's Communications Progam in January 1990. Beginning in November of that year, Firestone helped organize an especially fruitful partnership among Aspen, Markle, and the Carter Center's Commission on Radio and Television Policy. At the time, the Carter Center was working on a series of papers and forums to help the former republics of the Soviet Union develop democratically based television and media. Aspen hosted four such forums between 1990 and 1994 that explored television coverage of elections, new technologies, news coverage of minority groups, and radio and television autonomy from state control.

A string of conferences and publications on such topics as electronic town meetings and the future of electronic advertising helped Markle explore how new technologies might aid education and reconnect an alienated citizenry to the electoral process. In 1997, Markle provided nearly $50,000 for a strategic meeting with industry and policy leaders to discuss the goal of universal access to e-mail, one of the foundation's top communications priorities as the new century approached.

Morrisett, the convinced social scientist, had a personal affinity for research that colored his entire presidency. Heeding John Markle's injunction in the foundation's charter that it dedicate itself to "the diffusion of knowledge," Morrisett's pursuit of communications policy research was a central feature of his presidency. The foundation succeeded in identifying and breeding a close-knit network of scholars, lawyers, and analysts who, together, added factual and ethical dimensions to public debates about communications policy. Ithiel Pool at MIT, Leland L. Johnson and Walter Baer at RAND, Anthony G. Oettinger, Gerald Lesser, and Howard Gardner at Harvard, and Joel Fleishman and Ellen Mickiewicz at Duke produced a body of work on communications and the media that would not have been easily assembled, if at all, without the Markle Foundation.

High in that pantheon of communications thinkers were the three Markle Fellows: Henry Geller, Bruce Murray, and Monroe Price. As a member of the Carter Center's Commission on Radio and Television Policy, Price worked on model laws for leaders of former Soviet bloc nations. During the 1990s, he advised academic programs in communications in Budapest, Moscow, England, and Australia and continued his activism in regulatory and legislative issues in Washington, particularly in the area of children's television programming.

Murray had made history in 1965 when, as director of the National Aeronautics and Space Administration's (NASA's) Caltech Jet Propulsion Laboratory, he helped develop and interpret television images from the first Mars probe. In 1980, with the late Carl Sagan, Murray founded the Planetary Society, which is dedicated to the search for intelligent life in the cosmos. During the 1990s, he led Markle's "HyperForum" project that explored how to promote high-quality discourse on public policy issues on the World Wide Web.

Few personified the foundation's ideal of translating thought into practice better than Geller, whose career in government and public advocacy spanned forty-nine years. From 1979 on, with some $2 million in Markle funding, Geller became Washington's most widely quoted communications policy advocate and has filed literally thousands of legal briefs along the way. Although Markle, under Morrisett, generally eschewed Washington and avoided the limelight, Geller was there to turn up the volume occasionally and gather headlines for the causes, such as free airtime for candidates and debates, that Markle supported. Morrisett called Geller "a national treasure."[48]

Taken together, the body of knowledge produced by the many scholars at Markle-supported research centers provided crucial support for the belief that private profits and the public good need not inevitably be in opposition. Still, Morrisett's *institutional* goal of creating a critical mass of communications specialists and permanent institutions in which to house them was only partially realized. The failure to fully achieve that institutional goal raises questions about whether Markle's grants might have been misdirected in some respects. Might the foundation, for example, have spent less energy trying to establish permanent campus-based centers devoted to communications research and more on supporting such research within established departments of economics, history, or political science where the topic has been neglected?

Regardless, the programs at Aspen, Duke, and Harvard were still going strong in 2000. UCLA's Communications Law Center had a distinguished, if more limited, run. The dream of establishing a communications program at MIT came to life in 1999 after a nearly two-decade delay. The relationship between Markle and RAND continued through the 1990s, but Morrisett's hope of having a self-sustaining center of communications research at the think tank was never achieved. Despite these efforts, the community of serious scholars in media studies remains small, certainly when measured against the many challenges that cry out for objective study.

"It was a continuing frustration," Forrest Chisman said years later. "You just kept coming up with the same 50 or 100 people in the field, and that was it. It was a small world. It still is."[49]

NOTES

1. Ithiel de Sola Pool, untitled grant proposal to The Markle Foundation, 11 Jan. 1973, 1–2, Markle Archive Collection.

2. Shipan, "Keeping Competitors Out," 473.

3. Quoted in "The John and Mary R. Markle Foundation, Annual Report, 1969–70," 29.

4. RAND Corporation, "Administrative Report to The Markle Foundation," July 1974, 3.

5. Morrisett, interview, 17 Sept. 1997.

6. Etheredge, Lloyd S., "What Next? The Intellectual Legacy of Ithiel de Sola Pool" (article on web site www.media-in-transition.-mit.edu).

7. Robert W. Crandall, "The Economic Prospects for a 'Live from Lincoln Center' Pay Television Service," Center for Policy Alternatives at the Massachusetts Institute of Technology, 1 June 1975, 111–113.

8. Etheredge, "What Next?"

9. Oettinger, interview, 23 Oct. 1997.

10. Ibid.

11. "Program Publications, February 1997," published by the Center for Information Policy Research, Harvard University, contents page.

12. Oettinger, interview, 23 Oct. 1997.

13. Lilley quoted in ibid.

14. "A Perspective on Information Resources: The Scope of the Program 1973–74," booklet published by the Program on Information Technologies and Public Policy, Harvard University, 1.

15. John C. LeGates and Anthony G. Oettinger, "Prospectus for the Expansion of the Program on Information Resources Policy," Working Paper W-76–11, Harvard University Program on Information Resources Policy, Oct. 1976, 3.

16. Oettinger, interview, 23 Oct. 1997.

17. "Program Publications, February 1997."

18. Quoted in "Compliments Paid to the Program" (brochure, Program on Information Resources Policy, Harvard University), n.d., 5.

19. Quoted in ibid.

20. "Institute Retrospective: A Conversation with Joel Fleishman and Terry Sanford," *Duke Policy News* 22, no. 2 (1994):4.

21. Fleishman, interview, 13 Oct. 1997.

22. Ibid.

23. Monroe E. Price, "Public Interest Communications Law: A Proposal" (submitted to The Markle Foundation), 21 May 1971, 1, Markle Archive Collection.

24. Ibid., 2.

25. Ibid., 4.

26. Murray L. Schwartz, letter to Forrest Chisman, 17 Feb. 1972.

27. Geoffrey Cowan, "UCLA Communications Law Program, First Annual Report," Sept. 1973, 5.

28. Ibid., 6.
29. Ibid., 7.
30. Ibid., 15.
31. Richard W. Jencks, letter to Geoffrey Cowan, 14 Nov. 1973, copy in Markle Archive Collection.
32. Morrisett, interview, 16 July 1997.
33. "Entering the Eighties: A Progress Report of the UCLA Communications Law Program," (report to The Markle Foundation), 6, Markle Archive Collection.
34. Hyman, *Aspen Idea*, 238–9.
35. Ibid., 280.
36. Ibid., 281–2.
37. Douglass Cater, "Design for a Communications Media Institute" (file memorandum prepared for Aspen Institute), n.d., 8, Markle Archive Collection.
38. Lloyd N. Morrisett, file memorandum, 16 Apr. 1971.
39. Hyman, *Aspen Idea*, 285.
40. "Agenda: Aspen Program on Communications and Policy" (status report prepared for The Markle Foundation), 20 Oct. 1971, Markle Archive Collection.
41. In addition to Edward Barrett, Sig Mickelson, and Joseph E. Slater, the panel included Elie Abel, dean, Columbia School of Journalism; Harry Ashmore, president, Center for Study of Democratic Institutions; Charles Benton, president, Films, Inc.; Joan Cooney, president, Children's Television Workshop; Louis G. Cowan, journalism professor, Columbia University, and former president, CBS Television; Peter Goldmark, head, Goldmark Communications and a former CBS executive; Kermit Gordon, president, The Brookings Institution; James Hoge, editor, *Chicago Sun-Times*; James Killian, director, Corporation for Public Broadcasting, who chaired the commission that produced the landmark Carnegie Commission report on public broadcasting in the 1960s; De Vier Pierson, prominent Washington attorney; and Ithiel de Sola Pool, MIT. (Grant Report, The Markle Foundation, Program on Communications and Society, Aspen Institute and Academy for Educational Development.)
42. Lloyd N. Morrisett, press release announcing The Markle Foundation's grant to Aspen Institute, 8 Dec. 1971.
43. Douglass Cater and Stephen Strickland, "A First Hard Look at the Surgeon General's Report on Television and Violence" (unpublished paper prepared for Aspen Institute and Academy for Educational Development), March 1972, 9, Markle Archive Collection.
44. Ibid., 2.

45. Douglass Cater, "Communications and Society—Prospects for the Aspen Program" (internal memorandum, Aspen Institute), 15 Nov. 1972, 3, Markle Archive Collection.

46. Workshop on Uses of the Cable, Walter S. Baer, Director, Grant No. AO-7951–73–18 (Progress Report for the Period June 1, 1972–August 31, 1972), 1–4.

47. Geller, interview, 22 Sept. 1997.

48. Morrisett, interview, 17 Sept. 1997.

49. Chisman, interview, 8 July 1997.

4

The Coming of Cable

FROM MORRISETT'S EARLIEST DAYS as Markle's president, cable television was on his mind. Like other observers during the late 1960s and early 1970s, he was convinced—a bit prematurely as it turned out—that the young industry was poised for a takeoff that would transform overnight the landscape of broadcasting.

Between 1963 and 1969, the number of cable systems had tripled. Even at that growth rate, however, cable was just a blip on the screen compared with the established networks. When Morrisett became president of Markle, only 6.3 percent of America's households had cable.[1] Its technological ancestor, "community antenna television," had appeared twenty years earlier in rural Astoria, Oregon, and shortly afterward in Lansford, Mahanoy City, and Pottsville, Pennsylvania. CATV's original purpose was to bring better reception to remote areas.[2] It barely existed in urban areas. Consumer rates were often high, and connection fees of $100 or more were not unknown.[3] To Americans accustomed to thinking of commercial television as being as free as the air—which of course it never truly was—"pay television" was an utterly alien concept.

Still, Morrisett sensed an opportunity for his small foundation to have social impact on a rising new sector of the communications field while young and malleable. Markle, he believed, could help demonstrate how the new cable technology might offer the diverse and high-quality programming that seemed so foreign and prohibitively expensive at established commercial networks. Morrisett acknowledged from the start that any increase in program choice by cable operators "is likely to be accompanied by added trivia and trash as well as by programs of real value."[4] Yet, he also pictured a dozen new "Sesame Streets" on entire channels dedicated to children. He imagined hours of programming geared to the needs of underserved groups, such as the older population. With cable's capacity for two-way communications, he believed that it might make possible "electronic town halls" where policy issues could be meaningfully discussed and viewers could let their opinions be instantly known to decision makers.

Would the coming of cable merely expand the boundaries of TV's wasteland? Or could "more" also mean "better?"[5] Morrisett felt that his foundation had to act quickly and boldly before the public service objectives that he had in mind for the new medium were trampled in the inevitable rush for profits and competitive advantage.

Between 1970 and 1980, The Markle Foundation spent $4.1 million on cable television projects. In several of those efforts, it had a powerful ally in the Ford Foundation. For Morrisett, the overarching goal was to foster diversity and openness. He hoped to encourage cable operators to include as much community-oriented and educational programming as possible within their new channels and to serve groups in society that had been neglected by the established networks.

In support of those larger goals, four strands of foundation activity emerged through the 1970s. Markle sought, first, to fill the research void that existed concerning the economic, technical, and regulatory climate of cable. Solid research was needed to balance the arguments of industry lobbyists and economists-for-hire who were driving the policy debate in Congress and at the Federal Communications Commission. The foundation also established and supported a national information clearinghouse for state and local officials suddenly faced with the legal and economic complications of cable franchise negotiations. Markle hoped to launch a model urban cable system in Washington, D.C., to demonstrate cable's capacity to make more readily available a range of quality programming and city services. Finally, the foundation wanted to showcase the potential of public access cable—opening the airwaves for the first time to ordinary citizens and community groups to sound off on their concerns and observe, first-hand, the workings of government.

If the promise of cable seemed limitless in 1969, so were the obstacles faced by Markle as it entered the new arena. It was soon obvious that the foundation was wading into an economic and regulatory street brawl between one of the nation's most politically connected industries and a wily, threatening newcomer. In Washington, lobbyists representing cable operators, the established networks, and struggling UHF stations were jockeying for advantage in Congress and at the FCC as thirty-year-old regulations were being reconsidered to accommodate the new complexities of broadcasting. At the local level, the struggles to gain lucrative exclusive cable franchises were rife with backroom deals and even bribery in some cities and states. In that setting, Markle would be lucky indeed if its goals of program diversity, community access, and better children's programming made it past the peripheries of the policy debates.

In the midst of these skirmishes stood the FCC, the government's powerful, if occasionally bumbling, traffic cop of the airwaves. During the 1960s and early 1970s, the commission was deeply divided on the future of cable, and its actions were marked by indecision and susceptibility to political influence. Throughout the early 1960s, it refused to regulate cable at all on the grounds that it was not broadcast over the airwaves. Cable's gradual rise to prominence and the resulting collision with existing broadcasters forced the FCC to acknowledge its own jurisdiction. By the mid-1960s, the FCC was wielding a considerable and, for the most part, chilling influence on cable's growth. In 1966, the commission froze cable out of most big cities by banning the importation of distant signals into the largest markets.[6] It also sharply limited cable's ability to offer movies or sports.

Some, especially the leaders of the young cable industry, saw those actions as nakedly anticable, but the FCC's motives were more complicated. To be sure, some commissioners were intent on protecting the broadcast industry's turf. Other commissioners, as well as members of the FCC's legal staff, sought not to stop cable's growth but to rationalize it within the existing broadcast and programming setting that included commercial, public, and UHF stations. Chief among the "rationalizers" was the FCC's general counsel, Henry Geller, a prime architect of the commission's cable strategies.

Geller was, in fact, only too glad to see the new industry thrive with a minimum of regulatory interference. What rankled him and others at the commission was the cable industry's claimed right to transmit television programs snatched via satellite from networks or local broadcasters and relay them to distant markets without paying a dime for the right to do so.

San Diego was the most glaring example. In 1961, cable operators built a tall antenna capable of picking up Los Angeles television one hundred miles away and, for a small monthly fee, offered Los Angeles television programming to San Diego viewers.[7] By the end of the decade, San Diego had the largest number of cable subscribers of any U.S. city, but the local cable operator was paying nothing for the right to relay programs from Los Angeles. Such programs, cable operators insisted at the time, fell outside copyright laws because they were not, strictly speaking, "performances."

In effect, according to Geller, cable operators were asserting a legal right to steal. "We told the cable industry that if they would only come within the competitive market, we'd be there for you tomorrow," Geller recalled years later. "How can you stand outside the market? How can you move programs all over and make this chaos? In order to get programming, you have to bid and pay for it. They were simply taking the signal from satellites and sending it all over. This was nothing but piracy."[8]

Geller and other staff members at the FCC sought to end the chaos by freezing cable's growth in major markets until the copyright dispute could be decided by the Supreme Court. The strategy backfired. On June 10, 1968, the U.S. Supreme Court, in *U.S. v. Southwestern Cable Company*, upheld the FCC's right to freeze cable in big cities. But, in a crucial second decision issued seven days later in *Fortnightly Corp. v. United Artists Television, Inc.*, the justices decided that cable operators were not liable for payment of copyright royalties. The FCC had won its freeze but was denied the more important verdict on copyright payments. The commission considered such compensation essential before it could safely loosen its regulatory shackles on cable's spread.

The FCC, meanwhile, was under mounting public and political pressure to reconsider its restrictive stance toward cable. By the late 1960s, the Nixon White House had come to regard the three major networks as ideological enemies and was only too willing to use the threat of unleashing cable's growth as a weapon in its wars with commercial and public broadcasters. A growing body of research sponsored by Markle and other foundations was providing powerful arguments for allowing the free market, rather than government regulators, to dictate cable's growth. Finally, the public, especially in cities, was intrigued by cable's possibilities and increasingly impatient with the regulatory roadblocks to its spread.

To the broadcast world's heavy hitters, Markle's decision to inject itself into their turf wars was hardly viewed as an epochal event. Still, one network chief who did take notice was Arthur Taylor, president of CBS, and he didn't like what he saw. At a tense lunch, he let Morrisett know that he and CBS regarded Markle's efforts to explore the bright promise of cable television as an unfriendly act.

"He said, 'You're supporting work on cable television, aren't you? Well, I take that as clearly an antibroadcasting agenda,' " Morrisett recalled. "Afterward, I never heard anything about it again. But it was bizarre. I marched back across the street and wondered, why is this network thinking about the Markle Foundation as being important enough to do this?"[9]

Whatever minor ripples Markle caused with its entry into the cable fray, Morrisett clearly regarded the coming of this new technology as too rich an opportunity for the foundation to resist. "It is possible," Morrisett wrote in 1971, "that this different and seemingly prosaic method of transmitting television will bring about changes in opportunity for entertainment, education and ideas as vast as those brought about by the introduction of television itself."[10]

THE RAND REPORTS

On September 3, 1969, Morrisett's second day as Markle's president, a proposal from The RAND Corporation to study the regulation of cable programming landed on his desk. It led to the first of dozens of reports on cable that the Santa Monica think tank eventually completed with Markle funds during the early 1970s. The timing for the collaboration was propitious. Morrisett was developing personal ties at RAND, former FCC head Newton N. Minow was RAND's board chairman, and RAND was in the midst of assembling a team of communications research experts. The Ford Foundation also agreed to be a partner with Markle in supporting such research.

The RAND proposal's young author, Franz Allina, soon caught Morrisett's fancy.[11] At age thirty-seven, Allina had been a media-savvy writer and planner with CBS and Straus Broadcasting Group. He had been a speechwriter at the Agency for International Development since 1967 and knew his way around Washington. Allina's knowledge about the vagaries of cable impressed Morrisett, who was not nearly as well versed. At their first meeting on October 9, 1969, Allina bluntly told Morrisett that the industry was full of experts in cable hardware—television "grease-monkeys," as he indelicately called them. But hardly anyone in cable, he said, knew or cared much about the technology's potential for creative programming.[12]

More than three dozen RAND studies on cable poured out under Markle and Ford grants.[13] Their most immediate and lasting importance, as RAND's communication research leader Leland L. Johnson stated years later, "was to help the FCC come to the sensible decision that it ought to deregulate cable's growth."[14] By 1970, Allina had joined the Children's Television Workshop. He became a confidant of Morrisett's and an important player in both the workshop's and Markle's projects in cable television and children's programming over the next decade.

RAND's painstaking econometric models helped put to rest some of the fears among federal regulators that the rise of cable threatened the survival of local VHF and UHF broadcasters. To the contrary, the research demonstrated that cable might help UHF broadcasters by allowing them to overcome their biggest handicaps—poor signal quality, small audiences, and limited geographic reach.

In 1972, Rolla Edward Park, a leading economist and a member of RAND's research team, analyzed the effects of the FCC's newly enacted rules regarding "exclusivity"—rules that protected the monopoly of local commercial stations on such programming as syndicated series or feature films. He concluded that under the 1972 FCC rules, "about half of all distant programmings would have to be blacked out on the cable. . . ."[15]

That same year, RAND offered the first serious analysis of how FCC rules might affect the ability of cable operators to transmit different kinds of programming to distant markets.[16] It also wrote and distributed a cable television handbook that became a standard for municipal governments and other entities facing decisions on how to use cable.[17]

The caliber of RAND's work was never in doubt. But some communications experts, Henry Geller, for example, considered RAND's tactics in promoting its findings in Washington ineffective. Johnson argued that the RAND work was influential in softening the FCC's regulatory positions toward cable's growth. He and others at RAND spoke frequently with commissioners and FCC staff who were "quite receptive" to the research findings, Johnson said. Geller, for his part, left the RAND team after two years partly out of impatience with what he considered its unaggressive lobbying and its reluctance to engage in the kind of legal action that was his specialty. Minow told the author that while the work at RAND on cable was certainly well done and important, "it was not as recognized as it should have been."[18]

In 1972, Park produced a detailed analysis of the role that research had played in shaping cable regulatory policy. He decided that research of the sort produced by RAND was playing, at best, a "supporting role." Nonpartisan research, he found, was generally seen as more trustworthy than research by interested parties. The kind of work that RAND produced had, in fact, established a framework for policy discussions and helped to allay many of the commission's fears about cable's emergence as a competitor to others in the broadcast field.[19] Still, Park concluded that the intricate arguments and econometric models produced by RAND and others were simply too complex for most of the FCC staff and its embattled commissioners to grasp.[20]

BRINGING CABLE TO THE CAPITAL

In July 1970, the Children's Television Workshop hired Allina to work on a new and bolder cable venture. Morrisett, wearing his two hats as CTW's chairman and Markle's president, wanted to help create America's first truly "wired city" by obtaining a cable franchise in Washington, D.C.—"right under the nose of the FCC," as Allina put it years later.

The would-be project had four principal players. The Markle Foundation led and financed the effort. CTW, which was developing plans to enter the cable market, would contribute its creativity, name recognition, and reputation for wholesome programming. RAND, along with the Mitre Corporation, a McLean, Virginia, research organization with strong credentials in cable television and federal policy work, prepared the financial and technical feasibility analysis. With a $300,000 Markle grant in 1971, Mitre produced a report on wideband telecommunications cable systems that examined how an advanced cable system might be useful to police, fire, school, municipal government, and federal government operations.[21] Although the project focused on the nation's capital, Mitre's report aimed to provide a model for cable development in other metropolitan areas.

The collaboration produced fresh research on the economic practicalities of urban cable systems. Nonetheless, Markle's larger goal of bringing a model cable system to Washington never got off the ground. Mitre's final study, "Urban Cable Systems," completed in June 1972, discussed the feasibility of a range of one-way and interactive cable services—from educational TV and programming for ethnic groups to local library reference services, health service directories, and even ticket sales and restaurant reservations. The report was well received nationally: more than five thousand copies were distributed to cities around the country. Mitre's forecasts about the high capital costs of the project, however, had a chilling effect on the Washington venture.

Local politics undid the Washington cable project. Meetings between CTW and Markle representatives and Washington political operatives and lawyers in 1971 left Morrisett with the distinct impression that local politicians in the District expected payoffs—seats on the board, jobs for friends, perhaps even kickbacks—in return for the franchise.

There were also differences among the workshop's leaders about the wisdom of the project. Morrisett strongly favored cable as an important avenue toward economic self-sufficiency for the workshop. Joan Cooney was cooler toward the project. Another board member, Richard Steadman, worried that engaging in such a competitive commercial cable venture might tarnish the workshop's image. In late 1971, CTW formally withdrew from the Washington project, thus effectively killing it.

The net result of Markle's misadventures in Washington was a body of well-received research by Mitre. The larger dream of creating a model cable system in the nation's capital went unfulfilled. The Children's Television Workshop, meanwhile, kept its cable ambitions alive by forming CTW Communications, which successfully bid for franchises in other locations, including Dayton, Ohio, and Hawaii, with backing from the Ford Foundation.

FRANCHISE WARS: THE CABLE TELEVISION INFORMATION CENTER

The gold rush among cable operators for local franchise contracts picked up speed during the late 1960s and quickened during the 1970s as the FCC gradually relaxed its obstructionist stance on cable growth in large cities. With the stakes so high for both cities and cable companies, the dealings were, at best, difficult and, at worst, unsavory or even illegal. Using their regulatory clout, cities could demand from cable operators that were bidding for franchises such "sweeteners" as community access channels, free service to hospitals or schools, or two-way capability. Less scrupulous city officials used their leverage to gain percentages of cable's local profits, or bribes, for themselves.

Cable operators, for their part, were often willing to promise cities anything to gain exclusive municipal franchises, whether or not they had the technical or financial resources to deliver. The result was that cable systems often had poor signals. Some charged exorbitant rates. Others served only affluent neighborhoods. Few provided two-way communications or served schools or hospitals. And most local officials lacked the knowledge to ensure that cable companies fulfilled the educational, social, and civic potentials of the new technology.

Morrisett decided that a national clearinghouse was needed to spread reliable information for city and state officials to help them in their complex dealings with cable operators. In November 1971, Markle teamed with the Ford Foundation to establish the Cable Television Information Center at the Urban Institute, a nonprofit organization serving the needs of local authorities. Markle provided an initial two-year, $500,000 grant and, over the next decade, supported the center with another six grants totaling $1.2 million. The Ford Foundation added its own four-year, $2.5 million grant.

The center soon became, as one Markle staff memorandum put it, "the only public interest group operating effectively on a national level in the field of cable television."[22] Morrisett said its purpose was "to open up the options of municipal governments in the cable field by putting existing information at their disposal and developing new expertise which is particularly applicable to their problems."[23] Through 1980, the center provided economic and legal help to more than 1,800 local governments.

During the center's first five years of operation, cities seeking guidance tended to be small because FCC regulations still inhibited cable's growth in larger municipalities. Clients included Burbank, California; Eugene, Oregon; Wichita Falls, Texas; and Altoona, Pennsylvania.[24] Eventually, as cable spread to larger cities, the center offered assistance to officials in Minneapolis, Cincinnati, Boston, Indianapolis, Dallas, Fort Worth, Omaha, and Kansas City, Missouri.

In its later years, the center assumed a policy role and testified before the FCC and Congress as the federal government reexamined its restrictive stance toward cable during the 1970s. It also conducted a number of in-depth studies of the needs of individual cities, beginning with Jacksonville, Florida, in 1973.[25]

Jacksonville had recently consolidated to a city-county form of government and saw cable as a means of uniting its sprawling new metropolitan area. Previously, the city had negotiated infamous deals with local cable franchisers, such as awarding thirty-year franchises in exchange for 20 percent of their profits. A losing cable operator had successfully challenged that deal in court.[26] In its next go-round with cable, the Jacksonville city government asked the Urban Institute's information center for a study of design alternatives for a cable system. The result was an econometric model that was eventually used to test the feasibility of cable systems in numerous other cities, including Newark, New Jersey; Hartford, Connecticut; Fort Wayne, Indiana; and Syracuse, New York.[27]

Despite such successes, the center was sometimes criticized for being vague and overly cautious. One independent evaluation found that local officials occasionally found the advice received as "too benign, too neutral and too cautiously rendered."[28] The analysis of Jacksonville's cable options, for example, was judged to be thorough and well-researched but overly bland.[29] Such criticisms, although reasonable enough on the surface, also might have been naive in light of the difficult legal and political lines that the center was straddling during the height of the local cable franchising wars.

By the end of the 1970s, both Ford and Markle put the center on notice that the end of their funding was at hand. It would have to find ways to be self-supporting, such as selling its services to governments at market rates. On January 1, 1980, the center separated from the Urban Institute for a brief existence as an independent, nonprofit organization. That same year, it lost its tax-exempt status but successfully converted to a commercial consulting firm, CTIC Associates, Inc. It was still operating in Olympia, Washington, in 2000 and had provided consulting services to some three thousand local governments.

COMMUNITY CABLE AND A WOMAN NAMED RED

On April 14, 1997, show host Rosie O'Donnell and writer-filmmaker Nora Ephron were honored with Matrix Awards for distinguished work by women in the media at the Waldorf-Astoria Hotel. Alongside those better-known celebrities was another winner—Red Burns, a New York University (NYU) professor whose name matched her flaming hair.

Twenty-six years earlier, Burns had been a young adjunct instructor of filmmaking at NYU. In 1971, Morrisett decided to support her pioneering work in public access cable television, which gave ordinary citizens the ability, for the first time, to take to the airwaves as writers, editors, producers, actors, and social and political commentators. In the field of mass communications, Burns also proved to be a rarity—a humanist not infatuated with technology. "I've always had a healthy disdain for technology, and I still do," Burns told the author. "People become dazzled by the technology, by the speed, the color, the jazziness. They lose sight of the fact that it's really about people. But the technology has to be in place in order to make it happen."[30] Burns had offered some of the first and most convincing demonstrations of cable's potential to deliver social services and address the needs of ordinary citizens—from getting a traffic light fixed in a Manhattan intersection to helping senior citizens in Reading, Pennsylvania. "Television of the people, not just for the people," as McCandlish Phillips of *The New York Times* neatly, but optimistically, characterized community cable.[31]

Nicholas Johnson, then a commissioner at the FCC, expressed similar high hopes in a 1971 speech: "Perhaps as never before has technology given us the opportunity for a new 'meeting of men, meeting of minds' in our unworkable inner cities."[32]

The earliest documented experiment in public access cable in the United States took place in Dale City, Virginia, in 1968. The station was made available to the Dale City Jaycees, who took full financial responsibility for its operation. The experiment soon collapsed, however, because of poor equipment and lack of financing.[33]

The FCC's eventual rule requiring cable operators to set aside channels or broadcast time for use by communities or public users was not fully implemented until 1977.[34] Even without a government mandate, cable franchisers were offering public access as a bargaining chip to gain municipal contracts during the early 1970s. New York City made such deals with TelePrompter and Sterling Cable in 1971. To Red Burns, those franchising deals presented an opportunity to experiment with the untapped civic potential of cable television.

Burns's three-decade adventure with communications technology began in 1969 when someone handed her a Sony Porta-Pak camera, the first to take instant pictures with inexpensive, half-inch videotape. The camera was so simple that anyone could use it. "It was one of these epiphanous moments," Burns said. "I said to myself, this is going to have some impact. It was just incredible that nonprofessionals could make their own documentaries. Now I wondered, how can they do it?"[35]

Burns and an NYU colleague, Professor George Stoney, began taking film students into New York communities to develop innovative cable broadcasts. In the spring of 1970, NYU students filmed anti–Vietnam War protests, as well as Puerto Rican community activists fighting the city for better low-income housing. That fall, Burns made a presentation about her work at Automation House, a nonprofit labor center in New York. Forrest Chisman, Morrisett's program assistant, happened to be in the audience. As Burns left, he suggested to her that they talk further.

The challenge facing Burns was how citizens with no television training might be taught to produce programming that was technically sound, interesting, and informative. Could public access programming be advanced from spotty local experiments to a national model? In their proposal to Markle, "How to Do Something about Cable TV before It's Too Late," Burns and Stoney argued for a preemptive strike at cable TV before it became awash in commercialism:

> The kind of information (or diversion) sent out via cable TV for the next twenty years is going to be determined, we believe, in the next two or three years. . . .
>
> Right now there is a great deal of talk . . . about "community programming," "public service," "immediate and unrestricted access." . . . In fact, what we are more likely to have is a series of cable stations coining money with program formats composed of syndicated tapes of national sports events, old-time movies, a revolving drum that carries the time of day, the weather, stock quotations and a plethora of advertisements. . . .
>
> Once such an easily potted, profitable format becomes established it will be almost impossible to change, as impossible, say, as persuading radio stations to give up the "Top Pop 40" format.[36]

In fact, the timing could not have been better for making a match between Markle and Burns and her idea for an Alternate Media Center at NYU.

"This is very much a race against the clock," staff members wrote to Markle's board in endorsing the grant request. "While cable operators are presently receptive to experiments in programming, they will soon be courted by a great number of distributors of more conventional television shows; thus, if they are not presented with the possibility of trying new formats in the near future, they may simply fill up their presently existing excess channel capacity with more of the same kind of programming now carried over the air."[37]

In the climate of furious competition for municipal franchises, local cable operators had indicated that they would cooperate in giving community-minded or experimental production material a try. Still, it would be naive, Burns argued, to rely indefinitely on good intentions alone: "Perhaps not until the FCC puts muscle behind its 'public responsibility' and 'community programming' rhetoric can we expect a majority of the cable managements to be fully cooperative. But we dare not wait to act; now is the time to devise new and imaginative ways of public service programming that will be available when the day comes."[38]

In March 1971, Chisman called Burns with the news that Markle was awarding $260,000 to open the NYU center—the first of four grants totaling $845,000 through 1977. The new center opened shop one flight above the Bleecker Street Cinema in Greenwich Village, but eventually moved to the NYU campus.

Under the center's guidance, New York City became an early national pacesetter in community access cable. It produced hundreds of hours of programming for use on New York cable channels, including school board meetings and artistic programming, and published guides on public access. Burns and other center staff served as consultants to a number of organizations, including the Mitre Corporation. Under a partnership arrangement with a number of cable operators, the center trained scores of students and citizens in cable television production. It helped establish public access facilities in other cities, including Bakersfield, California; DeKalb, Illinois; Cape May, New Jersey; and Reading, Pennsylvania.

Burns's work in Reading was especially fruitful. Monroe Rifkin, president of the cable firm, American Television and Communications Corp., had read reports of Burns's early efforts in community cable. He contacted Burns, and their conversation led her to visit Reading where Rifkin's company operated a cable franchise. Burns offered to provide training for local residents in cable production if Rifkin would put up the money.

The result, *Community Video Workshop*, was an immediate success. More than fifty residents were trained to run editing machines and cameras and more than one hundred usable tapes were produced in three months. Community demand, from business people to housewives with messages to broadcast, became so heavy that the amount of taping equipment had to be doubled. In 1972, the Reading project was voted the nation's best local origination program by the National Cable Television Association.

In 1975, the project took a crucial turn when Burns received $1.75 million from the National Science Foundation to demonstrate the value of two-way cable technology in meeting the needs of Reading's older citizens. To ensure strong community involvement, Burns established a community board to oversee the operation. She met with the board every month so that eventually the community could assume responsibility for the senior citizen project. The result, Berks Community Television, survived, and the organization is still serving the needs of Reading's older citizens.

In 1979, NYU's Alternate Media Center had grown into a full-scale graduate program—the Interactive Telecommunications Program. During the next two decades, its enrollment grew from twenty students to more than two hundred a year. Their backgrounds varied from computer science to biology to dance, which reflected Burns's belief in the interdisciplinary nature of communications study. Over the years, students have produced video programs on global warming for the American Museum of Natural History, as well as a variety of interactive CD-ROM games and cable programs that allow viewers to control the action with touch-tone telephones. Graduates of the program have taken their technical knowledge and the center's humanistic perspective about the uses of technology to positions at Microsoft Corporation, TimeWarner Cable, and many other profit and nonprofit communications organizations.

As successful as the Alternate Media Center was in demonstrating the potential of public access cable in Reading and elsewhere, the national landscape for such broadcasts remained generally dreary. School board meetings, local sports events, town council hearings, and a fair amount of silliness and "vanity video" have made up the standard fare on most public access stations. There was, for example, the notorious "Dirty George," a New York City public access cable personality whose idea of community service broadcasting was inviting women to strip naked on the air.

As Morrisett observed: "Like public television, local origination and local access suffers from the idea that there is really a wealth of talent that can work with the economics of local television. It's really almost impossible, because local access channels are competing with all the other cable channels. So you really have to have a kind of community organization like the one Red developed in Reading, or you need a local source of funds that will keep it going. And there's practically none of it."[39]

If public access was, in large part, a disappointment, Morrisett never abandoned his search for ways to use communications technology to build a sense of community and give ordinary citizens a larger voice in shaping government decisions. To achieve those social goals, Markle turned during the 1990s to a new technology that was less expensive and more global in its reach: the Internet.

MORE, AND BETTER?

Morrisett had hoped that the coming of cable would spawn television programming that was not merely more plentiful but of better quality and of greater educational, civic, and cultural value than regular network TV fare. Cable undoubtedly produced "more" on viewer dials. Whether it was better, through Markle's efforts or otherwise, is debatable.

The body of research that Markle supported at RAND and Mitre Corporation provided much of the economic, legal, and technical justification for easing the FCC's early restrictions on cable's growth. Indeed, by the mid-1980s, President Ronald Reagan and Congress were deregulating the airwaves with a vengeance. New federal laws further freed cable from the FCC's grip and placed more power over franchising in the hands of local authorities. Thereafter, with only such rare exceptions as the 1990 Children's Television Act that affected all broadcasters, the spirit of deregulation was firmly in place.

Unquestionably, bad luck and timing played a part in thwarting many of Markle's cable initiatives. The recession of the early 1970s occurred at the height of Markle's attention to cable. The result was an interruption in cable's growth spurt and an increase in the already high front-end capital costs of new cable systems. Between 1972 and 1973, the market value of the stock of the largest cable corporations declined by approximately two thirds. During the first half of the decade, few big cities had any cable stations. Not until the 1980s did cable finally begin two decades of phenomenal growth. By the mid-1990s, according to the National Cable Television Association, some 162 networks were being broadcast on 11,200 cable systems to more than 65 million U.S. household subscribers.

What remained largely unaccomplished were two things Morrisett had most hoped for with the coming of cable: an explosion of fresh educational children's television with quality approaching that of *Sesame Street,* and widespread exploration and use of cable's two-way interactive capacity.

A few scattered experiments in interactive cable took place during the 1970s, most notably a short-lived program called QUBE by Warner Cable in Columbus, Ohio. Years later, in September 1993, Markle funded an electronic "town meeting" on health care in San Antonio, one of the few cities with a cable operator, Paragon Cable, that offered interactive capability and was enthusiastic about trying a social experiment. Titled "Condition Critical: San Antonio Deliberates Health Care," the program aimed to use interactive cable to go beyond sound-and-fury talk shows and offer a forum for group deliberation that allowed home audiences to join in. By most measures, the experiment worked. Using cable modems, viewers voted on various policy options during the two-hour discussion on KBL-TV. About eighteen thousand people tuned in, and an astounding 100 percent of those polled after the show said they would like to see similar electronic town meetings on other subjects.[40]

Despite the warm reception for the San Antonio experiment, few U.S. cities have developed two-way cable systems. Hardly any new ones are on the horizon because they have not proved themselves to be moneymakers. With the laudable exception of C-Span and, stretching the point, home shopping channels, Morrisett's hopes that cable might be a means of connecting people more effectively to the institutions that most affect their lives have not been realized.

Morrisett was similarly dissatisfied with what cable had accomplished in children's programming.[41] The Discovery Channel, Learning Channel, History Channel, and several others have provided interesting educational fare. The cable industry points with pride to its *Cable in the Classroom* program, begun in 1989, which provides commercial-free programming to seventy thousand schools at no cost. More often, however, cable has become the place on the dial where the undead among network sitcoms, such as *Bewitched* and *The Brady Bunch*, rise each weeknight to feed on the time and attention of fresh generations of children.

Of course, it can hardly be laid at Markle's doorstep that the cable industry proved to be as captive to commercial and market considerations as network television. Still, fresh hope emerged in 1998 with the announcement that Children's Television Workshop and Nickelodeon had entered an agreement to create a commercial-free educational children's network, Noggin, which began broadcasting in January 1999. Whether it eventually offers children the steady diet of appealing educational experiences that Morrisett dreamed about for cable nearly thirty years earlier remains to be seen.

NOTES

1. Data compiled by the National Cable Television Association, Washington, D.C.
2. Gillespie, *Public Access Cable Television*, 20.
3. Grant, *Cable Television*, xiv.
4. Lloyd N. Morrisett, "Cable TV: Can More Be Better?" (President's Essay in "The John and Mary R. Markle Foundation, Annual Report, 1970–1971"), 3.
5. Ibid., 12.
6. Sloan Commission, *On the Cable*, 29–30.
7. Park, *Role of Analysis*, 82.
8. Geller, interview, 22 Sept. 1997.
9. Morrisett, interview, 16 July 1997.
10. Morrisett, "Cable TV," 3.
11. Lloyd N. Morrisett and Leland L. Johnson, RAND Corporation,

telephone conversation, 5 Sept. 1969, written record, Markle Archive Collection.

12. Allina, interview, 17 Sept 1997.

13. Some of the most widely circulated and well-publicized RAND reports produced with Markle funding include Leland L. Johnson, "Cable Television and the Question of Protecting Local Broadcasting," Oct. 1970, R-595-MF; Leland L. Johnson, "Cable Television and Higher Education: Two Contrasting Experiences," Sept. 1971, R-828-MF; Rolla Edward Park, "Cable Television and UHF Broadcasting," Jan. 1971, R-689-MF; Michael R. Mitchell, "State Regulation of Cable Television," Oct. 1971, R-783-MF; Park, "Prospects for Cable in the 100 Largest Television Markets," Oct. 1971, R-875-MF; and Walter S. Baer, "Interactive Television: Prospects for Two-Way Services on Cable," Nov. 1971, R-888-MF. (Copies of these reports can be obtained from RAND Corporation, Santa Monica, Calif.)

14. Johnson, interview, 25 Sept. 1997.

15. Rolla Edward Park, "After Exclusivity Blackouts, What's Left on the Horizon," *TV Communications*, Aug. 1972, 48.

16. Rolla Edward Park, "The Exclusivity Provisions of the Federal Communications Commission's Cable Television Regulations," R-1057-FF/MF, June 1972, cited in "Annual Progress Report: The John and Mary R. Markle Foundation Grant to the RAND Communications Policy Program" (prepared by Leland L. Johnson, principal investigator), 1 July 1972–30 June 1973, 2.

17. RAND Corporation, "The Importance of Flexible Funding in Communications Policy Research," memorandum to The Markle Foundation, 19 Feb. 1973, 2.

18. Minow, interview, 18 Sept. 1997.

19. Park, *Role of Analysis*, 74.

20. Ibid., 78.

21. Mitre Corporation, "Summary of Work Conducted under Grants from The John and Mary R. Markle Foundation," 14 July 1972 (file memorandum), 1.

22. The Markle Foundation, staff memorandum to Board of Directors, recommending continued support in the amount of $250,000 for the Cable Television Information Center, November 1972, 14, Markle Archive Collection.

23. Lloyd N. Morrisett, "Cable Television Information Center," speech, 11 Jan. 1972, 2.

24. Urban Institute, "1977 Annual Report," 51.

25. Urban Institute, "1972 Annual Report," 37.

26. Urban Institute, "Activities of the Cable Television Information

Center, 1972–75: Report to The Ford Foundation and The John & Mary R. Markle Foundation," 10.

27. Ibid., 22.

28. Herbert S. Dordick and Allan Talbot, "The Cable Television Information Center—Summer 1973, A Status Report" (confidential unpublished report prepared for The Markle Foundation), 17, Markle Archive Collection.

29. Ibid., 13.

30. Burns, interview, 11 Aug. 1997.

31. McCandlish Phillips, "TV of the People Operating on Cable," *The New York Times*, 23 Sept., 1971, 62.

32. Nicholas Johnson, untitled address presented at Urban CATV Workshop, Washington, D.C., 26 June 1971 (issued as a public notice by the Federal Communications Commission), 13.

33. Gillespie, *Public Access Cable Television*, 36, 59.

34. Ibid., 7.

35. Burns, interview, 11 Aug. 1997.

36. "How to Do Something about Cable TV before It's Too Late" (proposal for an Alternate Media Center at New York University prepared by Professors Red Burns and George Stoney on behalf of the faculty of the Undergraduate Division of Film and Television in the School of the Arts), January 1971, 1.

37. The Markle Foundation, staff memorandum to Board of Directors, Markle Archive Collection.

38. "How to Do Something about Cable TV," 6.

39. Morrisett, interview, 12 Aug. 1997.

40. Kathie Johnson, Public Agenda Foundation, "Final Narrative on Markle Grant for Electronic Town Meeting Project" (unpublished memorandum prepared for The Markle Foundation), 8 Feb. 1993.

41. Lloyd N. Morrisett, "Paying for Children" (President's Essay in "The John and Mary R. Markle Foundation, Annual Report, 1980–1981"), 4.

5

Messages to the Media

DURING THE LATE 1960s when the Markle Foundation decided to explore whether unbiased criticism could lift the performance of the media and help restore the public's flagging confidence in journalism, a siege mentality existed in America's newsrooms. The messages to the media from the public and politicians were alarming—so much so that many observers, including Morrisett, feared that the nation was drifting toward repression of journalistic freedom unless the historic bonds between press and public could be repaired.

The festering anger toward the nation's news gatherers found its most strident expression on the evening of November 13, 1969, in Des Moines, Iowa. Vice President Spiro T. Agnew, until that night a rather unprepossessing figure in the Nixon Administration, delivered a headline-making speech accusing the press of being dominated by "a tiny, enclosed fraternity of privileged men elected by no one and enjoying a monopoly sanctioned and licensed by government."[1] He invited listeners to tell the news networks what they thought of their coverage. Within hours, thousands across the country did exactly that.

The presidents of the three major networks quickly denounced Agnew's speech. Julian Goodman of NBC called it "an appeal to prejudice."[2] Dr. Frank Stanton of CBS accused the White House of not so subtle blackmail, "an unprecedented attempt . . . to intimidate a news medium which depends for its existence upon government licenses. . . ."[3] Leonard Goldenson of ABC coolly assured viewers that his network would "continue to report the news accurately and fully, confident in the ultimate judgment of the American public."[4]

In fact, there was no reason for any such confidence.

Agnew, the Nixon White House, and the press itself quickly grasped that the Des Moines address had tapped a deep vein of public discontent. Agnew had deftly blamed the messengers for the recent outpouring of depressing news from Vietnam. He had deflected attention from revelations of the massacre of hundreds of Vietnamese civilians, including women and children, by U.S. forces in the village of My Lai. The warm public reception for Agnew's press attacks demonstrated to any doubters how widespread mistrust of the media had become. From that day on, press bashing became a standard staple of politics.

For the next four years, Agnew continued to batter away at the news media. With alliterative ammunition supplied by, among others, White House speechwriter and future *New York Times* columnist William Safire, the vice president branded reporters "nattering nabobs of negativism."[5] The message found its mark. In 1966, a Louis Harris poll reported that only 29 percent of the public had confidence in the press. Just five years later, in 1971, the press's approval rating had shrunk to 18 percent.[6]

Presidents from George Washington to Lyndon Johnson had had their feuds with journalists. But the raw animus during the late 1960s and early 1970s among the president, the press, and the public was different—and deeper. Days after Agnew's Des Moines address, James Reston, dean of political columnists at *The New York Times*, wearily observed: "It is not only that we [in the news media] are 'unfair' and 'inaccurate'—as God knows we sometimes are—but that we are 'subversives' . . . even pro-Communist."[7]

A large percentage of the public had evidently come to regard journalists as troublemakers who never admitted their mistakes because the First Amendment seemed to say they did not really have to. The growing fear of government interference in press freedom, however, was no fantasy. As tapes and documents from the Nixon archives would reveal years later, the White House was plotting a war of intimidation against the press, threatening television license renewals, barring reporters from public meetings, drawing up "enemies lists," and weakening the laws shielding reporters from libel suits.

Longer-term changes within the press itself also threatened to erode public confidence. Ownership of major news outlets was concentrating in fewer and fewer hands. By 1973, 97 percent of American communities were served by one newspaper or by chain-owned newspapers, according to Ben H. Bagdikian, a leading journalist and scholar who produced shocking documentation of this media monopolization with research funded partly by Markle.[8]

The monopolization of local newspaper markets was only a symptom of a far larger phenomenon brewing in the news business. Aided by new technologies and a largely complicit government, a small number of corporate information and entertainment empires—TimeWarner, Inc., Sony Corporation, Rupert Murdoch's News Corporation, The Walt Disney Company, *The New York Times*, Gannett Company, Inc., Viacom, General Electric Company, and a few others—were swallowing up entire chains of newspapers, magazines, publishing houses, and cable and television networks.

In 1981, Bagdikian wrote in the first edition of his classic book, *The Media Monopoly*, that forty-six corporations controlled the majority of business in daily newspapers, magazines, television, books, and movies. By 1996, the number of dominant media firms had shrunk in half, to twenty-three.[9] The largest media merger in 1983 was a $340 million deal between Gannett Company and Combined Communications Corporation. Thirteen years later, in 1996, the merger of Walt Disney and Capital Cities/ABC, Inc. was valued at $19 billion, and produced a media monolith consisting of newspapers, magazines, books, radio, television, cable, movies, records, videocasettes, and even telephones. In 1999, Viacom and Columbia Broadcasting System (CBS) announced a $37 billion proposed merger, only to be dwarfed later that year when Internet upstart America Online, Inc., announced the biggest media marriage in history: a proposed friendly acquisition of Time Warner, Inc., for an astounding $156 billion in stock.

This conglomeratization of the media and information industries had several consequences. Newspaper publishers such as William Randolph Hearst and Walter Annenberg, as well as broadcasters, had long possessed and freely used their power to help or to hurt political careers. But these emerging media conglomerates, by virtue of their increasing stranglehold on all avenues of public information, multiplied their political clout geometrically and became, collectively, one of the undisputed powerhouses of Washington lobbies. Single corporations controlled the airwaves, opinion magazines, news pages, and editorial pages in entire media markets. They therefore exercised unprecedented power, not only over the political destinies of elected officials from the president on down but over the democratic process itself.

Over the next two decades, the nation's press and broadcast barons would win victory after victory in Washington as they aimed to remove regulatory barriers to even further power, profit, and monopolization of the airwaves. In time, that power would grow so formidable that, in 1997, broadcasters managed to secure the passage—from a Republican Congress ostensibly dedicated to free markets and competition—of a federal giveaway of publicly owned high-definition digital channels on the broadcast spectrum that were worth billions of dollars. *New York Times* columnist William Safire likened it to "giving Yellowstone National Park to timber companies."[10]

Along with their virtually unmatched political influence, the media's monopolization raised fresh questions about the trustworthiness of news content itself. As the mentality of the boardroom seeped into newsrooms, the time-honored wall separating newsgathering decisions from the interests of publishers and, by extension, advertisers was crumbling fast. In setting news priorities, the concerns of the truth-seeking reporter seemed often to be growing more and more trivial when weighed against the interests of advertisers or shareholders.

Finally, as Morrisett noted in the early 1970s, the changing values and professional habits of journalists themselves were fueling doubts about their objectivity and fairness. A far more personal, occasionally even fictionalized, brand of reporting dubbed "new journalism," was vying for legitimacy alongside more traditional, "objective" methods of news gathering.

In the politically incendiary climate of the late 1960s and early 1970s, the media's near-paranoia about any criticism, whatever the source, might have been understandable. Still, it was that very hypersensitivity to criticism that would thwart much of what Markle attempted during the next dozen years to help restore public confidence in news gatherers. Morrisett was convinced that informed, objective criticism, coupled with more, not less, public accountability, was the best answer to ideologically motivated attacks on the media. The harsh truth was that the media's critics, regardless of their motives, were making points that no longer could be casually dismissed.

What much of the press had apparently forgotten was that its First Amendment shield from government interference was always intended as a means, as well as an end. The constitutional mandate of a free press was designed to create a vigorous, independent check on government power. The 1776 Virginia Bill of Rights, which foreshadowed the U.S. Constitution, described freedom of the press as "one of the great bulwarks of liberty." More recently, media scholar Timothy E. Cook has argued that the First Amendment "focuses on the rights of citizens to information, not on the rights of those in the media industry to disseminate what they want."[11]

Over time, however, at least some members of the press seemed to regard the First Amendment less as a public trust than as a constitutional shield from public accountability. In 1970, average citizens who felt wronged or damaged by news reports had little recourse short of libel suits. Although newspapers were slowly accepting the idea of printing corrections of errors in their news pages, television newscasts seldom admitted mistakes prominently, if at all. The stock replies to public calls for accountability—that people could always stop buying offending newspapers or tune out shallow TV newscasts—rang increasingly hollow as media monopolization further homogenized the news and quelled diversity.

"Today the press is becoming ever more important as an extension of the eyes and ears of the citizen," Morrisett wrote in his 1972 annual essay, "Press Credibility—The Citizen's Dilemma." "It is indeed becoming as important as its champions have always thought it to be. However, at a time when the citizen is in ever greater need of a credible press, his confidence in it has diminished.[12]

Morrisett was never motivated by hostility to the press, but he was certainly no blind apologist, either. In the early 1970s, a flip remark by Turner Catledge, executive editor of *The New York Times*, that "I'd steal a photograph off my grandmother's mantle for a story" struck Morrisett as the "quintessential attitude" of the working press.[13] To Morrisett, such comments typified his view that, as with members of any profession, some journalists were thoughtful and judicious, but many were not. The constitutional safeguards for press freedom had been vindicated in history many times over. He was equally convinced, however, that regular criticism of press performance was a way to restore the public's trust and banish the specter of government intrusion into newsrooms. Film, books, art, music, and theater were routinely criticized. Where, Morrisett wondered, were the magazines, television shows, or daily columnists whose mission was to keep print and broadcast journalism on its toes?

For the first dozen years of his presidency, Morrisett supported research that probed the media's habits and qualifications and explored ways to improve the training and professional preparation of practicing journalists. A second and even greater challenge was to create, if possible, new outlets for objective media criticism that would be accepted by both the public and the press.

In furtherance of these goals, Markle first rescued the financially ailing *Columbia Journalism Review* in 1971, which enabled it to become the most respected magazine of press criticism. From 1971 to 1973, Markle financed a well-received but short-lived public broadcasting series of press criticism called *Behind the Lines*. It supported the small but gutsy Fund for Investigative Journalism in Washington that provided freelance journalists with the money needed to produce courageous reporting on topics overlooked by mainstream publications. Markle also became a leading force in the growing "press council movement" that led, in 1973, to the establishment of the National News Council that sought unsuccessfully to offer the public a neutral forum for grievances against news organizations.

The media certainly had been receiving powerful messages from the White House and the public during the late 1960s and early 1970s. Now, Markle was preparing to send its own messages aimed at promoting the four principles that had governed Morrisett throughout his entire presidency: access, equity, quality, and improved content.

MEDIA RESEARCH AND TRAINING

The diminished credibility of the press in the eyes of the public, Morrisett was convinced, was in large part a product of ignorance about the profession itself. As usual, therefore, research for Morrisett and his staff was the natural entre into this new field of philanthropic interest. "Although there is currently a great deal of discussion about the state of journalism and the proper role of journalists, little information is available about the men and women who report, write and edit the news," he wrote early in his presidency.[14]

Markle provided more than one hundred research grants totaling more than $4 million on a range of media topics. Ben Bagdikian studied the increasing concentration of newspaper markets. Father Andrew Greeley of the University of Chicago received support to examine the nation's "ethnic" newspapers serving Polish American, African American, Puerto Rican, and other ethnic communities. During 1972 and 1973, Markle supported an investigation of First Amendment issues in political coverage by Benno Schmidt and Fred Friendly of Columbia University. A string of grants on how news coverage affects the political process also went to the Social Science Research Council, the University of Michigan's Institute for Social Research, and political scientists Thomas Patterson at Syracuse University and James David Barber at Duke University.

In 1971 and 1972, Markle provided $188,000 for a follow-up study to gather data on journalists' backgrounds and beliefs. The project was led by John W. C. Johnstone, a sociologist and expert on adult education at the University of Illinois at Chicago. The results, published in 1976 under the title, *The News People: A Sociological Portrait of American Journalists and Their Work*, revealed that men outnumbered women by four to one at the time in the news industry as a whole, and by more than nine to one in the broadcast field.[15] Fewer than 4 percent of all news professionals were black.[16] A surprisingly high 42 percent of the profession had not graduated from college.[17] More than one in four journalists believed that reporters displayed lack of objectivity, and about the same percentage thought their profession was guilty of superficiality in its coverage. More than 11 percent believed the press overemphasized sensational crime news, and 17 percent said the media habitually neglected international news or minority affairs.[18]

Early on, Markle also set out to improve the education and

training of journalists—a path already well-worn by other foundations. For three years beginning in 1971, Markle supplied $330,000 to expand an urban affairs internship program at the University of Chicago at a time when the problems of American cities were enjoying a brief period in the media spotlight. Soon after Markle ended its funding, the program folded—undone through lack of sustained interest by either participating journalists or their bosses at the newspapers.

Markle's interests in improving journalists' training led briefly to an exploration of the needs of minority journalists. The problems were evident: fewer than 100 of the 38,000 reporters and editors at daily newspapers in 1968 were nonwhite. A decade later, their ranks had risen to 1,700, but nonwhite journalists still accounted for a bare 4 percent of the total workforce.[19] Markle provided $100,000 to support a new office of minority affairs at the National Association of Educational Broadcasters, whose purposes included more minority hiring in educational broadcasting and more and better programming concerning minority issues. Morrisett himself served in 1978 and 1979 as a member of a National Association of Broadcasters's task force whose goal was to increase the number of minority-owned broadcast facilities.

In 1978, the foundation also gave grants totaling nearly $236,000 to support the Washington, D.C.–based Institute for Journalism Education, founded and led by *Oakland Tribune* editor Robert Maynard, the highest-ranking African American print journalist in the nation at that time. Eventually renamed the Maynard Institute for Journalism Education after his death, it established an employment service for minority journalists in 1978 called Job/Net and operated a summer program for minority journalists. Nonetheless, the mood in the news industry about diversity in its ranks has remained pessimistic. A survey in 1998 by the American Society of Newspaper Editors found that more than 11 percent of the nation's reporters, editors, and photographers were from nonwhite ethnic groups, triple the percentage in 1978. By 1998, however, progress had stalled. From 1997 to 1998, the growth in minority presence in newsrooms was a mere 0.10 percent, and the talk in the industry was of "diversity fatigue."

THE RESCUE OF THE *COLUMBIA JOURNALISM REVIEW*

Markle's first concerted effort at promoting objective media criticism centered on the rescue of the financially ailing *Columbia Journalism Review* (*CJR*). The magazine was founded just as a young media star, John F. Kennedy, was rewriting the rules that had long governed relations between news gatherers and news makers. Kennedy's mastery of media imagery, beginning with his 1960 debates with Richard Nixon and carrying through his subsequent presidential news conferences, transformed those relationships forever. The capacity of the press to manipulate, and to be manipulated in turn, demanded thoughtful scrutiny. Leaders of Columbia University's Graduate School of Journalism decided that they were uniquely positioned, by dint of their credibility and stature, to start an objective national journal of press performance. In the fall of 1961, the first edition of *CJR* went to press.

During its first decade, the magazine was well regarded by many people in the news industry but was considered esoteric by many others. Because it was published only quarterly, its tone and content were more scholarly than topical, and circulation was well under ten thousand. Also, it was not universally welcomed by the news business. James Boylan, the magazine's original editor, recalled years later that such veterans of the profession as Wes Gallagher, the gruff, bushy-browed general manager of the Associated Press (AP) in those days, never warmed to the notion of being critiqued by a "J-school" magazine.[20] Still, the *Review* slowly gained prestige, if not readership, through the 1960s.

By 1969, however, *CJR*'s readership had stagnated at less than twelve thousand.[21] To safeguard its editorial purity, the *Review* accepted no advertising. A five-year grant from the Ford Foundation that averaged $39,000 a year would soon expire, and Ford officials made clear their disappointment with the *Review*'s financial progress. Subscription revenues covered less than half of the magazine's $123,000 annual expenses. Much of the rest was made up with modest foundation grants, and Columbia University had lent the magazine money each year to cover a cumulative deficit of some $30,000. Now, with mounting financial problems of its own, Columbia was growing reluctant to continue bailing out a magazine that was seen by some as a misfit in its academic setting.[22] Unlike most academic publications, *CJR* was not peer reviewed, did not offer a forum for faculty research or writing, and therefore had few academic bona fides.

As its tenth anniversary approached, the magazine could claim to be the nation's most prestigious outlet of press criticism. But its survival was still in doubt.

In 1969, Edward Barrett, then dean of Columbia's graduate school of journalism, invited Alfred W. Balk to become the *Review*'s visiting editor for a year. Balk, a thirty-nine–year-old Iowa native, was a veteran reporter, editor, and freelancer who had worked for the *Saturday Review* and *Chicago Sun-Times*, and had recently completed a study for the Russell Sage Foundation that exposed scandals in property tax exemptions. He accepted Barrett's offer and stayed on for four years as *CJR*'s editor and the magazine's only full-time staffer.[23]

"Here was a marvelous vehicle that society and the media needed, but the marvelous vehicle was in jeopardy and needed to move to a next stage of editorial and financial development," Balk said in looking back on the challenge that he had accepted. "Clearly it had acceptance and prestige by journalists and opinion leaders outside journalism. But there weren't that many of them, so the circulation was not large."[24]

In Balk, the magazine had found an editor who could lift it to a new level, but it still needed a financial angel. Louis G. Cowan, a former president of CBS and chairman of *CJR*'s Publishing Committee, phoned Morrisett in March 1970, and they arranged a meeting at Markle the following month.

Ten months later, Markle agreed to provide a $204,000 grant, enough to ensure the magazine's immediate survival. Just as critically, the money allowed the magazine to publish bimonthly and thereby assume a less scholarly, closer-to-the-news tone. The funds also enabled Balk to attract top contributors, including Walter Lippmann, Theodore White, Edwin Diamond, and Ben Bagdikian.

In keeping with its custom, Markle never intruded into the editorial content of the *Review*. There was little need: Balk and Markle were on virtually identical wavelengths about the larger goals of press criticism. The magazine was an avid supporter of press councils. It began a special section highlighting the articles of other struggling regional journalism reviews, such as the *Chicago Journalism Review* and even its for-profit, more bombastic rival, *MORE Magazine*. Balk himself played a key role in starting the National News Council during the early 1970s, and, through 1981, *CJR* reported the council's deliberations faithfully and often alone.

As the original grant to *CJR* was expiring in 1973, Markle provided a fresh $80,000 award to raise salaries, make further editorial changes, increase the size of the staff, and hire professional management of the circulation department to help the magazine increase circulation from 20,000 at the end of 1972 to a long-term goal of 45,000.[25] Unfortunately, the optimism that was building at Markle about *CJR*'s seeming growth, however, was founded on a deliberate deception. As Morrisett related years later, the magazine's circulation manager had been inflating the numbers in order to make himself look good so that he could keep his job. The discovery was a double lesson to Morrisett. Not only had Markle been awarding grants largely on faith that *CJR*'s internal accounting was accurate and honest, but Morrisett learned that the university's financial controls and oversight were slipshod.

Barrett telephoned Morrisett to request a meeting at Markle and said only that it was serious. When Barrett and Cowan gave him the embarrassing news on August 13, 1973, Morrisett showed little reaction. "What could you say?" he recalled. "I mean, they felt so bad, you can't make them feel much worse than they already felt. The thing was done, the people are gone, there's very little one can say."[26]

Still, that experience with the magazine led Markle to tighten its financial oversight of grants, especially to universities.

Over the next two decades, the *Columbia Journalism Review* survived but was rarely free of financial woes. By 1975, circulation had grown to 35,000. Markle's major funding of *CJR* ended in 1976, but the foundation did grant the magazine $50,000 in 1997 to develop a home page on the World Wide Web and to beef up its coverage of technology issues. The magazine eventually dropped its self-imposed prohibition from taking advertising but continued to depend on support from foundations and other outside benefactors to stay alive. As of June 1999, circulation was 28,400, with journalists accounting for 62 percent of its subscribers.[27] Most of the magazine's financial support came from interest groups and corporations. With rare exceptions, such as The New York Times Foundation, the media themselves and most foundations concerned with the media ignored *CJR*'s repeated pleas for support.[28]

BEHIND THE LINES

Even as Markle was salvaging the *Columbia Journalism Review*, Morrisett understood that television was a far more powerful means to broadcast media criticism beyond the rarified group that might read professional magazines. Thus was born, on October 9, 1971, *Behind the Lines*, a public television series that examined the inner workings of the news media and criticized their flaws but, at the same time, defended them against politically motivated attacks from the Nixon White House and elsewhere. Operating on a bare-bones annual budget of about $500,000, the series appeared for four seasons.

Originally, *Behind the Lines* aired only in New York on WNET public television, where it gained critical acclaim and a respectable following. From the second year on, it was carried nationally by PBS. Markle appropriated $295,000 in June 1971 for the first twenty-six episodes and became the main source of funding for two of its four seasons with a total of $559,000 in grants. The Ford Foundation provided most of the balance.

The series was the creation of three people with strong and occasionally clashing personalities: James Day, president of Educational Broadcasting Corporation; John Jay Iselin, a former national affairs editor of *Newsweek* and newly named general manager of WNET; and Carey Winfrey, a young *Time Magazine* press correspondent (and years later, a news executive at *People Magazine*), recruited by Iselin to be executive producer of the series.

Winfrey could hardly have imagined what he was in for. During the first year, there was not enough money for a set. Shows were often written, shot, and edited in three days. "Every dollar we got barely kept up with the technological costs of production," Winfrey said. "Everyone on the staff was on the air. I put my secretary on the air. I put myself on the air because I worked for nothing and I worked very well with the executive producer, who was me."[29]

Winfrey and his Channel 13 bosses seized upon an incredibly opportune opening for the new series. In October 1971, PBS abruptly cancelled an edition of WNET's satirical series *The Great American Dream Machine*, which purported to show how undercover agents with the Federal Bureau of Investigation were acting as provocateurs to undermine the New Left movement. The show's cancellation brought cries of political censorship that were acutely embarrassing to PBS.

This intramural spat within PBS provided the perfect vehicle that same month for the first edition of *Behind the Lines*, which consisted of a two-hour critique of the decision by PBS to spike the program. Titled "Anatomy of a Decision," the premiere drew critical raves by signaling that the new series would turn a fearless eye not only on others in the media but also on itself and its public television bosses. The program offered National Educational Television (NET) a way to make public amends by broadcasting in full what had been previously censored. (The opening program also introduced New York audiences to a young Dallas reporter named Jim Lehrer, eventual cohost of the future *McNeil-Lehrer News Hour.*)

The first season's twenty-six broadcasts amounted to a wide-ranging apologia to the press's legions of political critics. Many of those first shows were designed to increase public understanding of how news is gathered and thereby serve, as Winfrey later said, as a "rebuttal to many of the things Mr. Agnew, Mr. Pat Buchanan and others in the [Nixon] administration were saying."[30]

The first programs included a look at the "new" journalism of Tom Wolfe and Gay Talese, the problems of black and Puerto Rican newspeople, the mechanics of wire service journalism, a farewell to the journalistic crusader I. F. Stone as he was retiring, and even an examination of the pornographic *Screw* magazine. One of the earliest programs critiqued the coverage by *New York Times* columnist Tom Wicker of the bloody Attica prison riot, during which Wicker became, rightly or not, a player in the story by joining the negotiating team seeking to end the crisis.

"We hope to make people more skeptical about the information they receive," Winfrey said as the series premiered, "but we'd like to have that skepticism based on an understanding of how the medium works rather than on some across-the-board assumption that its biases are conspiratorial."[31]

Behind the Lines ended its first season as the top-rated locally produced public TV show in the New York market—a modest enough distinction since even wildly successful public television shows attracted miniscule audiences compared with those of commercial offerings. Still, it was good enough for PBS to decide to offer the show nationally in its second season. It was also enough to earn the program a second $250,000 grant from Markle for its 1972–73 season that covered more than half the program's $410,000 total budget.

In its fourth and final season in 1975, the program was hosted by Harrison Salisbury, the venerable *New York Times* correspondent. But interest in the program waned as scant funding forced producers into a talking-heads format that lacked the immediacy and visual excitement of previous seasons. By then, too, the media's "Great Satan," Richard Nixon, whose presidency had provided much of the dramatic fodder for the show during its first seasons, was gone from office. *Behind the Lines* also suffered a common malady of public affairs programming during the mid-1970s. Foundations, particularly Ford, were pulling back their funding and were being replaced by corporate backers less inclined to risk offending viewers by supporting controversial programs.

During its brief run, *Behind the Lines* was a milestone in press criticism. It also fueled Morrisett's growing doubts about what Markle, as a small foundation, could reasonably accomplish in starting and sustaining educational TV programming. In several respects, Markle should have been a dream partner for public television. Unlike federal agencies and most other foundations, Morrisett and his staff never intruded into editorial content. Winfrey said, in fact, that Morrisett was always "very amiable, supportive and hands-off. He was very careful not to tell us what to do."[32]

Still, the chemistry was never quite right. Markle, like many foundations, saw itself as a pump primer, rather than a long-term source of sustenance for public television. Morrisett was also increasingly disenchanted with public television's eccentricities, its chaotic decision-making processes, and its slavish devotion to audience ratings that made it only marginally different, in his mind, from commercial stations. To some public broadcasting executives, however, Morrisett's withdrawal from the program suggested overcaution and even naivete about the time needed to start and sustain public service programs.

The mutual misunderstandings evidently simmered long after the program ended. Following a lunch with Iselin, then president of Educational Broadcasting Corporation, in April 1976, Morrisett felt obliged to write a three-page letter to make clear that Markle was not about to be the savior of public television:

> . . . [A]s I'm sure you are aware, our concern is with mass media and information technology generally. Television is, therefore, only one part of this broad field in which we are working. Here our concern is with the advancement and improvement of "television"—public television is again only part of this concern. Obviously, it is impossible for us with a small staff and limited funds to try and deal intensively with this entire area of mass media. . . .
>
> With this perspective, I think it is clear that no public television institution can look upon the Markle Foundation as a steady source of support. We simply don't have that much money, nor are we involved with public television in that way. . . .
>
> What I want to do is to give you some understanding of the way we work so that you need not feel continually frustrated by the idea of Markle being in communications but making few grants to Channel 13. Our agenda and set of purposes are bound to be quite different from yours most of the time. I would expect, however, that from time to time there will be some mutuality of interest as there has been in the past.[33]

Years later, after leaving television to assume the presidency of Cooper Union, Iselin continued to find Markle and its president inscrutable: "I never had the sense that Markle was in there to see a series [like *Behind the Lines*] go," he told the author. "I'll take it a step further. Does Markle understand what it means to deal with electronic broadcasting? You've got to stay with this cumulatively because you've got to keep going back again and again and establish a presence in the minds of people. That comes about through repetition. I found myself cumulatively more and more mystified as to what a foundation [with a mandate to improve and criticize the media] would do to make a real mark. I still am mystified.

Lloyd was always a perfect gentleman, but I'm just damned if I can figure out what Markle has been up to."[34]

If *Behind the Lines* proved to be an early instance of the foundation's rocky history with public television, it also demonstrated the popular appeal of objective press criticism and self-examination. The program won an Emmy Award in 1974 for a segment titled "The Adversaries" that focused on the relationship between President Nixon and the media. The evident appeal of media watching was not lost on others. In years to come, Hodding Carter hosted a PBS program of media commentary, and press behavior became a regular staple of other programs, including CBS's long-running *60 Minutes*.

Along the way, *Behind the Lines* also helped establish the right to present overt political commentary on public television. The Nixon Administration, in suing the program for delivering an on-air editorial against the President's handling of the media, challenged it on the grounds that the broadcast was using public money to engage in partisan politics. The federal courts sided with public television's freedom to comment.

Behind the Lines eventually passed into the mists of forgotten television series and has been overlooked even in recent histories of public broadcasting.[35] Still, the program that Markle brought briefly to life should be remembered as one of the first efforts by television to dispel myths about the media at a time when such mythology was being spread by the nation's highest officials.

As Winfrey told the author, "What *Behind the Lines* has done is to destroy a bunch of old shibboleths that needed busting a long time ago: that the press was incapable or unwilling to look at itself, that a general audience wouldn't be interested in a program about journalism." And finally, he said that a program about the press could even be fun to watch.[36]

THE FUND FOR INVESTIGATIVE JOURNALISM

During the late 1960s and early 1970s, "investigative journalism" emerged as a romantic idea that meshed neatly with the public's cynicism about all powerful institutions in society. Unlike the old "who-what-where" brand of reporting, this new kind of journalism promised to dig behind the headlines and expose the corrupt and the comfortable in public and corporate life. The allure of investigative reporting rested on its self-described freedom from ideological motives or political ax-grinding.

Embedded in the phrase *investigative journalism*, however, was also a thinly veiled swipe at the somnolent state of much of daily news gathering. The very term suggested that there was something called *journalism*—the routine nuts and bolts of most news accounts. *Investigative* journalism, by contrast, was what resulted when reporters dug energetically and fearlessly for the whole story and its meanings—doing, in other words, what they should have been doing all along.

Only three things, of course, prevented most mainstream reporters from regularly reaching that investigative ideal: lack of time, lack of money, and lack of support from editors or publishers for reporting that might offend powerful persons, institutions, or—worst of all—advertisers. Despite the short-lived patina that the Watergate saga conferred on journalism during the mid-1970s, reporting à la Bob Woodward and Carl Bernstein of *The Washington Post* was never the industry norm.

In 1968, James Boyd, a forty-year-old political scientist turned magazine and book freelancer in Washington, established the Fund for Investigative Journalism in the hope that it might supply at least two of the three missing ingredients of hard-hitting reporting: time and money. Boyd received an initial $50,000 grant from the Stern Family Fund and, with a staff of two—himself and his wife— began operating the fund out of his Washington home. He assembled an impressive board of directors: Milton Viorst, *Washington Star* columnist; Julius Duscha, director, Washington Journalism Center; Clayton Fritchey, nationally syndicated political columnist; Richard J. Barnet, codirector, Institute for Policy Studies; the Reverend David Eaton, pastor, All Souls Unitarian Church, Washington, D.C., and local radio and television personality; and Karl Hess, former speechwriter for conservative Republican Barry Goldwater and a top Republican Party operative.

The fund's underlying assumption, Boyd wrote at the time, was "that the 'watchdog' role of the press is essential to effective democratic government, but is inadequately performed today because it is inadequately financed. Our goal is to promote, within the periodical press, an increased emphasis on investigative reporting. Our method is to make financial grants to journalists to compensate time and expenses devoted to specific projects aimed at the disclosure of malfeasance, malfunction, or non-function on the part of public or semi-public bodies."[37]

Between 1969 and 1971, the fund issued sixty-five small grants, from $100 to $1,000, to freelance journalists that resulted in sixty published articles—a 90-plus percent success rate that reflected its policy of approving grants only to projects that had publishing agreements securely in hand. In the process, the fund helped nurture important journalistic careers. Early work that it supported included an award-winning cover article in the September 1969 issue of *Atlantic Monthly* by Ronald Dugger on the power of the oil lobby and another *Atlantic Monthly* article in November 1969 by Brit Hume, future ABC White House correspondent and Fox News editor, that revealed corruption in the United Mine Workers union. Ralph Lee Smith published a lengthy article in the May 17, 1970, edition of *The Nation.* Titled "The Wired Nation," it discussed the potential of cable television, as well as efforts by media monopolists to thwart the promise of that new technology. Most important, the fund enabled Seymour Hersh, a young freelancer whose work had been rejected by several magazines, to produce his Pulitzer Prize series of syndicated newspaper articles in November 1969 that exposed the My Lai massacres of Vietnamese civilians by American troops.[38]

On the strength of the fund's growing reputation, Markle's Forrest Chisman called Boyd during the summer of 1971 and invited him to write a proposal. Boyd suggested that Markle funding could be used to expand work in an area near and dear to Morrisett's heart: fostering well-aimed criticism of the press by the press.[39] The fund had already supported exposés in the *Chicago Journalism Review* on censorship of the media by large law firms and the police practice of posing as newspaper reporters.[40] It had also provided start-up money for *MORE Magazine*, a feisty journal of press criticism, in 1971. In March 1972, Markle provided a two-year $100,000 grant and, during 1974–75, another two-year $60,000 grant to the Fund for Investigative Journalism to help broaden its investigative activities.

Markle's support for the fund was modest, but it proved to be the lifeline that it needed to survive its first decade and gain further national credibility. In 1973, Dugger reported on construction profiteering at the University of Texas. Richard Hebert published an article in *The Nation* titled "AMTRAK: Asleep at the Switch," detailing the foibles of the public railroad's first year of operation in 1972. The fund granted $30,000 to James Polk, a journalistic expert on political financing, to spend a year in covering violations of political fund-raising laws. His award-winning dispatches were carried in newspapers across the country.

The fund survived but never financially thrived. By the late 1990s, it was a one-person operation led by Margaret ("Peg") Lotito, a former chain newspaper journalist in Annandale, Virginia. Its annual budget, about $75,000, came from small foundation grants and individual contributions, enough to provide $500 to $3,000 grants to freelance journalists.[41] In January 1997, Lotito approached the Markle Foundation one last time for a $50,000 grant. Morrisett's reply was that journalism was "no longer a main priority" at Markle.[42]

"What I find frightening," Lotito said, "is that we have these multinational corporations controlling the media, and yet there are fewer and fewer foundations willing to support good investigative journalism."[43]

GUARDING THE GUARDIANS: THE NATIONAL NEWS COUNCIL

On April 3, 1972, Arthur O. ("Punch") Sulzberger, publisher of *The New York Times*, summoned a half dozen of his top news and editorial page executives to lunch in the publisher's dining room on the eleventh floor of the paper's 43rd Street headquarters. The topic: What position the paper should take on the proposal for a National News Council, a new media watchdog organization taking shape with the backing of the Twentieth Century Fund and The Markle Foundation. Founded on August 1, 1973, and buried unceremoniously eleven years later, the council never gained enough support from the press, the public, or the philanthropic world to last. Its failure had many causes, but the council's fate was almost certainly sealed even before it was born—by the internal politics and clashing personalities within the nation's "newspaper of record."

The press in the early 1970s badly needed a credible, neutral defender against the attacks from both the political left and the political right. Morrisett and others who supported the council believed that an impartial forum for airing public grievances would, in time, rebuild the public's trust in news gathering. The case for an unbiased national news council was stated by Alfred Balk, of the *Columbia Journalism Review*, who became a key player in drafting the council's early plans:

> Press performance now is, and always had been, publicly discussed, but most often from either an uninformed or partisan viewpoint. There has been no place where the citizen without benefit of special office, organization or resources can take questions and complaints, and no national mechanism to which the public and the news media can look for detached and independent appraisals when fairness and representativeness is questioned. The press council . . . would provide a forum for both criticisms of press abuses and defense of press freedom. . . .[44]

The first serious talk about press councils in this country began following World War II, after the successful precedent of the British Press Council established in 1951. Not until 1967, however, when a few local councils were funded by the Newspaper Guild, did the movement begin to bear fruit in this country.[45] A further milestone occurred in 1970 when Elie Abel, dean of the Columbia University School of Journalism, delivered a speech in Minneapolis that inspired newspaper owners in Minnesota to set up a state press council the following year.[46] As the Nixon White House stepped up its attacks on the media's credibility, the notion of a national news council gained more supporters.

The prime force behind the council was not Markle, but the smaller Twentieth Century Fund. Its leader, Murray Rossant, was a talented but quirky former *New York Times* staffer with a distinguished career as an economic columnist and editorialist. But his coverage had fallen into disfavor with Sulzberger, who worried that his newspaper had acquired an antibusiness image.

In 1971, Rossant established a Twentieth Century Fund task force to explore the feasibility of a news council. The group included academics, several judges, top broadcast and newspaper executives, and, most notably, John B. Oakes, editorial page editor of *The New York Times* and the newspaper's most enthusiastic proponent of a news council.[47]

By 1972, the task force had established the broad principles that would govern the fund's operations during its early years. It would be entirely nongovernmental. To avoid any conflict, it would not accept financial support from the news industry. To avoid spreading itself too thin, it would concern itself mainly with the national rather than local media. The council would be chaired by a nonjournalist to ensure its credibility with the general public. Cooperation with the council would be entirely voluntary. Although its deliberations would be quasi-judicial, its power would rest solely on the credibility of its decisions and the publicity that the press itself chose to give the council's decisions.

Rossant turned to Balk of *CJR* to act as rapporteur for the task force. Along with writing the final report, Balk sought to build a network of supporters for the council in the news business—or, at minimum, to quell any outright opposition.

Balk's missionary work met with some success, but it also revealed deep divisions within the news industry. A number of major newspapers, including the *Denver Post*, the *Cleveland Plain Dealer*, the *Milwaukee Journal*, and the *St. Louis Post Dispatch*, supported the council idea. One of the most steadfast procouncil publishers was Barry Bingham, an original task force member, whose *Louisville Courier-Journal* opined that the council "will perform an essential service for us all."[48]

Of the three networks, CBS was by far its warmest supporter. The president of CBS News, Richard Salant, was an early task force member and would eventually lead the council. ABC, by contrast, opposed the council as unnecessary. NBC was relatively neutral. Katherine Graham, publisher of *The Washington Post*, said that she had nothing in principle against the idea but deferred to Ben Bradlee, *The Post*'s vice president and executive editor, who opposed the council.

In January 1973, a month after a Washington press conference announced plans for establishing the council, the American Society of Newspaper Editors found opinion among its membership running against the idea by a 3–1 margin.

Wes Gallagher, then AP president, was never fond of the council but agreed to report its deliberations on the news wire.[49] H. L. ("Steve") Stevenson, editor of United Press International (UPI), was more sympathetic and assured Balk that his news wire would print the council's findings faithfully if it ever got off the ground.[50] Time, Inc., publicly opposed the council. The *New York Daily News* editorial page blasted the council idea as "a sneak attempt at press regulation, a bid for a role as unofficial news censor."[51] Some years later, the *News* softened its stance and printed the council's rulings.

Then there was *The New York Times*.

The news executives who gathered around the elegant oval table at the April 1972 lunch in the publisher's dining room fully understood the power that *The Times* held in determining the fate of the proposed news council. Its support would set the pattern for the rest of the news industry. Even neutrality might clear the way for major financial supporters in the philanthropic field to aid the council. Opposition, on the other hand, would wound the nascent council grievously, possibly fatally.

The lunch was a stormy affair. Oakes, the council's champion within *The Times*, considered it "a device to enhance credibility, contact, and accessibility."[52] He argued that a boycott of the council by the paper would fuel the public's perceptions of the press as arrogant and self-serving.

Oakes's position enraged two other *Times* executives, Clifton Daniel, managing editor during the 1960s, and his successor, A. M. ("Abe") Rosenthal. The latter, in particular, felt that Oakes's support was just one more sign that the newspaper, and the editorial page in particular, had drifted too far to the political left. He even suggested there was something faintly treasonable about Oakes's service on the Twentieth Century Fund task force, even though, as Oakes later reminded Sulzberger, he had done so with the publisher's full knowledge.[53]

Rosenthal had made no secret of his opposition to the council. Even after the council was launched, Rosenthal would say repeatedly that it was "a waste of time and money and, more important, it diverts attention from real problems confronting the press, courts and the public about the flow of information."[54]

The problem, he said, was that there was no possible single yardstick of fairness to measure the performance of the panoply of news organizations. Even if such a standard could be arrived at, enforcing it would only serve to undermine the independence and variety of American journalism. Further, a news council composed of editors sitting in judgment of other editors was a conflict of interest on the face of it. Finally, Rosenthal told Rossant and Morrisett that if the council wanted to make a national reputation, it would undoubtedly concentrate its fire on the biggest media targets, especially the *Times*—a position Oakes regarded as "paranoic."[55]

On January 16, 1973, seven months before the council officially opened for business, Sulzberger publicly rendered his verdict in his own news pages. He announced that the paper "would refuse to cooperate with the press council being set up . . . to monitor the performance of the national news media."[56]

Oakes's editorial page, of course, never came out against the council, but, even there, opinion was divided. Columnist Tom Wicker wrote in 1973:

> That the press council would aim to keep the press "free" by making it more "responsible" is a contradiction in terms. If the press is truly free, it follows that it will not always be "responsible"; and anything that tends to enforce its "responsibility" necessarily makes it less than free.[57]

The Times's public opposition had two immediate and devastating effects on the young council's prospects. It lessened the chances for gathering broad support within the news industry. Less directly, it contributed to cutting off the council from its most important potential financial source, the Ford Foundation. Along with other foundation executives whom Rossant approached, Fred Friendly of Ford claimed to be personally sympathetic but was in no apparent hurry to make a decision. In correspondence to Rossant, Friendly had suggested that the council idea was still too half-baked for Ford to commit to it. Friendly had heard inklings of Sulzberger's lack of enthusiasm for Rossant, and, over lunch with Rosenthal and Morrisett, he learned firsthand where *The Times*'s volatile managing editor stood.

Nonetheless, Friendly commissioned Balk to fly to England and write a report for Ford on the British News Council. Friendly himself, after spending the summer of 1972 canvassing leading print and broadcast executives, was convinced that the majority of national news suppliers opposed the idea of a council.[58] Morrisett volunteered to help Rossant garner support from other foundation leaders in hopes of drawing Ford into the fold. The final verdict, however, was inevitable. On December 14, 1972, Rossant dropped Morrisett a note with the news that Ford would not go along with the council. Fresh from being raked by Congress in the 1960s for its politically tinged grant-making practices, Friendly and his boss at Ford, McGeorge Bundy, apparently saw little to be gained, and a lot to lose, in alienating the country's most powerful newspaper.

Despite those early letdowns, the council's planning committee pressed ahead through the winter and spring of 1973 as it prepared for its August opening. "The stronger the attacks," wrote Rossant's assistant, Matthew L. Fox, to his fellow committee members, "the more determined we are that the council is needed."

A fresh disappointment related to the council's early leadership. To establish public credibility, the founding board had decided that the chairman of the council should be a prestigious jurist rather than someone from the news business. One name mentioned was that of former Supreme Court Justice Arthur Goldberg. Although Goldberg expressed interest, the majority of the board members felt that such an overpowering appointment might turn the press council into a cult of personality—in effect, a "Goldberg commission."[59]

Eventually, the council departed from its early policies and turned to journalists for leadership—first, Norman E. Isaacs, the highly respected former president of the American Society of Newspaper Editors, and, later, Salant of CBS News. With the exception of Isaacs, however, the council suffered from uninspired, reactive leadership that was never able to cope effectively with its chronic financial crises (its average annual budget was just $250,000), never attracted sustained public attention to its deliberations, and tended to be preoccupied with trivia rather than matters of national significance. During its eleven years, the council considered 242 complaints. Especially during its first years when it was so important to capture the attention and confidence of the public, the council wasted time and resources adjudicating such matters as a complaint by a Charlotte, North Carolina, reader who was upset that his local paper did not print a letter to the editor "as is." (The council dismissed the complaint.)[60]

The council had its finest moments under Isaacs's six-year term as chairman. A sixty-eight-year-old dynamo when he took office in 1976, he dropped the sweet talk and let the council know what was increasingly obvious to everyone—that it had squandered its first years of existence by being overcautious and had thus remained largely irrelevant in the news business. In a letter to his colleagues on the council, he stated:

> Members of The Council draw comfort from warm comment made by monitoring teams for the various news organizations. They have applauded the thoughtful deliberation that has gone into the hearing of grievances. May I suggest that there may be another aspect to this praise? Might it not be relief that The Council has not been as forthright and strong as was feared by so many when the agency was launched? Our No. 1 critic, A. M. Rosenthal . . . has been silent about us. It is likely that he shares the opinion of Ben Bradlee of *The Washington Post* that what we do or say is of no concern because we are insignificant in journalistic affairs.[61]

Under Isaacs, the council secured a deal with the *Columbia Journalism Review* to print its deliberations regularly. Isaacs abandoned the council's policy against taking money from news organizations and managed to get modest funding from a number of them. Most of all, he encouraged the council to change its policy forbidding it from taking cases unless a complaint was made, a policy that had made the organization reactive rather than giving it the freedom to tackle matters of genuine consequence to the journalism profession and to the public.

In 1977, a publisher of a Michigan-based chain of newspapers called Panax, owned by John McGoff, handed Isaacs the high-profile crusade for which he had been yearning. In June of that year, Panax's New York bureau chief wrote a pair of stories insinuating that President Jimmy Carter condoned staff promiscuity and was grooming his wife for the vice presidency in 1984.[62] The articles were accompanied by orders from McGoff to his chain of papers to run the stories on page one, unedited, and send the clips to him personally. It turned out that this publisher freely and frequently dictated editorial content in his papers. When articles containing the letters "MG" came in, Panax editors understood that the letters were a code for "McGoff," or "must go," meaning, print the articles without change or question. When the editors of two upstate Michigan papers refused to run the "MG"-coded articles about President Carter, they were promptly fired.[63]

Without waiting for a complaint, Isaacs plunged the council into the case. It issued an opinion that McGoff, as a publisher, had intruded improperly into the editorial content and integrity of his papers. Only one council member, William Rusher of the conservative magazine *National Review*, dissented. McGoff was infuriated and launched a counteroffensive in the pages of *Editor & Publisher* and *CJR*. He threatened to sue the council and campaigned for its abolition. Isaacs could not have been more pleased. The Panax case, he said, had "proved the value of the News Council and its mettle."[64]

The National News Council would have a few more high points during the years ahead but never enough to draw sustained public support. Besides the McGoff case, perhaps the clearest demonstration of the need for a news council came in 1981 in a case involving *Time Magazine*. *Time* had published an article erroneously accusing several child psychologists of endorsing sexual relations among children. It refused to admit its error or print letters of correction that cleared the names of the psychologists whose views had been misrepresented. Not wanting to go to the expense of a legal action, the doctors went to the council. The council sided with the doctors, but the magazine refused to cooperate with the decision—a public demonstration of the occasional arrogance that made an impartial news council so essential to the credibility of the press.

Still, few in the news industry stepped forward with funds or public words of encouragement to keep the council alive as Markle's support was ending. Even the council's most faithful press outlet, the *Columbia Journalism Review*, stopped printing council news in 1982, a move that some council members believed might have been a payback for an unfavorable decision rendered by the council eighteen months earlier against *CJR* in a dispute with

UPI.[65] In any case, the loss of its regular spot in *CJR* was a sign that the council was on its deathbed.

After the council disbanded in 1984, its archives were consigned to the University of Minnesota, financed partly with $20,000 in unspent Markle grant funds. Its foes saw the council's demise as the welcome end to a failed idea. The sudden, if temporary, recovery of public confidence in the media after their exposure of the Watergate cover-up also lessened the urgency of the council's work.

For the Markle Foundation, the council was an early display of Morrisett's willingness to carry on, at least occasionally, a losing fight in the face of clear opposition or indifference from other foundations and key players in the news industry. How, after all, could a foundation billing itself as a leading proponent of media reform show feet of clay by not supporting the National News Council? In fact, Markle, not the Twentieth Century Fund, proved to be the council's most steadfast financial backer. Between 1972 and 1983, Markle provided seven grants worth more than $1.2 million to start up and sustain the council. Morrisett even persuaded his Children's Television Workshop friend, Joan Cooney, to add her prestige to the cause by joining as a council member in 1973.

Regardless of the foundation's high-minded intentions, Markle's staff had few illusions about the council's prospects for long-term success. They considered it merely a "good gray grant," in the words of Kendra O'Donnell, the program officer who handled the council's grant portfolio for much of its existence.[66] In 1976, even as Morrisett was recommending to Markle's board a further three-year grant of $300,000 to the council, on top of the $325,000 that it had already approved since 1972, his endorsement was guarded. The council, he wrote, might eventually prove itself as a constructive force in journalism, but only if it gained enough support from the industry and the public, and if it were not so chronically cash starved. "It is clear," Morrisett added, "that the Council has so far made a good, if unspectacular, beginning."[67]

"We hung in there for awhile, because the council had good folks with a good mission," O'Donnell told the author. "But we knew we were going to get out of it gracefully over time. We weren't going to let anybody down, and we weren't arguing that the need wasn't there. But we knew this wasn't going to have a huge impact. We weren't startled or upset."[68]

During its brief life, a number of foundations such as the Gannett Foundation, the Edna McConnell Clark Foundation, and the John D. and Catherine T. MacArthur Foundation, tossed the council modest grants, but their total was not even close to the $500,000 a year that Morrisett considered necessary to sustain the council. As early as January 1973, six months before the council even opened for business, Morrisett had warned Rossant that "a hard look should be taken as to whether the council could be started" unless the Twentieth Century Fund were willing to guarantee the council's inevitable financial shortfalls for at least the first three to five years.[69]

The vacuum of unbiased criticism left by the National News Council's demise in 1984 remained through the 1990s, even as scandals involving another sitting president raised fresh questions about the quality and proportionality of press performance. The Minnesota News Council survives as the only vestige of the news council movement of the 1970s. Historian and former *New York Daily News* editorial writer Patrick Brogan's epitaph of the news council, written a year after its demise, still seemed on target as the century closed. The council's failure, he wrote, "was so complete that . . . there seemed very little hope that any other philanthropy would try soon to recreate it, but the proposition that a news council is needed is as valid now as ever it was."[70]

NOTES

1. Vice President Spiro T. Agnew, address to the Mid-West Regional Republican Committee, Des Moines, Iowa, 13 Nov. 1969, as transcribed in *The New York Times*, 14 Nov. 1969, 24.

2. Replies to Vice President Agnew's speech by networks, *The New York Times*, 14 Nov. 1969, 24.

3. Ibid.

4. Ibid.

5. Vice President Spiro T. Agnew, speech, San Diego, Calif., 11 Sept. 1970.

6. Lloyd N. Morrisett, "Press Credibility—The Citizen's Dilemma"

(President's Essay in "The John and Mary R. Markle Foundation, Annual Report, 1971–1972 [reprint]), 3.

7. James Reston, "Washington: The Voices of the Silent Majority," *The New York Times*, 28 Nov. 1969, op-ed section, 38.

8. Ben H. Bagdikian, "A Study of Causes of Death among American Daily Newspapers," n.d. (typed grant proposal submitted to The Markle Foundation), Markle Archive Collection. Markle granted Bagdikian $106,000 over a period of two years to support the study. The research led to Bagdikian's *The Media Monopoly*, one of the most authoritative books ever written on the corporatization of the press. The first edition was published by Beacon Press in 1983.

9. Bagdikian, *Media Monopoly*, 21.

10. William Safire, "Broadcast Lobby Triumphs," *The New York Times*, 23 July 1997, a21.

11. Cook, *Governing with the News*, 180.

12. Morrisett, "Press Credibility," 4.

13. Morrisett, interview, 12 Aug. 1997.

14. Excerpt from a description of grant to the University of Illinois at Chicago and the National Opinion Research Center in "The John and Mary R. Markle Foundation Annual Report, 1970–1971," 27.

15. Johnstone, Slawski, and Bowman, *The News People*, 22–23.

16. Ibid., 26.

17. Ibid., 32.

18. Ibid., 121.

19. Kendra O'Donnell, staff memorandum, 27 June 1978.

20. Boylan, interview, 17 Nov. 1997.

21. Alfred W. Balk, transmittal of subscription figure taken from "*Columbia Journalism Review*: A Proposal," to Lloyd N. Morrisett, 23 Apr. 1970, Markle Archive Collection.

22. Balk, interview, 11 Nov. 1997.

23. Ibid.

24. Ibid.

25. The Markle Foundation, staff memorandum to Markle Board of Directors, recommending further support of $80,000 to *Columbia Journalism Review*, to be paid July 1973, n.d., 29–30, Markle Archive Collection.

26. Morrisett, interview, 12 Aug. 1997.

27. Giza, interview, 30 Nov. 1999.

28. Foundations and other nonprofit organizations listed as *CJR* supporters have included Edna McConnell Clark Foundation, The Freedom Forum, Kaiser Foundation, Rockefeller Foundation, Twentieth Century Fund, and U.S. Committee for UNICEF. Media supporters

included ABC News, Agence France-Presse, Allnet Communications Services, Dow Jones, New York Times Company, *The Boston Globe*, and The Tribune Company.

29. Winfrey, interview, 19 Nov. 1997.

30. Carey Winfrey, "Reflections of a Two-Faced Press Critic," *Image*.

31. Quoted in WNET, "Television's First Look at ALL Media—Including TV Itself—on Channel 13," press release, 1 Oct. 1971, 3.

32. Winfrey, interview, 19 Nov. 1997.

33. Lloyd N. Morrisett, letter to John Jay Iselin, President, Educational Broadcasting Corporation, 26 Apr. 1976.

34. Iselin, interview, 30 Oct. 1997.

35. Two such recent histories, David Horowitz and Lawrence Jarvik, eds., *Public Broadcasting & the Public Trust* (Los Angeles: Second Thoughts Books, 1995), and, more surprisingly, James Day, *The Vanishing Vision: The Inside Story of Public Television* (Berkeley: University of California Press, 1995), make no mention of *Behind the Lines*.

36. Winfrey, interview, 19 Nov. 1997.

37. Fund for Investigative Journalism, descriptive brochure, 1969.

38. Fund for Investigative Journalism, "Our Grants and What Happened to Them," a listing prepared by James Boyd, executive director of the fund, of newspaper articles produced with backing from the fund between 1 Aug. 1969 and 1 Aug. 1971, 1–2. Rockefeller Archive Center.

39. James Boyd, letter to Forrest P. Chisman, 13 Oct. 1971.

40. Ibid., 9.

41. Fund for Investigative Journalism, Inc., Web site: www.FIJ.org.

42. Lloyd N. Morrisett, letter to Peg Lotito, 13 Feb. 1997.

43. Lotito, interview, 4 Dec. 1997.

44. Alfred W. Balk, "Report of Twentieth Century Fund Task Force for a National Press Council," unpublished typed manuscript, n.d.,4, Markle Archive Collection.

45. Alfred W. Balk, "The Voluntary Model: Living with 'Public Watchdogs,' " in *Media Freedom and Accountability*, ed. Everette E. Dennis, Donald M. Gillmor, and Theodore L. Glasser (Westport, Conn.: Greenwood Press, 1989), 67.

46. Ibid.

47. Twentieth Century Fund Task Force members were an eclectic group and generally well disposed toward the council in principle. They included Barry Bingham, Sr., Chairman, *Louisville Courier Journal*; Lucy Wilson Benson, President, League of Women Voters; Simson Bullitt, President, King Broadcasting Company, Seattle; Hodding Carter III,

Editor, *The Delta Democrat–Times*, Greenville, Miss.; Robert Chandler, Editor, *The Bulletin*, Bend, Ore.; Ithiel de Sola Pool, Massachusetts Institute of Technology; Hartford N. Gunn, Jr., President, Public Broadcasting System, Washington; Richard Harwood, Assistant Managing Editor, *The Washington Post*; Louis Martin, Editor, *Chicago Defender*; C. Donald Peterson, Justice, Minnesota Supreme Court; Paul Reardon, Associate Justice, Supreme Judicial Court, Boston; Richard Salant, President, CBS News; Jesse Unruh, former Speaker of the California Assembly; and Douglass Cater, Head, Aspen Communications and Society Program.

48. *Louisville Courier-Journal*, editorial commentary. Excerpt reprinted in *Columbia Journalism Review*, March/April 1973, 56.

49. Boccardi, interview, 25 Nov., 1997. Boccardi was the AP's managing editor when the National News Council was formed; Wes Gallagher had died earlier in 1997. (Personal note: The author, an AP reporter from 1974 to 1991, knew both Boccardi and Gallagher and was assigned on several occasions to report on the council's deliberations.)

50. Balk, interview, 15 Nov. 1997. (Personal note: The author, a business reporter at UPI from 1972 to 1974, worked for H. L. Stevenson.)

51. *New York Daily News*, editorial commentary. Excerpt reprinted in *Columbia Journalism Review*, March/April 1973, 57.

52. John B. Oakes, private memorandum to Arthur O. Sulzberger, Publisher, *The New York Times*, 3 Apr. 1972, which was written after the lunch. (Copy supplied to the author.)

53. Ibid.

54. A. M. Rosenthal, letter to The Honorable George Edwards, Committee to Evaluate the National News Council, 11 Aug. 1975.

55. Rosenthal and Oakes, interviews, 1 Dec. 1997 and 9 Jan. 1998, respectively.

56. Quoted in David Shipler, "*The Times* Bars Support to Panel for Monitoring News Media," *The New York Times*, 16 Jan. 1973, 39.

57. Tom Wicker, "Publish, and Be Damned," *The New York Times*, 30 Jan. 1973, op-ed section.

58. Fred W. Friendly, letter to Lloyd N. Morrisett, 4 Aug. 1972, Markle Archive Collection.

59. Brogan, *Spiked*, 23–24.

60. The National News Council, Inc., report to The Markle Foundation, March 1974, 9.

61. Norman Isaacs, letter to "News Council Colleagues," 11 Nov. 1977.

62. Celeste Huenergard and Jane Levere, "Panax Controversy Heats Up," *E&P Magazine*, 16 July 1977, 7.

63. Kendra O'Donnell, internal memorandum to Lloyd N. Morrisett that summarized the Panax dispute, 1 Nov. 1978.

64. Brogan, *Spiked*, 56.

65. Ibid., 61.

66. O'Donnell, interview, 19 Nov. 1997.

67. Lloyd N. Morrisett, memorandum to Markle Board of Directors, recommending a $300,000 grant payable in three installments from 1977 through 1979, n.d., 31, Markle Archive Collection.

68. O'Donnell, interview, 19 Nov. 1997.

69. Lloyd N. Morrisett, Murray Rossant, and Twentieth Century Fund colleagues, record of meeting, 12 Jan. 1973. Markle Archive Collection.

70. Brogan, *Spiked*, 100.

6

Changing Channels

THE END of Morrisett's first decade as president of The Markle Foundation signaled a period of introspection about programs and methods. It was also a time of fresh upheavals within the communications world itself.

Morrisett's larger goals remained intact. He still regarded Markle as a force for improving the performance of the media and increasing the quality and diversity of their products and practitioners. His faith in social scientific research as a means of informing the public debate about the complexities and social possibilities of the Information Age was unshaken. Despite sobering experiences with television, he had not abandoned his plans to explore how traditional media might be channeled to serve more equitably all groups in society, from children to the elderly. To the contrary, Morrisett was preparing to explore the neglected social and educational possibilities of two of the oldest existing mass media—film and radio.

Still, by the late 1970s, new technologies also beckoned. After a recession-related delay earlier in the decade, the long anticipated takeoff of cable television was occurring with a vengeance. The stunning impact of communications satellites and affordable personal computers was too obvious to ignore. For the balance of his presidency, Morrisett would look increasingly toward those newer computer-based communication tools to fulfill his foundation's social goals.

With the communications field in upheaval, Markle's philanthropic methods were also about to take on a new, bolder, and more focused look. Morrisett's first decade had been a kind of smorgasbord. Markle's grant portfolio had been filled with a variety of small- to medium-sized grants as Morrisett and his staff probed many corners of the communication field to test where a small foundation might make the most difference. Armed a decade later with more knowledge and some hard-won lessons about the possible points of leverage for social action, Morrisett was ready to place fewer, larger, and more daring bets. Henceforth, Markle would be interested not simply in dispensing money and hoping for the best but in investing and institution-building. These activities, in turn, would demand different kinds of knowledge and management expertise beyond that displayed by most foundations, along with a far more sustained level of involvement in their projects by Morrisett and his staff.

Where the foundation had earlier sought, for example, to improve media performance by salvaging the *Columbia Journalism Review,* it was laying plans in 1978 to start an entirely new magazine of television criticism, *Channels of Communications*, that eventually would cost nearly $3.5 million in foundation funds and many hours in Markle staff time. And even as *Channels* was being launched, Morrisett was hatching a second, multimillion dollar long-shot venture aimed at developing a brand new television rating system designed to measure not merely the size of audiences but the quality and audience impact of programs.

The size, cost, and complexity of these projects demanded new ways of funding and managing them. Increasingly, the foundation would view itself as a quasi-venture capitalist, but, unlike usual financiers, Markle would measure its success in social benefit, first and foremost, ahead of profit. Although continuing to allow grantees considerable latitude to pursue their work, Morrisett and his staff would become more engaged with business and management issues in order to increase the odds of their projects' long-term survival.

If the communications arena was still not as well stocked as the education, art, and health fields with potential philanthropic partners to help carry out Morrisett's ideals, then Markle was now prepared to take a far more active hand in creating durable new institutions, both nonprofit and profit, to translate its social ideals into action.

A FORAY INTO FILM: OPENING DOORS TO WOMEN

Even as the foundation was beginning to shift its gaze toward newer technologies, Morrisett and his staff remained on the lookout for neglected corners of the traditional communications field. Markle began two such explorations in the late 1970s—film and radio. Might either of those venerable media be more flexible and economical vehicles than television had proved to be in providing more educational, diverse offerings to mass audiences?

Filmmaking certainly fit legitimately within Markle's mission. Its reach and popularity were undeniable. Forrest Chisman, Morrisett's first program officer, had an interest in film and had led the foundation to undertake a few modest research projects during the early 1970s. Markle's most interesting foray in the film world, however, came later with the arrival in 1976 of a new program officer, Jean Firstenberg. Under her guidance, Markle supported a new Hollywood center dedicated to opening the male-dominated field of film directing to women and thereby, it was hoped, to some fresh and more open perspectives.

Firstenberg had long-standing family ties to the movie industry. Her father and grandfather were executives with Loew's, Inc., which owned Metro-Goldwyn-Mayer. The business end of filmmaking fascinated Firstenberg, and she had spent her early career in television production and advertising. Paul Firstenberg, her husband at the time, was a board member of the Children's Television Workshop. Joan Cooney introduced Firstenberg to Morrisett, who offered her a job at Markle. One of her first assignments was to explore how the foundation might carry its social and educational goals into filmmaking.

She found her answer in a small program called the Directing Workshop for Women at the American Film Institute. The workshop was begun in 1974 by Dr. Mathilde Krim, the Swiss-born wife of United Artists Chairman Arthur Krim. In her later years, Dr. Krim became a leading international spokesperson for AIDS research. She had founded the directing workshop because, in an age of awakening women's consciousness, film directing remained a male domain. With her connections to the foundation world, she arranged a $35,000 start-up grant from the Rockefeller Foundation for the first year and a $100,000 grant to keep the workshop going for a second year.

Led by Jan Haag, the workshop attracted a stellar group of actors and writers eager to try their hands at directing: Maya Angelou, Anne Bancroft, Marsha Mason, Susan Oliver, Lee Grant,

Dyan Cannon, Kathleen Nolan, Gail Parent, and Ellen Burstyn. Firstenberg's sister-in-law, Nessa Hyams, a Columbia Pictures executive, also had been a participant. Using video cameras, professional casts, and crews supplied by the workshop or by donors, the women completed a number of short films, from an eighteen-minute comedy to an hour-long drama, shot for as little as $350 apiece. Such a star-studded cast guaranteed press attention. Still, by 1976, the workshop was struggling.

At Firstenberg's urging, Markle provided $150,000 to upgrade the workshop and sustain it for a third year. Although the workshop was never a major priority at the foundation, Morrisett and his staff saw it as an engaging grantee. The workshop and the media attention that it garnered were effectively shaming the image-conscious movie industry into hiring at least some of its big-name participants. By 1976, Lee Grant, Marjorie Mullen, Maya Angelou, Dyan Cannon, and Ellen Burstyn were getting their first directing assignments for television or the movies.

One film was especially successful. A short subject by Dyan Cannon, *Number One,* a gentle look at children growing up and discovering their sexuality, received an Oscar nomination and respectful reviews in *The New York Times* and other leading papers. Morrisett and Firstenberg decided it would be a nice touch to have Cannon appear at the Markle board dinner on April 6, 1977, to show what women film directors could do. That night, when the sultry world of Hollywood met the staid world of philanthropy on the second floor of the St. Regis–Sheraton Hotel, became one of the most surreal in Markle's history.

"Dyan Cannon arrived in a tight gold lamé pants suit with a zipper that was down to her navel," Morrisett recalled. "In terms of the Markle board and their wives, she was, to put it mildly, an exotic flower."[1]

After a brief talk by Cannon, Firstenberg showed her film, *Number One.* As older members of the Markle board looked on aghast, the film depicted a group of prepubescent schoolgirls wandering into a boys' lavatory and asking to see the boys' genitals—a natural and innocent display of childish curiosity. Still, between the sensuously clad Ms. Cannon and her film, at least one elderly board member, Jarvis Cromwell, had seen enough. For the next six weeks, he peppered Morrisett with phone calls demanding to know if the Markle Foundation was financing "child pornography."

"When Lloyd told me about it, I was never so shocked in my life," Firstenberg said. "But Lloyd was an absolute champion. Cromwell was an important trustee, but it didn't bother Lloyd at all."[2]

That minor maelstrom finally passed after Morrisett wrote Cromwell a lengthy letter assuring him that the workshop and Dyan Cannon's film "have clearly passed the tests of taste, good judgment and high moral intent."[3]

"It was a yoke around my neck that I thought I would never get rid of," said Morrisett, looking back on the misadventure. "Now it's all very funny."[4]

Markle's brief but interesting excursion in film had helped achieve the laudable goal of expanding opportunities for women. Morrisett's decision to back the workshop was almost certainly more a pragmatic one, rather than a display of ideological feminism. The point for him, as in so many ventures, was to widen the foundation's circle of outsiders and mavericks of all stripes who might act as change agents in the media world. The Directing Workshop for Women was still operating in 2000. Since its founding, more than 130 women have participated. Thanks to the workshop and Markle's support, female directors are no longer the oddities that they were twenty-five years ago. Firstenberg left the Markle Foundation in 1979 and has since continuously served as director and chief executive officer of the American Film Institute.

Beyond the success of that program, however, it was never clear to Morrisett how a fairly small philanthropy in New York could realistically expect to influence, in a sustained way, a communications medium whose power base was three thousand miles away, whose distribution system was tightly controlled, and which had few nonprofit organizations willing to act as potential partners or grantors. For those reasons, the foundation's involvement with film never went beyond a flirtation.

WAKING THE GIANT: MARKLE AND RADIO

Over lunch one afternoon during the mid-1970s, Markle board member D. Ronald Daniel mentioned to Morrisett that radio seemed a strange absentee in the portfolio of a foundation dedicated to improving mass communications.[5] Morrisett readily acknowledged that his point was well taken.

The cognitive psychologist within Morrisett was soon intrigued by the demands that radio placed on human listening, thinking, and imagination compared with the mental passivity and spoonfed visual images of television. Equally intriguing to him was the relative inexpensiveness of quality programming on radio compared with that on television. If a hundred Sesame Streets or a welter of cultural or public interest programming would not easily bloom on TV, could Markle help that to happen on radio? And could visionary leaders in the radio world be found who would work with the foundation to realize those ideas?

Beginning in 1975, the foundation undertook a seven-year, $3.1 million exploration of the social, educational, and cultural potential of what Morrisett dubbed the "sleeping giant." He stated the possibilities and paradoxes of radio in a 1976 annual essay heralding Markle's growing interest in the older medium:

> Four hundred million radio sets and eight thousand stations add up to a wealth of opportunity to listen to radio, but critics contend that this wealth is largely imaginary because the range of available programming is extremely small. With the exception of NPR stations and some others, the programming that is presented is popular music and headline news. Little attempt is made to exploit other forms of programming—drama and the arts, education, programming for children, the elderly—programming that reflects the range and variety of human taste and interest. . . .[6]

Markle's radio initiative, though relatively brief as with film, was more calculated and costly than the latter. Between 1978 and 1983, the period of highest activity, Markle spent nearly $3 million on a variety of radio grants. Aside from supporting the occasional public service or cultural offering, few members of the philanthropic community had ever paid such sustained attention to the educational potential of radio. To most of the listening public, radio was simply there, in the shadows of television—a way to fill the sensory void of car travel or housework or to provide unobtrusive ambience in the workplace.

Radio stations, for the most part stuck in narrow program ruts, offered news and weather and set music formats. Listeners with a taste for rock-and-roll, country and western, or breaking news, might be reasonably content with what radio delivered. Contrasted to what it *could* be doing, however—offering creative children's programming, drama, and documentaries or serving the needs and interests of such special audiences as minority groups and the elderly—radio's programs were, Morrisett believed, well below par. As with television, radio was yet another medium held captive to the corporate dictates of commercialism and entertainment, with education and the public interest in a distant second place.

National Public Radio (NPR), founded in 1970, was supposed to fill much of that void. By the mid-1970s, NPR had grown to 190 stations. Yet, many cities lacked public radio. The system as a whole was cash starved and a perennial weak relation to public television in competing for scarce federal and foundation funds. Public radio was getting less than 20 percent of the Corporation for Public Broadcasting's program money.[7] Some members of the broadcast industry considered NPR's program philosophy to be elitist, narrow, and unresponsive to local community needs.

Still, radio as a medium was far from the dead relic that it was sometimes presumed to be during the late 1970s. It was, in fact, a $3 billion growth industry, with 7,700 commercial and 1,000 noncommercial stations, that commanded large audiences and considerable amounts of local, if not national, advertising. The audience for radio had increased some 25 percent during the 1970s. The average American adult spent nearly three and one-half hours per day in listening to the radio, according to the Radio Advertising Institute, an amount not much less than the average TV viewing time.[8]

What, then, might a small foundation do to awaken the educational and civic potential of the sleeping giant?

Morrisett's first impulse was to explore how radio might address the needs of underserved groups, especially children. But the advice that came back from his own staff and from trusted advisers, such as Franz Allina, was discouraging. Kendra O'Donnell, the program officer at Markle who managed many of the foundation's radio initiatives, told Morrisett that her soundings from the industry argued against spending significant time or energy on children's radio.

"The message was that this was not the place to start, that this would be the most difficult nut to crack," O'Donnell recalled years later. "Not only did we have a medium that was not amenable to alternative programming, but it was a medium that had no audience in the youngest age group. I remember saying to Lloyd that radio is a great opportunity for us, but it is not going to be children's radio."[9]

Another natural outlet for Markle's assistance was public radio. From the late 1970s to the mid-1980s, the foundation sent roughly $1 million to National Public Radio and its public radio affiliates for special projects. A $225,000 grant to Eastern Public Radio in 1981 aimed to promote regional cooperation among public radio stations to produce higher-quality and more economical programming. A $221,000 award to Western Public Radio that same year helped expand that organization's training programs in radio writing, voice techniques, and engineering. In 1982, Markle provided National Public Radio with $300,000 at the height of a fiscal crisis caused by a recession and shrinking federal funding.

Still, propping up public radio was never a prime motive for Morrisett. He was more interested in whether the foundation could stimulate program diversity in commercial radio with its far larger audiences. Morrisett hoped, first, to identify and coalesce visionary industry leaders willing to provide their listeners with a more varied menu of cultural and educational programming. Second, he sought to organize and support the "little guys" in the radio industry—community broadcasters who were disunited and economically weak but were producing some of the most innovative, locally minded programming on the dial. Third and most ambitiously, Markle sought to create from scratch an organization that would support freelance radio writers and producers whose work was highly imaginative but often unrecognized and underfinanced.

The job of identifying and mobilizing public-spirited commercial radio operators went to a newly formed New York–based philanthropy, Center for Public Resources, Inc., whose specialty was bringing the talents and resources of the business world to bear on public issues.[10] The center was headed by James F. Henry, an acquaintance of Morrisett's, who was just completing five years as president of the Edna McConnell Clark Foundation. In 1977, Markle gave the center $35,000 to study how to broaden commercial programming, including Morrisett's idea of providing federal tax incentives to radio stations that did so.

Henry's study, submitted in 1978, concluded that radio was essentially a "ma-and-pa" industry populated with owners mainly interested in protecting their turf. Few displayed any potential for leadership in promoting better, more diverse programming. As matters stood, the prospects for diversifying commercial programming seemed limited, at best, because of the competitive concerns among the owners about the formats that they used and the ratings that determined their income. Nonetheless, the center proposed that an organization of broadcast leaders be formed to stimulate industrywide support for greater programming diversity. Markle provided $471,500 between 1979 and 1981 to try to create such a group.

The effort never succeeded. Station owners and managers were willing enough to attend meetings and listen politely to the foundation's ideas. The Center for Public Resources and Markle cosponsored several such conferences, including a three-day gathering of industry and academic leaders in October 1979 at the Seven Springs Center in Mount Kisco, New York. What never emerged was a solid commitment to lead the industry to concrete action. As one frustrated participant put it:

> There is a need for leadership, guts, and controversy, and for programming that involves the listener. What better vehicle could an advertiser want than a responsive listener? If you have leadership in broadcasting—that's the huge if—that's what this conference is about: the focusing of leadership on what radio can uniquely do to reach its audience.[11]

After Markle failed to attract much interest from leaders in the mainstream commercial field, its second target of opportunity was the small but growing number of community broadcasters and independent radio professionals. Between 1976 and 1983, the foundation provided five grants totaling $245,000 to the National Federation of Community Broadcasters, a fledgling lobbying organization.

When the federation was founded in 1975, twenty-nine noncommercial educational radio stations, known as community broadcasters, existed. Unlike most public radio stations, community broadcasters operated independently of municipal or educational institutions and were almost entirely supported by listener contributions. Such stations, located in cities that included Miami, Florida; Cincinnati, Ohio; Santa Cruz, California; and Juneau, Alaska, typically provided outlets of information and programming for minority groups, women, and the young who were neglected by other stations, including public radio. Thomas J. Thomas, the federation's executive director, told Morrisett at the time that community broadcasters were getting scant help from the Corporation for Public Broadcasting. Instead, he said, the corporation was spending its money "unimaginatively" on large, university-affiliated public stations whose programming consisted mainly of classical music and national news.[12]

In short, community broadcasters occupied a strange netherworld. Scornful of NPR's programming as elitist and uninteresting, such broadcasters nonetheless had to cooperate with the Corporation for Public Broadcasting to increase the pool of public radio funding on which their survival depended. They and the corporation also had a common interest in putting some semblance of order into the allocation of increasingly scarce FM spectrum space.[13]

With Markle's help, low-wattage community broadcasters successfully organized under the umbrella of the National Federation of Community Broadcasters, gained an effective voice in Washington, and elbowed into the noncommercial radio picture alongside the much larger NPR. In doing so, these stations were able to provide a range of cultural, educational, and local programming not available elsewhere on the dial. When the federation first opened a Washington, D.C., office in 1975, it represented barely a dozen stations. At the time of Markle's final grant in 1983, the number of community broadcasters had risen to about 170. By the mid-1980s, the federation had become an effective, self-sustaining national voice for allocating FM spectrum space, opening new minority-operated public radio stations, and obtaining a larger share of the public radio pie from the Corporation for Public Broadcasting and NPR. Relocated since 1995 in San

Francisco, the federation was still operating in 2000, with more than two hundred members serving markets from New York to Spanish-speaking California farming communities to Native Lakota tribes in South Dakota.

Another of Markle's more interesting initiatives involved radio's most disorganized and, in many ways, most creative group—freelance producers and writers. Although not affiliated with any single radio station, these men and women managed to produce—on their own and with little financial support—some of the most remarkable drama, comedy, documentaries, and children's programming to be found anywhere. They included, for example, Lynn Chadwick, who ran the Feminist Radio Network in Washington; Himan Brown, producer of CBS's *Mystery Theater* in New York; and Joe Belden of the Pacific News Service in San Francisco. Nobody knew how many such independent producers existed, but California, New York, and Chicago were the main centers of their creativity.

That this diffuse and individualistic group might be the change agents in radio for whom Markle and his staff were looking first occurred to O'Donnell in 1977 when she learned about WFMT, a haven for such producers in Chicago. The station's listeners, some 300,000 strong, could listen to the bright, witty talk and interviews of Studs Terkel, or opera, or original dramatic programming from the Chicago Radio Theater led by Yuri Rasovsky.

Having already produced well-received renditions of such classics as *A Tale of Two Cities* and stories by Edgar Allen Poe, Rasovsky now sought Markle's support to produce a thirteen-part series based on Homer's *The Odyssey.* Markle's board approved a two-year, $133,500 grant in 1977 to finance the research and pilot production phases of the *Odyssey* project. Rasovsky later received $300,000 from the National Endowment for the Humanities. As Rasovsky said at the time, he didn't simply want to retell Homer's story, Hollywood style: "We want to give the feeling of Homer as well as tell the story, balancing good theatricality, good poetry, and good scholarship." To assure the latter, he took the unheard-of step in radio production of assembling an advisory group of six classics scholars.[14] The resulting series, starring Irene Worth as the goddess Athena and Barry Morse as Odysseus, premiered on January 14, 1980, to critical raves.

The *Odyssey* project was, for Markle, "a way into the radio game," O'Donnell said. The project also raised broader questions. How many Yuri Rasovskys were there in radio-land? Could Markle organize this ragtag group of individualistic artists into a national force for program diversity? "My sense then was that independent producers could not only be a force in their own right, but could be insinuated into public radio and commercial outlets—a 'farm system' for a new breed of broadcast artists," she told the author.[15]

That notion led Markle to host a get-together for about thirty independent radio producers at Automation House, the old union headquarters in New York City, in October 1978. In between wining and dining at the Tavern on the Green restaurant in Central Park, the group swapped stories about their often difficult dealings with NPR, getting their productions on the air, and getting fair pay for their work. The upshot was a unanimous agreement that they should try to organize themselves in order to get a fairer shake from the commercial and public broadcasters. By the spring of 1979, the producers who attended the meeting presented a formal proposal to Markle. Thus was born Audio Independents, Inc., an organization representing independent radio producers that Markle kept alive with three grants totaling $612,000 from 1979 to 1983.

The grants to Audio Independents marked an important milestone for the foundation. They were the first step in a new philanthropic strategy—an attempt to establish, from scratch, a separate nonprofit organization to carry out Markle's social goals. It also quickly became, in O'Donnell's words, "a complete headache," a harsh lesson in the difficulties that Markle would repeatedly face during subsequent projects in finding the right leadership and expertise to move a newly created nonprofit entity from foundation dependence to self-sufficiency.

From the beginning, the organization had serious management problems that Markle's staff found themselves powerless to correct. The radio organization's board forced out its first executive director when he proved inept, and its new leadership decided to move the organization from its original Lincoln Center office to San Francisco.

Still, that early experiment in institution building was not entirely in vain. Audio Independents perked up considerably under its second leader, Michael Toms, founder of the highly innovative New Dimensions Radio in Yukiah, California. Under his leadership, the organization became an effective advocate for independent producers in their often difficult dealings with NPR. What was never achieved was economic self-sufficiency. Reflecting on those experiences years later, Toms insisted that Audio Independents might have survived had Markle been willing to fund it for two more years.[16] By 1983, however, such support was unlikely given Audio Independents's record of shaky management. The organization folded in 1983 almost immediately after Markle's funding ran out. A successor group, the Association of Independents in Radio, was founded in Washington several years later and assumed many of the functions of its ancestor.

O'Donnell, who left Markle in 1979 for a career as a foundation and academic leader, offered this assessment in hindsight:

> Long-term, Audio Independents had to find ways to support itself. Members have to support it through dues, and there had to be valuable enough income-producing services for its members. It just never was going to work financially.
>
> But if we hadn't done it, the radio field wouldn't be where it is. There is still such an animal called independent producers. Because of Audio Independents, they have far more access to money, to station money, to NPR money, and in some instances, foundation money. They got respectability, access, and they learned about each other and shared with each other.[17]

Markle's attention to radio during the 1970s was one of the few times that the social and educational potential of this neglected medium received sustained attention from a foundation aside from grants for specific broadcasts. As with its film initiatives, Markle sought out mavericks as a possible force for diversity and constructive change. By the late 1990s, some 150 community radio stations were in existence, many relying on the creativity and volunteer work of several thousand independent producers. Owing partly to Toms's lobbying, the Corporation for Public

Broadcasting set aside an annual $3 million in program support for use by independent producers.

Markle's withdrawal from the radio arena also contained something of an irony. Morrisett had turned to radio in 1976 with the conviction that the potential of that medium had been tragically overshadowed by television. By the mid-1980s, mammoth new foundation projects in television and computer-based media would once again crowd radio out of Markle's priorities.

ADVANCING THE ART OF CRITICISM: *CHANNELS OF COMMUNICATION* MAGAZINE

In 1981, some two hundred new consumer magazines were founded in the United States. For most, life would be brief: just two out of ten could expect to survive for four years or more.[18] One of those newcomers, which premiered in April of that year, was *Channels of Communications*—commonly known as *Channels*— a magazine that sought to advance the art and the reach of objective television criticism. Founded and financed by The Markle Foundation, it defied the magazine actuaries and survived for nine years. Still, the magazine's combination of noble purposes and iconoclastic tone eventually made it a hard sell to both general and industry readers.

As early as the mid-1970s, Morrisett had been toying with the idea of starting some kind of publication devoted to probing, objective television criticism—something modest, perhaps a newsletter, aimed mainly at TV writers and producers. His reasons were almost identical to those that had previously led to Markle's involvement with the National News Council: Morrisett considered the near absence of regular, credible criticism of television to be unhealthy for the medium and the public it served.

An opportunity to advance those ideas presented itself in the summer of 1978. A strike by pressmen had silenced New York's newspapers, including *The New York Times*, for eighty-eight days. Les Brown was *The Times*'s TV columnist, author of several acclaimed books, including a best-selling encyclopedia of television, and the acknowledged dean of television journalists. With his employer on strike, Brown suddenly found himself uneasily encamped two thousand miles away at a media seminar at the Aspen Institute funded by Markle and wondering what his next career move should be. Confiding his worries to Jean Firstenberg, who was at the Aspen gathering with Morrisett, he was told that Markle might have something for him.

When Morrisett learned that a journalist of Brown's stature might be available, he invited Brown to write an editorial prospectus. His report concluded that the general press, including his own paper, was contemptuous of television, whereas the trade press, with the exception of *Variety*, was a captive to it. This, Brown argued, suggested a possible opening for a broad-interest publication that would be respectful but critical of television.

What Brown envisioned was far bigger, costlier, and riskier than Morrisett's newsletter idea—a full-scale magazine to be called *Channels of Communication*. The title said it all—the magazine was to be a forum for public airing of broadcasting's economic, regulatory, political, and social issues. Above all, Brown hoped the proposed magazine would be a conduit of conversation between the television industry and the public that it was supposed to serve. Such a magazine, Brown asserted, might have a potential general readership of 100,000 or more.

Of course, neither Brown nor Morrisett had any firm evidence that such a broad readership actually existed for serious television criticism. Still, a kind of euphoria set in. With an industry heavyweight like Brown as editor, Markle's staff and board of directors felt that it could be the start of something genuinely big and exciting—a credible vehicle for broadcasting serious, objective media criticism.

"There was a collective excitement," recalled David B. Hertz, a media-savvy friend of Morrisett's, who had discussed the magazine's feasibility with Morrisett early on and who was eventually named chairman of the Media Commentary Council, Inc., which Markle established to oversee *Channels*'s operations. "Television was big, and it should be monitored. And if you're a foundation and you do it, you can take credit," Hertz added.[19]

A memorandum to Markle's board by Jean Firstenberg in the spring of 1979 echoed those high hopes:

> The staff is keenly aware of the difficulties, expense and risks in such a business venture. However, the staff is confident that a publi-

> cation could be designed which would have an impact on the communications industry, an impact not unlike that of the *Scientific American*, *Chronicle of Higher Education*, *Rolling Stone*, *New York Review of Books*, or the *Harvard Law Review*, on their individual professional audiences.[20]

Whatever reservations Morrisett harbored about abandoning his more modest newsletter idea in favor of the far riskier magazine, he decided that *Channels* was worth a shot. "Once Lloyd got Les involved," recalled Ronald Daniel, chairman of Markle's board from 1979 to 1986, "the board was swept along by his enthusiasm."

A year later, in March 1980, the board approved an unprecedented $1.5 million grant to establish *Channels* as a not-for-profit magazine. The size of the grant spoke for itself. Markle saw *Channels* as its biggest bid yet to influence the broadcast world at a moment when cable, satellites, and other technological advances were posing historic challenges. Brown agreed to leave his cherished post at *The Times* to become editor of the new magazine.

"At no other time since the introduction of television in the late 40's has there been an opportunity to help to mold an emerging system so as to ensure that the future will profit from the mistakes of the past," according to a description of the new venture in the foundation's 1979–80 annual report. "A crucial role for this magazine would be to help set the agenda for the formation of enlightened public policy regarding television."[21]

Markle set up Brown in a small, windowless office at the Children's Television Workshop during the initial months of planning. Armed with formidable writing skills, keen intellect, and unparalleled knowledge of the television industry, Brown was nonetheless a neophyte in designing, planning, marketing, and managing a magazine. For that matter, so was practically everyone else connected with *Channels* during its formative stages.

To help on the business side, the foundation hired Lawrence Durocher, a magazine consultant, to draw up plans and create a "buzz" in the industry for the magazine's launch. It also established a nonprofit corporation, the Media Commentary Council, Inc., to act as de facto publisher of the magazine as well as its adviser and financial overseer. Besides Hertz, council members included Morrisett and Mary C. Milton, Markle program officer, along with Al Balk of the *Columbia Journalism Review*; veteran publisher Jack Nessel; Thomas B. Morgan, a founder of *New York* magazine; and, eventually, advertising maven Jerry Della Femina.

The early governance structure for operating the magazine soon proved unwieldy. With a council, rather than an individual, serving as publisher and with a foundation looking over its shoulder, *Channels* was a magazine run by committee. Its members had little of the in-house expertise required in the magazine world and, above all, no definite sense of its readership—who they might be or how to reach them.

Brown, however, drew upon the best media talent throughout the magazine's life. The first issue, in April 1981, featured an article on PBS by John Hess, another by Ralph Lee Smith on the spread of cable to cities, and a piece by Jonathan Black describing the battles between CBS's *60 Minutes* and the corporations accusing it of faulty reporting. Despite the young magazine's internal woes, the print media showered it with praise. The *Chicago Sun Times*, called it "the best magazine about television today." Every issue "is like a blast of insight about a medium that intrudes on our lives in ways we seldom reflect about."[22] Markle board member Joel Fleishman, an ardent supporter of the project, wrote in 1983: "Not only should the Trustees of the Foundation be proud, but so should everyone who cares anything about the communications media."[23]

As the first year of publication drew to a close, the financial condition of the magazine looked precarious but not hopeless. Subscription renewals were at a healthy 50 percent, and articles from the magazine had been reprinted in more than fifty publications. One magazine analyst, Gail Pool, astutely sized up the key unmet challenges if *Channels* were to survive:

> *Channels* is a type of magazine that was founded on the basis of editorial purpose to fulfill an informational and educational need. A need, however, is not a market; and *Channels*, like many content-oriented publications, has paid too little attention to locating and reaching its market—with economic consequences. Unless a magazine has a sense of who its readers will be, it cannot afford to go after them, for subscriber solicitation by any method is expensive.

> Unless an advertiser clearly knows who a magazine's readers are, it will not advertise, unwilling to waste dollars on what may be an irrelevant circulation. Both finding a market and marketing itself have been among the major difficulties of *Channel*'s first year.[24]

The first to appreciate the full import of those problems were Hertz and Morrisett. Editorially, Brown had more than lived up to his billing, and the magazine had gained critical respect, but it was bleeding money. During its first year of publication, expenses exceeded combined advertising and subscription revenues by nearly four to one. Markle's $1.5 million investment in the spring of 1980 had been on a calculation that it would cover an anticipated $1.25 million cumulative deficit over the magazine's first five years. By November 1981, Hertz informed fellow council members that those losses would be reached not in five years but in two.[25] If something wasn't done to rationalize management, lower costs, increase revenues, or make the magazine attractive enough to investors or a potential buyer with deep pockets, *Channels* was headed for an early grave.

In January 1982, Morrisett hired a full-time publisher, George Dillehay, to take charge of the business aspects of the magazine. Dillehay, a North Carolina native, previously had been publisher of the Children's Television Workshop's magazines and assistant publisher of *The Village Voice*. The hiring of a respected publisher was also a necessary prelude to the next major step that Morrisett had in mind—launching the magazine as a for-profit venture. Still, as 1983 approached, the magazine was nowhere near commercial viability. Paid circulation was barely 22,000.

By this time, too, the magazine's woes were a continuing drain on Markle's staff resources. Milton was spending considerable time in overseeing the magazine's management and design. After Hertz's departure in 1983, Morrisett himself assumed the chairmanship of the Media Commentary Council.

With uncertainties about its prospects mounting, Markle put the magazine on a tight financial leash and strung out payments month to month, with close scrutiny on how those funds were spent. While injecting a needed dose of management accountability, the heightened vigilance further strained the energies of foundation staff and hindered long-term planning at the magazine.

The question of readership also remained ethereal. Subscription rates stagnated, and it became clear that the audience for serious TV commentary existed primarily among industry insiders, rather than the broader readership originally envisioned by Brown and Morrisett. Further, the magazine's bimonthly publishing cycle was too infrequent to produce copy current enough to satisfy a more knowledgeable readership. At least some industry insiders were also growing annoyed at the magazine's occasionally acerbic commentaries on TV programming. Brown might well have started with the intention of maintaining a tone of respectful criticism, and indeed, under his editorship, *Channels* was certainly more ready than most of the print media to celebrate television's strengths. Still, Brown could never entirely resist the occasional Olympian swipe that made *Channels* seem, at times, just another snobbish print critic out to portray television as mindless. The October 1985 issue, for example, was largely devoted to a "Salute to Excellence." Yet, it also contained a slash-and-burn portrait of *Entertainment Tonight*'s cohosts Rob Weller and Mary Hart: "Both wear an unearthly sheen, as if they'd been dipped lightly in plastic. It's like Ken and Barbie finally got their own show. . . ."[26]

The lack of clear definition of readership or basic identity was not lost on potential advertisers. Dillehay outlined the problem in a 1982 memorandum to the Executive Committee of the Media Commentary Council:

> During the past year *Channels* has been constantly put on the defensive within the advertising community at large. Everywhere one turned the question as to *Channels*' positioning philosophy was being questioned. What is *Channels*? Is it a trade magazine or a consumer magazine? Who is your audience? During the past years, *Channels* bounced around on the issue and did not consistently respond to these inquiries.[27]

By mid-1983, with some $2.5 million in foundation money already spent, Morrisett and the council decided that it was time to move the magazine closer to self-sufficiency. The council transferred *Channels*'s assets and liabilities to a new, for-profit subsidiary, Channels of Communications, Inc., and proposed a plan to capitalize it by selling shares through a limited partnership arrangement. In making the switch to a profit-making enterprise and seeking private investors, Morrisett hoped the magazine might raise about $1 million, enough to break even and make the critical leap from six issues a year to monthly publication. To no one's great shock, the limited partnership concept attracted few takers.

By mid-1984, Morrisett and the rest of the magazine's board had reached several blunt conclusions. Its editorial quality was high but of limited appeal. It was, in effect, a trade magazine trying to compete with more established and accepted publications. To reach a wider readership, it would have to reinvent itself editorially. Even if it did, there was considerable doubt that a more consumer-oriented magazine could reach profitability on circulation of less than 250,000.[28] Annual paid circulation in 1984 was only 18,330.[29] Milton told Morrisett that, in her opinion, the choices had dwindled to a painful few—put out a smaller magazine, give Brown and Dillehay a chance to raise money to keep it going on their own, or suspend publication and convert it to a newsletter.[30]

Time was clearly running out. By mid-summer of 1984, a hunt began for single buyers to bail out the magazine. In July, Brown visited his old friend Norman Lear in North Bennington, Vermont. He and Lear, the wealthy producer of the groundbreaking television comedies *All in the Family* and *The Jeffersons*, had long admired each other as kindred spirits of social conscience. When Brown broached the subject of buying *Channels* over a country breakfast, Lear replied simply, "I'm your money."[31]

By the spring of 1985, Lear agreed to take over the four-year-old magazine. At first, the arrangement seemed to promise a happy solution. Markle had found a buyer with a social conscience and deep pockets. Lear had gained a small but prestigious magazine and seemed willing to pump in enough capital to upgrade its appearance and publish it ten times a year. Also, he was retaining Brown and Dillehay as editor and publisher, respectively.

Before long, however, *Channels*, under Lear's newly formed magazine company, shifted dramatically from its early public service orientation to one focused almost entirely on the business aspects of broadcasting. For Brown and Dillehay, it was a painful departure from the magazine's original mission. In 1988, Brown left the magazine's editorship and stopped writing his column "The Public Eye." Thereafter, *Channels* enjoyed modest success but published its last edition in December 1990 when Lear decided to shut down his entire magazine operation in the midst of the national recession.

In the end, the motivations and ideals at Markle that gave rise to *Channels* collided with tough practicalities. Morrisett had placed a bet on an excellent person with an idea worth trying. With Brown at the helm, the magazine was consistently well written, informative, independent, and provocative. Once *Channels* tried to make the transition from a foundation-supported publication to a commercial venture, its strengths became its handicaps. Its socially conscious orientation did not endear it to the industry on which it depended for survival. Even after it adopted a more pro-industry tone under Lear, the magazine was never able to attract a sufficient audience or advertising base to survive.

As Dillehay said years later, "That was the delusion, the great denial, that we thought we were independent of the industry we were writing about. In truth we were not. We couldn't be."[32] Brown, for his part, had nothing but praise for Markle's generosity, but he added that wasteful promotional and advertising spending, coupled with the inability from the onset to publish more often than bimonthly, wounded the magazine's chances for survival.

Despite the unresolved problems that sealed its eventual fate, *Channels* lasted nine years and continued to be recalled respectfully by historians of magazine publishing. "Lloyd was being very far-reaching in a way," Hertz said. "It did get certain people in the broadcasting world to think for a minute, if not for a whole hour, about what they were doing."[33] Still, it was never clear, even years later, whether more time and money or better business leadership might have saved the magazine—or whether the idea was misguided from the start.

MAKING QUALITY COUNT: TELEVISION AUDIENCE ASSESSMENT

Through the first dozen years of his presidency, Morrisett had learned through hard experience about what makes television tick and what a foundation, whether large or small, could and could not do to influence the medium. He had hosted conferences of broadcasters and had urged them to embrace statesmanlike ideals of diverse programming, including more educational and cultural content. Markle had funded research about the effects of programming on children and adults. Through *Channels*, Morrisett had tried to use objective criticism as a prod for better programs. Through several adventures and misadventures with public television, he was convinced that his foundation did not have pockets deep enough to fund programming on its own. Whatever those past efforts had accomplished collectively and singly, they were simply not getting at the heart of the matter.

Years later, Morrisett recalled the words, though not the identity, of an advertising executive who framed the dilemma precisely at a meeting of broadcasters in the mid-1970s: "You don't understand what business we're in," the ad man had said. "We're in the business of delivering audiences to advertisers. That's our only business, our only interest. That's the only thing we do."

So there it was. Those who worked in television were apparently captive to an economic system that was performing, with great efficiency, exactly the job it was designed to do—not educate, not even entertain, but to collect the largest audiences possible, deliver them to advertisers, and reap huge, reliable profits for both the networks and Madison Avenue.

The television community might allow a Lloyd Morrisett and his co-founders to get away with a once-in-a-lifetime aberration like *Sesame Street*. But if "delivering audiences" was what this medium was about, then probably no amount of research and no appeal to reason or conscience could accomplish what he had had in mind all along—making quality count in determining what appeared on television on a large scale.

Morrisett decided that it was time to change the fulcrum on which economic decisions in the television and advertising industries turned. That fulcrum, Morrisett was rapidly coming to believe, was the rating system used to measure audience size.

Carried over from the radio era, the dominant audience ratings for television were those produced by A. C. Neilsen & Co. (later called Neilsen Media Research) and Arbitron. They were, as Morrisett put it, the "lingua franca of the television marketplace," a market ruled by broadcasters, Madison Avenue, and corporate sponsors.[34] Ratings determined everything that really counted—the value of a minute of advertising on different programs, whether shows stayed on the air, and what time of day they would be broadcast.[35]

The very word *ratings*, however, was a fascinating misnomer containing both the challenge that Morrisett now perceived and its possible solution. The Neilsen and Arbitron numbers didn't *rate* anything, nor did they claim to. They told nothing about the quality of shows or whether audiences liked them, were moved by them, or learned anything of value. They did not even indicate for certain that anyone was actually watching a specific show, only that a particular set was switched on to a given station at a given hour. For the purposes that television broadcasters and advertisers had in mind, that seemed to be enough. But was it?

A few industry mavericks, such as former CBS news chief Fred Friendly, believed that the iron grip of audience ratings was responsible for networks perennially ignoring quality in favor of bland formulas. There was, he asserted, "a conspiracy of limited choice in which a 0.0016 percent sample of the total population is given the equivalent of choosing between dinner at Burger King, McDonalds, or Kentucky Fried Chicken. That sample is subsequently projected in a closed-market model by which it is automatically concluded that 35,471,984 Americans love to eat Big Macs."[36]

What Morrisett was pondering by the late 1970s was both radical and staggeringly difficult. Change the ratings, he believed, make quality count as much as quantity in measuring TV audience preferences, and perhaps Markle could finally amend the iron laws of broadcasting.

The foundation, following its accustomed script, began with fact-finding and research. In 1978, Morrisett turned to Carolyn E. Setlow, executive vice president of the opinion research firm of Louis Harris & Associates and soon-to-be director of corporate planning for Newsweek, Inc. Morrisett also consulted with a fellow psychologist from the London School of Economics, Hilde H. Himmelweit, whom he greatly admired.[37]

Himmelweit's research, "The Audience as Critic: An Approach to the Study of Entertainment," offered evidence that television audiences could reliably and honestly rate the quality of television shows. Her work also suggested the possibility of a twofold framework for measuring audience responses to program quality: (1) whether viewers are captivated by what they are watching and (2) the degree to which they are moved by its content.[38]

Setlow's research for Markle, "Quality Television Ratings: Who Cares?" concluded that developing a better rating system was an idea worth trying, and it might win over enlightened members of the broadcasting and advertising industries. Yet, she was prescient in pinpointing the likely obstacles—the economic conservatism among most broadcasters and advertisers and the skepticism that would greet any radical change in ratings.

Would broadcasters, Setlow asked, welcome the chance to "free themselves from the tyranny of the numbers, the contest that causes network executives to lose many a night's sleep and maybe even their jobs? Would they welcome the chance for more creative and experimental programming in place of the familiar but safe spin-offs and copies of last year's rating hits?"[39] And what about advertisers? Would a General Foods or Procter & Gamble rather have their products linked to programs that viewers thought were worthwhile?

"Unfortunately," Setlow wrote, "the answer to all of the above questions is a resounding NO. . . . Today, squeezed out of their once close identification with and participation in program content, advertisers coldly regard programs as interchangeable vehicles for carrying their commercial messages."[40]

Procter & Gamble's chairman, the late Owen ("Brad") Butler, typified the indifference that many advertisers felt, at the time, about program quality as vehicles for selling his products: "I have no feeling that my commercial on *Kojak* is less positive than on *Mary Tyler Moore*. The average consumer sees my commercial over and over again. How can it have a positive effect on one show and a negative one in another?"[41]

The skepticism about the value of quality-based ratings, Setlow concluded, was rooted in at least two broad objections. First, there was the widely held suspicion that such polls would give false readings. People might say that they dislike violent programs. What really mattered, as the marketing director of McDonald's put it, was "what they watch, not what they like."[42] Second, even if one accepted that the average ratings poll respondent was candid in reconciling stated preferences with actual viewing habits, there was still no proof that that really mattered.

In other words, it was by no means obvious that advertising on a well-regarded program was any more effective in helping Procter & Gamble sell its soap than a commercial on a mediocre program. Indeed, some thought the opposite: If audiences were too engrossed with a program, they might be more likely to use commercial breaks to get a snack or head for the bathroom.[43]

Any new rating system would thus collide with some deeply entrenched beliefs—some valid, some perhaps not. A well-researched case had to be made that the television audience's perceptions of program quality could be reliably measured. Markle would then have to prove that this new and undoubtedly more complicated rating system would help broadcasters and advertisers economically or, at the very least, not hurt them. Ideally, Markle hoped to prove to Madison Avenue's doubters that high-quality programs "sold more soap" than mediocre ones.

Even with such research in hand, the true tests would still lie ahead. Markle would have to find a way to field test a new ratings system. In the best of worlds, the foundation would help establish a new ratings system as a successful commercial venture that could exist alongside the much larger Neilsen and Arbitron ratings. Failing that, Morrisett hoped that an existing rating company might buy or adopt the idea of qualitative ratings. At minimum, he hoped that a compelling case for qualitative ratings would change the way that advertisers and broadcasters made programming decisions.[44]

In short, Markle was about to take on what was certainly the boldest gamble of Morrisett's presidency to date—convincing two prospering and self-satisfied industries, network broadcasting and advertising, that a serious problem existed where very few in those industries perceived one and then offering a solution that all parties would find too economically compelling to ignore. As Setlow's paper put it, Markle would be attempting to "change the rules in the middle of a winning game." Nonetheless, in 1979, Morrisett believed that new technologies were changing the broadcasting game itself and that the time was ripe for his foundation's attempt to change the coinage of television program decision making.

As Morrisett later wrote:

> It was an opportune moment. The status quo in broadcasting was crumbling due to growing competitive pressures from cable television, VCRs, and other new video delivery systems. As the three major networks' share of viewing declined and commercial prices rose, leading national advertisers began demanding new solutions to the worsening "underdelivery" problem. . . . In the heated debate over the meaning of the shortfall, Nielsen and Arbitron came under heavy fire for failing to adequately track this critical hemorrhaging of upscale viewing households. Advertisers were on the lookout for better ways of pinpointing who really watched what, when, and how.[45]

The venture might have seemed "a trifle hubristic," as Morrisett so delicately put it.[46] But the potential rewards were irresistible. For the next seven years, through 1986, Television Audience Assessment (TAA) became Markle's biggest preoccupation and cost $3 million. As much as anything that the foundation had ever attempted, this would be Lloyd Morrisett's "baby."

Following a two-day meeting in New York City in early January 1979 with Himmelweit, Setlow, Elihu Katz of Hebrew University, and a half dozen other communication experts, Morrisett was ready to take the first major step. In March 1979, a start-up grant of $100,000 was approved by Markle's board to establish Television Audience Assessment, Inc., a nonprofit organization that would conduct essential research and field testing and, if all went well, devise an entirely new rating system. The Ford Foundation added its own small start-up grant of $35,000.

Morrisett's first task was to find the right leader for TAA, someone with solid connections in the television industry, with entrepreneurial and management skills. This person also had to be comfortable in the parlance of cognitive research. He believed that he found that person in Elizabeth J. Roberts.

Roberts knew her way around television. During the early 1970s, she had served as director of the children's television unit at the FCC. She had founded Population Education, Inc., an organization in Boston devoted to the study of human sexual development.[47] Between 1977 and 1979, Markle had given her organization several small grants to hold workshops for broadcasters on a range of topics related to television and sexuality. Through these conferences, Roberts had further widened her contacts in the broadcast world. She had impressed Morrisett as a bright, personable leader.

In the spring of 1980, Roberts accepted the assignment to lead the new TV ratings project. That December, Television Audience Assessment, Inc., based in Cambridge, Massachusetts, was formally incorporated as a nonprofit entity, with Roberts as president and with a five-member board of directors.[48] In March 1981, the Markle board allocated $415,000 to produce research to overcome the industry's skepticism. TAA's Cambridge location was fortunate because the corporation could draw on the talents of Harvard and MIT graduate students.

The first of TAA's research, shared with Markle's board on October 16, 1981, quickly shattered two bedrock myths about ratings. Based on a telephone survey, conducted in June 1981, of 1,600 representative TV viewers in Springfield, Illinois, Roberts showed that satisfied viewers are the most attentive. Such audiences were, in fact, more likely to watch a program to the end, more likely to watch it week after week, and less likely to engage in such distractions as cooking, schoolwork, or conversation while the program was on. Most crucially, the survey demonstrated for the first time that highly enjoyed programs were more effective vehicles for advertising. Nearly seven out of ten viewers of such programs said that they stayed in the room during commercial breaks, compared with only 51 percent of viewers of less well-regarded programs.[49]

Armed with those findings, TAA proposed two new measures of audience response designed to supplement existing Neilsen and Arbitron "head-count" polls: (1) "Program Appeal," which asked viewers to rate, on a scale of 1 to 100, how much they enjoyed the show and whether they were likely to plan ahead to watch it; and (2) "Program Impact," which measured on a similar scale whether viewers felt that "it touched my feelings" or "I learned something from it." The second measure was meant to indicate how involved or distracted viewers were while the show was in progress.

What still remained to be proved was that the new ratings would measure how favorably and attentively viewers watched the commercials themselves. Unless such a link was convincingly established, advertisers and broadcasters would, in all probability, greet TAA's impeccable research with a collective "So what?"

The breakthrough came with two viewer surveys conducted during April and May 1982 in New Britain, Connecticut, and Kansas City, Missouri. The data established that programs with "high-impact" scores, such as *Hill Street Blues* or the critically acclaimed TV movie, *A Woman Called Golda* starring Ingrid Bergman, tended to keep viewers in the room during commercials more effectively than "low-impact," though highly popular, programs, such as *Dallas* or *Charlie's Angels*. On balance, TAA's researchers found, 42 percent of viewers surveyed said that they left the room during low-impact programs, compared with 26 percent of viewers who left during high-impact shows. The higher the appeal score, in other words, the more likely it was that viewers would regard commercials as believable, memorable, and likable.[50] The crucial link between audience appeal and the effectiveness of advertising seemingly had been found.

The research phase of the project had accomplished everything Morrisett had hoped. TAA's findings received extensive and, for the most part, respectful coverage not only in the broadcast and advertising press, including, unsurprisingly, *Channels* magazine, but also in *The Wall Street Journal*, *The New York Times*, and *Newsweek*. In a letter to Morrisett, Roberts wrote effusively of an "explosion of interest" in TAA.

The media hubbub and Roberts's painstaking missionary work aroused the curiosity, if not the unbounded support, of advertisers and broadcasters. TAA, she reported, had successfully raised $110,000 from six cable services to support its ratings studies. Early reactions from some ad executives were also encouraging. Ron Katz, an executive at J. Walter Thompson/USA, called TAA's methods and cost-effectiveness "as good as any that can come along." Other leaders from Madison Avenue firms, such as Doyle Dane Bernbach and Ogilvy & Mather, said that the TAA studies had opened the door to the possibility of qualitative ratings as a new industry standard.[51] TV executives were more skeptical, with several attacking its methodology and timeliness. CBS's research chief, David Poltrack, questioned whether viewers polled by TAA were giving socially desirable answers or truthful ones in stating their program likes and dislikes.[52]

Such reservations aside, Roberts argued that TAA's research had made its point—"the television audience is not . . . the universally satisfied mass of attentive viewers that traditional market structures and ratings practices assume it to be." More than that, TAA had proved that the wide variation among programs in audience appeal really mattered, or ought to, to broadcasters and advertisers.

"We certainly have a long way to go before the television industry is ready to buy a qualitative rating system," Roberts told Morrisett, "but I think we have scaled the first hurdle—visibility." After spending some $2 million to develop high-quality data on the economic value of its new ratings formula, it appeared that TAA and Markle might actually beat the odds.

At that high point in 1983, just as TAA was preparing to capitalize on its momentum and to begin the daunting process of converting from a nonprofit to a commercial enterprise, matters began to unravel. One of the worst developments came first. Roberts became seriously ill and assumed a scaled-back role as a board member and consultant. At the worst imaginable moment, the leader who had come to personify the new ratings system was out of the picture. The ensuing search to replace her took more than a year and effectively paralyzed TAA. Much of the excitement and momentum that had built by 1983 withered away. Worried that Markle was supporting an essentially leaderless project that lacked a well-defined business or financing plan, Morrisett tightened the reins on TAA. At Markle's November 1983 board meeting, he recommended a $200,000 grant covering only three months of TAA's operation. Through 1984, such stopgap funding became the norm and further complicated TAA's operating and planning capacities during an already difficult transition period.

TAA's leadership crisis worsened what was, in hindsight, a number of miscalculations. The decision in 1984 to convert TAA from a nonprofit to a commercial venture was almost certainly premature. TAA was attempting to attract business partners or potential investors with an unproved and untested product. As

Roberts bluntly told the TAA board in 1985, the decision was made in the absence of a long-term business plan or a full national test of the ratings and prior to making sufficient effort to help industry executives understand the product. With Roberts half-way out the door and no new leader yet selected, she told the board, "We were left short-staffed trying to finish one phase while starting another."[53]

Whether TAA's haste in changing to a for-profit organization was the product of Morrisett's growing uneasiness over TAA's costs, the length of the foundation's commitment, or the leader-ship vacuum caused by Roberts's illness, is hard to ascertain. Probably all of those factors were at work. Whatever the case, by the spring of 1985, the die was cast. The nonprofit TAA converted to a new, for-profit Television Audience Assessment, Inc., led by a pair of well-regarded researchers, Rolf Wulfsberg and Steven Holt, each of whom had previously helped to develop TAA's ratings.

In April, with a new TAA management team in place, Markle approved a program-related investment (PRI)—in foundation parlance, meaning a loan or equity purchase as distinct from a simple grant—in the amount of $560,000 to finance the new, for-profit organization for a six-month start-up period.

There was no longer any doubt where Markle stood. In its request to Morrisett for the PRI in March, 1985, Wulfsberg and Holt had estimated that TAA would need to raise $2.5 million in capital to survive the start-up period. In providing the $560,000, the foundation gave TAA just six months to find at least another $500,000 from outside investors and begin to build a client base—or face the likelihood of folding up.

The hunt for start-up capital and customers in 1985 was not going well. On the positive side, as Holt reported to Morrisett, there was still a considerable buzz about the concept of qualitative ratings in the advertising and broadcast industries. The best news was that there were solid expressions of interest from a number of leading TV advertisers—Anheuser-Busch Companies, Inc., Ralston Purina Company, Campbell's Soup Company, and Polar-oid Corporation—in subscribing to TAA's ratings. If TAA were eventually up and running, each would pay it a fee of $40,000. But that was where the good news ended. Holt informed Morrisett that most of Madison Avenue remained in the "wait-and-see camp"—interested in the idea of qualitative ratings but not committed enough to recommend the service to clients.[54] Network executives, although perhaps more favorably disposed to TAA's ratings than they had been three years earlier, were still not ready to switch to a new rating formula for their programming.[55]

Both TAA and Morrisett made several dozen further overtures to potential business partners, including NYNEX, New England Telephone, J. Walter Thompson/USA, Dun & Bradstreet, Gannett Newspapers, Knight-Ridder, Inc., and Dow Jones & Company, Inc. They also contacted a number of venture capitalists whom they thought might be willing to invest a couple of million dollars in the new firm and even sounded out A. C. Nielsen and Arbitron as potential investors. Those approaches went nowhere. As Holt reported to Morrisett, the search for outside capital was stymied by the mixed reviews that TAA's ratings had received from broadcasters and advertisers, the high start-up costs, the lack of a full management team, and, perhaps most important, the absence of solid evidence of the rating system's marketability along with doubts about TAA's probable short-term profitability.[56]

Looking back years later, Morrisett added that the search for potential partners and investors was naively pursued. The overtures were handled by TAA itself rather than by an experienced investment banker. TAA had the added burden of overcoming the skepticism of potential investors who saw the whole thing as a do-good project by a foundation.[57]

There were further blows. In the midst of TAA's marketing effort, new competition and new technology for rating TV programming came on the scene, notably the "people meters" that purported to reveal far more about the demographics and viewing preferences of people actually watching shows. In that increasingly competitive climate, advertisers were even more reluctant to commit to any new rating method until the dust settled. With many leaders in the advertising industry bedazzled by the new people-measuring technologies, TAA began to look like yesterday's news.

The last gasps came in November 1985. With a final $500,000 emergency grant from Markle, TAA conducted a five-day national daytime ratings sweep of three thousand viewers. It was the long-awaited test run of the product that was designed to demonstrate the commercial credibility and usefulness of its rating system. The results once again vindicated TAA's research—77 percent of daytime TV viewers watching high-impact shows stayed put during commercial breaks, compared with only 57 percent of those watching low-impact programs.[58] An added bright spot for Morrisett was that of the ninety-two programs rated by TAA for program appeal, *Mr. Rogers' Neighborhood*, *Electric Company*, and *Sesame Street* each ranked in the top ten among adults, even though they were geared primarily toward young viewers.

Wulfsberg and Holt struggled to capitalize on the November sweeps. Holt wrote Morrisett that TAA had in hand $215,000 in firm client contracts from Polaroid, Campbell's Soup, Ralston-Purina, and Public Broadcasting Service, as well as a verbal commitment from Lipton Soup (a division of Unilever Canada Limited).[59]

With no luck in attracting venture capitalists, business partners, or enough advertising clients, a planned Evening Sweeps in the winter of 1986 had to be cancelled. Following a farewell dinner hosted by Markle at the Four Seasons restaurant in Boston for TAA's staff, the venture went out of business on April 18, 1986.

There was a last hurrah, of sorts, in the spring of 1987, when PBS contracted to use TAA's methods to measure attitudes toward network, independent, and public television programming—a contest that, by TAA's qualitative standards, public television handily won.[60]

Still, Neilsen remained the dominant force in the ratings industry because it had the money, the technology, and the name recognition to set the terms of the television race. TAA's research had shown that its ratings might have been a boon to viewers yearning for more variety and quality. But the advertisers and the three networks were never convinced that ratings that measured not only the size but the attentiveness of audiences really mattered. As one postmortem of the project observed, Markle's research, as impressive as it was, stopped short of proving a crucial point—that greater audience involvement in commercials actually affects consumers' buying decisions or habits.[61]

Might TAA have succeeded with better luck, steadier leadership, and more time? Or was it doomed before it began? The failure of the TAA venture, having come so tantalizingly close to success, haunted Morrisett as much as any single project during his presidency. He devoted much of his final annual essay in 1997 to second-guessing himself on the collapse of TAA:

> To give TAA a fair chance, we should have continued our support for two years or more. The Foundation should have planned to provide approximately half the total expenses and supplement revenue from the initial six advertisers. Assuming some success, advertising revenue might have grown in the second year of operation and lowered the necessary subsidy. Our total investment might have risen to $5–6 million. While that would have been an extraordinarily large commitment, Markle would have avoided the sin of undercapitalization.[62]

Ron Daniel, Markle's board chairman during the TAA venture, offered a more pessimistic verdict: "Was TAA undercapitalized? I don't think capital was as important as timing. If we'd had four times as much to spend, we still wouldn't have been able to pull it off. I think there just was too much broadcaster resistance, and not enough advertiser and political support. I don't think TAA was ever able to form an effective partnership with the advertiser or agency world to counterbalance the resistance of the networks. . . . When a puny little foundation was trying to deal with broadcast networks, it was the equivalent of the National News Council being shut out by Abe Rosenthal [of *The New York Times*]. If the 'paper of record' doesn't want to play, you don't have a game."[63]

Television Audience Assessment was, beyond question, The Markle Foundation's most audacious attempt to alter the underlying values that drove decision making in the television industry. The social and educational goals of fostering better, more diverse programming—goals that once seemed so attainable when Morrisett and Cooney launched *Sesame Street*—were still very much alive in Morrisett's mind. Still, with the demise of TAA, they seemed increasingly like goals in search of a more willing and economical medium than television had proved to be.

Morrisett decided that it was time to change channels. For much of the rest of his presidency, the foundation devoted most of its energy to exploring the social, political, and educational potential of newer, less hidebound computer-based technologies—videodiscs, CD-ROMS, and the Internet. Once again, Markle would find itself a lonely philanthropic player in an uncharted new corner of the communications arena.

NOTES

1. Morrisett, interview, 17 Sept. 1987.
2. Firstenberg, interview, 29 Dec. 1997.
3. Lloyd N. Morrisett, letter to Jarvis Cromwell, 26 Apr. 1977, Markle Archive Collection.
4. Morrisett, interview, 12 Aug. 1997.
5. Daniel, interview, 7 Jan. 1998.
6. Lloyd N. Morrisett, "Radio-USA" (President's Essay in "The John and Mary R. Markle Foundation, Annual Report, 1975–1976"), 13.
7. Ibid., 11–12.
8. Ibid., 13.
9. O'Donnell, interview, 19 Nov. 1997.
10. Center for Public Resources, "Examination of the Potential of Radio in the 80's" (prospectus for the center's "radio project"), 1.
11. Conference Summary: "Radio Today." Minutes of meeting sponsored by Center for Public Resources, Inc., and The John and Mary R. Markle Foundation, Seven Springs Center, Mount Kisco, N.Y., 29–31 Oct. 1979, 8.
12. Thomas J. Thomas, letter to Lloyd N. Morrisett, 29 Oct. 1975.
13. Thomas J. Thomas, record of interview by Kendra Hamilton, 17 Oct. 1977.
14. Rogers Worthington, "Producing 'Odyssey' Was Odyssey into Imagination," *Chicago Tribune*, 14 Jan. 1980.
15. O'Donnell, interview, 19 Nov. 1997.
16. Toms, interview, 5 Jan. 1998
17. O'Donnell, interview, 19 Nov. 1997.
18. The author is indebted to Samier Husni, professor of journalism, University of Mississippi, and author of *Samier Husni's Guide to New Consumer Magazines*, published annually since 1985 by Oxbridge Communications, Inc., New York.
19. Hertz, interview, 13 Dec. 1997.
20. Jean Firstenberg, report to Markle Board of Directors concerning

initial $130,000 to study the feasibility of a magazine devoted to commentary, criticism, and analysis of television and related communications technologies, 42, Markle Archive Collection.

21. "The John and Mary R. Markle Foundation, Annual Report, 1978–1979, 1979–1980" (reports combined under single cover), 42.

22. John Teets, "Channels on Right Wavelength," *Chicago Sun Times*, 16 May 1982.

23. Joel L. Fleishman, letter to Lloyd N. Morrisett, with copies to Board of Trustees and Mary Milton, 23 Sept. 1983.

24. Gail Pool, "Magazines," Wilson Library Bulletin, April 1982, 618–9.

25. David B. Hertz, chairman, Media Commentary Council, Inc., report to the Board of Directors, 19 Nov. 1981, 3.

26. *Channels of Communication*, Sept./Oct., 1985, 68.

27. George M. Dillehay, memorandum to Media Commentary Council Executive Committee concerning 1982 publishing plans, n.d., 1, Markle Archive Collection.

28. Lloyd N. Morrisett, "Summary of *Channels* Board Discussion," 8 May 1984.

29. Media Commentary Council, "Summary Prospectus," 2nd draft, 13 June 1984 (prepared for prospective investors or buyers of Channels), 2.

30. Mary Milton, memorandum to Lloyd N. Morrisett, 24 May 1984.

31. Brown, interview, 28 July 1997.

32. Dillehay, interview, 19 Dec. 1997.

33. Hertz, interview, 23 Dec. 1997.

34. Lloyd N. Morrisett, "Television Audience Assessment," in "The John and Mary R. Markle Foundation Annual Report, 1985–1986/1986–1987" (two biennial periods contained in one publication), 8.

35. Ibid., 6–7.

36. Quoted in Television Audience Assessment, Inc., "Report: April 1982," vol. 1, no. 1, 2, Markle Archive Collection.

37. In his retirement speech, 29 April 1997, at Markle's annual dinner, Morrisett spoke admiringly of Professor Himmelweit as a personal friend and one of six "creators of knowledge" who had helped shape his thinking about communications. Prior to her paper that paved the way for Television Audience Assessment, Himmelweit had written about the positive and negative influences of television on children. Until her death in 1989, Himmelweit continued to advise Morrisett on a variety of Markle projects. Their close and sustained relationship became the model for Morrisett's Markle Scholars Program. Although she was never

formally named as such, Morrisett, in later years, often referred to Himmelweit as the first such scholar.

38. Hilde H. Himmelweit, Betty Swift, Marianne Jaeger Biberian, "The Audience as Critic: An Approach to the Study of Entertainment," in Percy H. Tannenbaum, ed., *Entertainment Functions of Television* (New York: Lawrence Erlbaum Associates, 1978), 38.

39. Carolyn E. Setlow, "Quality Television Ratings: Who Cares?" (paper prepared for The Markle Foundation), summer 1978, 5.

40. Ibid., 5–6.

41. Quoted in ibid., 11. In later public pronouncements, Butler appeared to have modified his views. In a speech in June 1981, for example, he advised the TV industry to listen to its critics, particularly those concerned with "excessive or gratuitous sex and violence."

42. Quoted in ibid., 15.

43. Ibid., 15–16.

44. Morrisett, "Television Audience Assessment," 9.

45. Ibid.

46. Ibid.

47. Ibid., 10.

48. Along with Roberts and Morrisett, TAA's original board members included Joel Chaseman, president, Post Newsweek Broadcasting; Ben C. Fisher, communications attorney; and Gerald Levin, group vice president, Video Division, Time, Inc., and, years later, chief executive officer of TimeWarner Inc.

49. Elizabeth J. Roberts, "Audience Attitudes and Alternative Program Ratings: A Preliminary Study," Executive Summary presented to Markle Board of Directors, 16 Oct. 1981, 4.

50. Morrisett, "Television Audience Assessment," 11.

51. "Qualitative TV Ratings Project Gets Agency Support, but . . ." *Television/Radio Age Magazine*, 6 June 1983, 37.

52. Ibid., 68.

53. Elizabeth J. Roberts, "An Evaluation of Television Audience Assessment's First Five Years of Operation" (report prepared for TAA's board of directors), February 1985, 9.

54. Memorandum to Morrisett from Steven A. Holt, general manager, Television Audience Assessment, Inc., concerning the general climate of receptivity to TAA, 14 Jan. 1985, 1.

55. Ibid., 2.

56. Ibid., 3.

57. Morrisett, interview, 14 Jan. 1998.

58. Television Audience Assessment, Inc., "Television Audience Assessment's Qualitative Ratings and the Daytime Viewing Environment: Executive Summary," 2.

59. Morrisett, "Television Audience Assessment," 15.

60. John W. Fuller, "Qualitative Ratings Report of a National Survey Conducted by Television Audience Assessment, Inc., April 30–May 13, 1987," 1.

61. Burston Marsteller, "Television Audience Assessment and the Ratings Industry" (report for The Markle Foundation) 4 Apr. 1988, 43.

62. Lloyd N. Morrisett, "Philanthropy and Venture Capital" (President's Essay in "The John and Mary R. Markle Foundation, Annual Report, 1997"), 14.

63. Daniel, interview, 7 Jan. 1998.

7

Electronic Everything

"The computers are coming," Morrisett wrote in his annual essay in 1982. With that simple, deadpan declaration, he heralded a feast of fresh possibilities and high-risk challenges that would occupy his foundation for much of the balance of his presidency. For the next fifteen years, Markle plunged into a world of software evangelists, quirky economics, mercurial communications technologies in vogue one year and out the next, and an argot of such terms as *multimedia* and *interactive* that everyone was loosely brandishing but few had bothered to analyze with any care.

Morrisett, for his part, was convinced that in the looming era of "electronic everything," very little would remain unaffected—from reading and writing to shopping, banking, sending mail, telling stories, voting, paying taxes, doing homework, and even learning the piano. He foresaw an era of convergence in which old media and new would eventually blend in both form and function. That blending, in turn, might open the way to richer multimedia products combining video, print, and sound experiences. Perhaps in time, these future products might be used to create rich new educational experiences at home and in schools.

"At the moment," Morrisett wrote, "most of us think of television, telephones, and computers as separate media. In the future, a single, interconnected system will form a communications network unlike anything previously known to mankind. For the future, individual choices in entertainment, education and information will be as boundless as the technological imagination that masterminded the new age in communications."[1]

In his 1985 annual essay, Morrisett unveiled four fresh priorities for his foundation that he judged to be "increasingly important to the public in coming years, but, at present, . . . were receiving relatively little attention from public interest organizations."[2] Two of those priorities are the subjects of this chapter: electronic publishing, which promised to transform the traditional world of print, and personal computer software, an area of vast promise but one also marked by slow market growth, undercapitalization, and generally disappointing results.[3] The third priority—how communications technologies might help the needs of the elderly—is discussed in chapter 8. The fourth priority—how these new tools might be used to revitalize electoral democracy—is the subject of chapter 9.

For Markle, 1985 was an especially opportune time to take a fresh look at priorities.[4] By the mid-1980s, *Channels* magazine was leaving the foundation fold for its brief afterlife as a for-profit publication. Television Audience Assessment was in its death throes, done in by the indifference of broadcasters and advertisers. After more than fifteen years of focusing mainly on traditional media, such as television, radio, and print, Morrisett felt that newer, computer-based tools of communications offered unexplored, potentially economical avenues for realizing his educational and social goals. The unmet challenge, as Morrisett saw it, was to sort out, with solid research, the economic, social, educational, and political implications of the computerized age. To the extent that any small foundation could, Morrisett was determined to promulgate a national discussion of the educational and social paths for this newest communications revolution.

Before the debut in 1971 of the microprocessor produced by Intel Corporation, computers had been commonly regarded as clunky, costly, and immobile machines hidden in sterile corporate and government back rooms. The public was left to worry: Would these remote, powerful machines be our servants or masters? In 1968, Stanley Kubrick's classic film, *2001, A Space Odyssey*, had portrayed a love-crazed, paranoid computer named HAL, whose terrifying plausibility to movie audiences spoke volumes about how remote from everyday life computers still were, even at that late date.

Over the next dozen years, economic and technical breakthroughs by the young computer industry transformed these alien tools into familiar appliances. The outer skins of personal computers shrank to desktop size. As Morrisett accurately foresaw in 1982, ". . . today's professional-model $30,000 dream machine is likely to be the $3,000 home machine of tomorrow."[5] Two years later, the easy-to-use, graphically arresting Apple MacIntosh, priced at $2,500, was unveiled, and it soon had a cult following in homes and offices. By the mid-1980s, the number of computers in American classrooms passed the million mark. Most presciently, Morrisett forecast that electronic mail would soon take the nation, and the world, by storm.[6] The goal of making E-mail universally available would become Markle's major preoccupation by the 1990s.

Although Morrisett was intoxicated by the possibilities of the computer age, he was also quite aware of its unsettling questions. Familiar rituals of life were about to be changed or even lost. Confidential medical and financial histories might be open to electronic Peeping Toms. Computers might live up to their highly touted promise of revolutionizing teaching and learning—or merely add pointless games and stultifying drills to classrooms. They might bring people closer together with electronic connections—or isolate them behind yet another glowing electronic screen. They might open new worlds of information and communication—or simply add one more commercially driven wasteland to those created by radio and television.

During the mid-1980s, for that matter, the case had yet to be made why most people even needed a computer. For the relatively few home computer buyers in the pre-Internet days, personal computers served mainly as glorified typewriters, bookkeepers, memory ticklers, or platforms for games of dubious entertainment or educational value. Why spend several thousand dollars for a device whose advantages were still so limited but that required hours of frustration to master?

The much-touted promise of computers as educational tools was similarly unrealized. Computer manufacturers were flooding schools with low-cost terminals and software during the 1980s, and newspapers were full of stories about an impending "classroom computer revolution." Still, many teachers who had lived through previous eras of "miracle teaching machines" were understandably skeptical and resistant. Only the rare school district took the time to train teachers in proper computer use. Educational software on the market was generally of the primitive "drill and practice" variety. Even during the 1990s, with more than three out of four U.S. schools wired into the Internet, questions were still being raised in educational circles about whether the billions of dollars invested in supplying classrooms with computers had actually paid off in improved student learning, or whether the pell-mell rush to wire the nation's schools was a multibillion dollar pig in a poke.[7]

As legitimate as were such concerns, they were never the prime focus at Markle. What mattered to Morrisett was that the educational, social, and civic possibilities of computer-based technology were a vast new target of philanthropic opportunity that had been largely overlooked as too risky and untested by such traditional sources of capital as banks and venture capitalists. Starting in the early 1980s, Markle sought to fill that breach and act as a "social venture capitalist" willing to risk its resources on computer products that promised social and educational benefits.

This blend of social purpose and entrepreneurship also led Markle to consider new methods of funding and managing its projects. In particular, the foundation turned to the program-related investment (PRI), a relatively seldom-used philanthropic device. The Ford Foundation pioneered its use during the 1960s for housing and community development projects. A PRI allows a foundation, in accordance with Internal Revenue Service regulations, to extend different forms of assistance beyond grants to nonprofit or for-profit organizations. In the case of for-profit organizations, a foundation can extend loans or lines of credit, purchase equity shares, or, more rarely, buy stock options or warrants provided that certain legal conditions are met.[8] For a nonprofit recipient, the PRI is usually in the form of a loan. A 1995 survey by The Foundation Center found that seventy-four foundations had disbursed a total of $718 million in PRI grants, loans, and equity investments during the three decades since Ford's earliest PRI. Of that amount, Ford and the John D. and Catherine T. MacArthur Foundation together accounted for 42 percent, or nearly $400 million, of outstanding PRIs.[9]

Unlike typical foundation grants that are, in effect, charitable gifts, PRIs are investments that demand more expertise and business savvy, as well as more active participation by a foundation's staff, to ensure the success of projects. "With an investment," Morrisett said, "it's my job to help make it work. Even though profit cannot be a primary motive in a PRI, there is a thought in the back of your mind that you may get some money back or, if you're very lucky, even make a profit. When making a grant, that's not your thought. It's a charitable gift."[10]

Markle's use of PRIs departed from that of most foundations, which had followed Ford's example and used them mainly to assist nonprofit organizations engaged in community development, housing, and health fields. Markle's use was more capitalistic in spirit. It extended PRIs to assist educationally oriented commercial enterprises whose ideas were considered too advanced or risky to attract loans or start-up capital from traditional sources.

Markle's first experiment with PRIs, in 1982, was a $300,000 start-up investment for a new corporation, Family Radio Programming, Inc., to develop syndicated commercial children's educational radio shows. The venture found few commercial takers and folded in 1987. Beginning in 1989, PRIs became an important funding tool for Markle to help several young struggling firms create multimedia and Internet-based products that sought to fill educational or cultural needs.

Markle also used PRIs to help nonprofit ventures convert to commercial enterprises. As noted in chapter 6, Markle provided PRIs totaling more than $1 million in its unsuccessful effort to convert Television Audience Assessment into a for-profit company. In 1990, the foundation invested $1 million to convert the British Broadcasting Corporation's Interactive Television Unit into a new, for-profit venture called Multimedia Corporation.

PRIs held a further attraction for Markle. In entering the high-cost, high-risk arena of computer technology and software development, PRIs offered the possibility of recycling scarce foundation assets rather than continually depleting them through grants. Loans repaid by recipients or profits earned through equity investments could be plowed back into the foundation's coffers and used again for other purposes.

PRIs, then, were not merely a different way of distributing philanthropic money. They were also management tools that placed a new onus on both the foundation and the recipient of aid to put a premium on sound administration. "Indeed," noted Karen D. Byers, Markle's chief financial officer, "it is this level of extra scrutiny that has caused many foundations to shy away from

PRIs. If you are doing a PRI to help start a new company, you have to do the same 'due diligence' that a venture capitalist does. Who are the people? What do they propose to do? Is there a market for this? What is the distribution mechanism? What are the marketing strategies?"[11]

By 1995, Markle ranked first among foundations in the number of outstanding PRIs supporting the arts, culture, and media fields and fifth in the dollar amount of those awards—no small feat for a foundation its size.[12]

To help manage these more complex projects, Morrisett hired a crucial new staffer, Edith C. Bjornson, in 1986. As vice president and senior program officer over the next dozen years, Bjornson's business acumen, appreciation of public relations, and wide-ranging knowledge of the media proved to be particularly valuable to Markle's new enterprises. Previously, she had been a consultant to PBS and had gained extensive television and radio producing credits, including the acclaimed *Omnibus*. She also had held executive positions, including assistant general manager of Channel 13 public television in New York City and corporate vice president for programming at Group W, Westinghouse Broadcasting & Cable.

PIANOS AND ELECTRIC HOCKEY: EXPLORING THE NATURE OF INTERACTIVITY

To Morrisett, an immediate issue crying out for research was the nature of interactivity itself. By the 1980s, commercial software publishers were flooding store shelves with games and a host of other "interactive learning products," that is, products demanding some sort of reasoned response from the participant learner. Yet, no one had convincingly shown whether interactivity in and of itself was, as Morrisett would later put it, "the 'open sesame' of information processing and human learning."[13] Between 1988 and 1997, Markle spent $1.5 million on studies aimed at assessing the potential of interactive learning—the use of computers as educational tools.

Carnegie Mellon University was a hotbed for such work. The Pittsburgh-based school was home to computer gurus Allen

Newell and Herbert Simon, whom Morrisett had known since his Social Science Research Council days of the late 1950s. During the 1980s, Newell and his colleagues were developing a computer-based architecture for simulating the entire range of human thought and intelligence. Called Project SOAR, it involved creating computer programs that imitated human thought processes. Their research excited Morrisett and, on a personal level, offered him a chance to flex his own dormant experimental psychology muscles. Markle provided some $816,000 to the team led by Newell until his death from cancer at age sixty-five in 1992. Thereafter, the research on the nature of interactivity was directed by a principal investigator of Project SOAR, Jill Fain Lehman.

Lehman's project involved the teaching of basic college physics by using a specially designed game of electric field hockey. The sights, sounds, and motions of the hockey game were governed by the same principles as the subject matter to be learned—in this case, the physical laws governing the behavior of charged particles. Using a keyboard and a mouse, students were asked to perform tasks and solve problems by using their skills in the electronic field hockey game whose patterns behaved along the same lines as the charged particles that the students were studying. Lehman and her colleagues thus sought to test the widely held belief that interactive game playing could, in and of itself, create a powerful learning situation.[14]

The experiment provided an important and debunking lesson. Mere interactive game playing was not the magic path to learning that had been commonly assumed in the education community and that commercial computer game publishers had touted. As Lehman explained to the author, "What our work showed was that it was possible to solve the problems [generated by the field hockey game] without actually learning physics. That's not the same as saying that they didn't learn anything. What it means is that you have to be very clear in designing these systems that students know the knowledge that they are supposed to be getting."[15]

In 1988, a second opportunity presented itself at Carnegie-Mellon to explore the nature of interactive learning. A team of computer experts and music instructors, led by Roger Dannenberg, was developing a computerized "piano tutor" designed to simulate the give-and-take between a piano teacher and student. The piano tutor aimed to speed the learning process and reduce frustration by acting as a silent observer able to critique a student when a live teacher wasn't there. Between 1988 and 1991, Markle provided six grants totaling nearly $635,000 to support Dannenberg's research.

The piano tutor's multimedia system worked by connecting a musical instrument to a computer equipped with special music recognition software. It could diagnose whether a student was playing the right note and holding the note for the correct length of time, and it could detect more subtle problems with rhythm. At the end of the lesson, the computer gave a remedial assignment based on the mistakes detected, thus allowing the student to progress at his or her own pace.

Dannenberg's research produced quick, promising results. Carnegie-Mellon students who tested the piano tutor were uniformly enthusiastic. By 1990, using videodisc technology, Dannenberg's team had prepared some fifty lessons and twenty supporting exercises and was planning to test it in the Pittsburgh public schools.

Ironically, those early successes gradually gave rise to mutual frustration between Dannenberg and Markle's staff. Commercial development was never in the forefront of Dannenberg's mind. He viewed his work purely as research on interactive learning, not product development, and hoped that Markle would judge it as such. To Morrisett and Bjornson, however, piano tutor seemed like a natural product for the consumer market. They pressed the idea on Dannenberg, but his lack of marketing expertise was soon apparent.

"Markle wanted us to do marketing studies, but we didn't have that kind of expertise," Dannenberg said several years later. "It was too bad. We were too successful too early. It would have been better to consider this as research and evaluate it that way."[16]

Dannenberg and his colleagues eventually published a number of scholarly papers on their work between 1990 and 1994. Dannenberg also managed to license his research commercially to CODA Music Technologies in Minnesota under the product name Smart Music several years after Markle funding ended in 1992. Piano tutor was ahead of its time compared with most computerized piano-teaching products on the market; however, its commercial fate, if any, remains uncertain.[17]

Was the work on interactive learning by Carnegie-Mellon computer scientists worth the $1.5 million that Markle invested? Morrisett, the devoted social scientist and amateur pianist, certainly believed that it was. Allen Newell's theoretical work on artificial intelligence and the nature of interactive learning was highly influential in computer research circles at Carnegie-Mellon, as well as at the University of Michigan, the University of Southern California, and other leading centers. Carnegie-Mellon's research by Lehman and others provided important caveats about the limitations of interactive learning. Unfortunately, that research had virtually no effect on the quality of educational software available to home and school consumers. As Lehman put it: "There is an enormous amount of junk out there. I don't believe any amount of journal articles is going to turn the tide on what's being sold on the shelves of Comp-USA."[18]

BBC AND THE BIRTH OF MULTIMEDIA

During the mid-1980s, the epicenter of creativity in multimedia software development was not Silicon Valley, nor was it even in the United States. It was an old movie lot owned by the British Broadcasting Corporation (BBC) in Elstree Centre, England, some forty minutes' drive from downtown London. Most of the lot was used to produce a popular British soap opera, *EastEnders*. It was also inhabited by BBC's newly formed Interactive Television Unit that included a team of production mavericks led by Peter Armstrong and Max Whitby, who were fascinated by the idea of blending television with the power of computers.

Armstrong's team was piecing together the first genuinely multimedia videodiscs integrating text, graphics, audio, and video content on a single format. In 1986, the BBC unit became the talk of the computer world with a videodisc called *Domesday*, a high-tech update of the identically named survey of Britain conducted exactly nine hundred years earlier by William the Conqueror.

Domesday was an astonishing feat, both technically and creatively. The material for the videodisc was gathered by volunteers from fourteen thousand schools, hundreds of other organizations, and more than a million individuals. The resulting inventory of modern Britain's population, culture, resources, and industries proved to be, as Armstrong later told the author, "a huge conceptual success and a huge commercial flop." Intended mainly for schools and libraries, the £2,000 sterling price tag set by its producer, Philips Electronics, "crucified sales," Armstrong said, because it was affordable to only a relative handful of libraries and the wealthier schools.[19]

To Morrisett, *Domesday*'s disappointing sales were beside the point. An unabashed Anglophile since his Carnegie days, he had always found the British refreshingly adventurous in their approach to creativity, in general, and computer technology, in particular.[20] He also felt an affinity to the educational and cultural orientation of the BBC, to say nothing of its massive library of material that might provide endless grist for educational computer products.

Morrisett was convinced that the BBC was, at that time, the world's leader in multimedia educational products. He was even beginning to imagine a kind of BBC-affiliated Children's Television Workshop, where the educational potential of new disc-based interactive television might be researched and produced. "I suggested that we provide them with some R&D funds," Morrisett recalled. "They had production funds, but in terms of having a research component—I was analogizing with *Sesame Street*—they didn't have it."[21]

Following several transatlantic visits by Morrisett to meet Armstrong and Jan Maulden, head of BBC's Interactive Television Unit, Markle's board approved a three-year, $972,000 grant in March 1988 aimed at boosting the research capacities of the unit. The decision came just as the BBC was strapped for cash and under political pressure from the Thatcher government to trim its spending and its sprawling activities.

By 1989, the BBC unit had added impressively to its disc library. Among its products were *Countryside*, a comprehensive guide to farming. A joint project with Oxford University Press titled *Volcanoes* allowed a simulated exploration of major volcanoes. *Gallery* gave students a step-by-step tour of how *EastEnders* was produced.

By that time, too, a divorce between the BBC and its young Interactive Television Unit seemed increasingly inevitable. With Europe in the grips of recession and with interactive television still years from mass market reality, the futuristic unit might have been admired by BBC's brass, but it was also considered a corporate misfit and money drain. By July 1989, the BBC had agreed in principle to a buyout that would permit the Interactive Television Unit to become an independent commercial enterprise. That same month, Maulden and Armstrong asked Morrisett for an investment in the new corporation. Markle's board obliged in November with a $1 million PRI in exchange for a 20 percent equity stake in the new company, Multimedia Corporation. As part of the deal, Morrisett became a director of Multimedia.

"At the beginning," Armstrong told the author, "we thought we had enough to make it. We had software. We had alliances with Philips Electronics and Apple Computer. We had access to the BBC library. We thought we had a winning combination."[22]

As hopeful as everyone was about Multimedia's prospects, it soon became clear that both Multimedia and Markle were in for an economic roller-coaster ride. Within months of its founding in February 1990, the company was awash in financial troubles. As a result of the recession and the weak market in educational CD-ROMS, Multimedia reported losses of nearly £400,000 pounds sterling in 1990. By the summer of 1992, the company was clinging precariously to life. Markle provided a £25,000 emergency line of credit and extended it in October 1993. At Morrisett's and Armstrong's urging, top management was shaken up and expenses sharply trimmed.

Just as abruptly, in 1993, the company's fortunes turned for the better. The market for multimedia products revived along with the world economy. Multimedia produced *3-D Atlas*, by far its biggest moneymaker, which won international awards and sold more than 2.5 million copies. Nearly on its deathbed months earlier, Multimedia was now regarded as a hot young company by venture capitalists who had rarely given educational software firms a second glance. In January 1994, British venture capitalist

David Rowland agreed to buy a 40 percent share of the corporation for £1 million.

By mid-1995, at Rowland's urging, Multimedia prepared a public offering of its stock. "Multimedia was very sexy on the British stock market," Armstrong said, "and Rowland probably thought they could put their million in, float the company, get a lot of other money, and get out themselves."[23]

That belief proved correct, at least for a short time. Through the first half of 1996, Multimedia's stock soared. From an initial public offering price of 24 pence per share, it nearly tripled to the 70-pence range. From Markle's viewpoint, a highly risky PRI investment now looked as if it might become a great success story, philanthropically and financially. After consulting with Markle's board, Morrisett decided to sell the foundation's stake in Multimedia. In March 1996, Markle sold its shares for 65 pence each, for a total of $2,980,000 in American currency, which roughly tripled the foundation's original investment. Morrisett resigned his seat on Multimedia's board in January 1997, thus ending his formal ties to the company.

For Markle, the timing of the stock sale proved incredibly lucky. By the end of 1997, Multimedia's fortunes had collapsed again. The company was essentially put in mothballs, no longer producing new software but finishing up contracts and selling off its intellectual property. Share prices plunged to under 5 pence. From a purely financial standpoint, Morrisett's "social venture capital" strategy had reaped a few million dollars for Markle. But his philanthropic goal of creating an innovative, durable CD-ROM company that turned out top-notch educational multimedia products had failed.

What happened?

By Armstrong's reckoning, the rapid rise in the popularity of the Internet in the mid-1990s effectively killed the multimedia CD-ROM market in the space of a year. Multimedia Corporation was simply too small and undercapitalized to weather such an abrupt shift in technology. "We weren't unique in this," Armstrong said. "We gambled and lost on CD-ROM technology. If you're wrong on that basic gamble, it doesn't really matter how well or badly organized you are."[24]

Morrisett agreed that timing and unpredictably shifting markets were behind Multimedia's downfall. He also cited profligate spending and the part-time status of many of the principals running Multimedia. Still, he said in retrospect, "I'd have to say it was a worthwhile investment, and I'd do it again. It's like *Channels*. We created a viable magazine that had a nine-year run, and I feel fine about that. You have to put both of these things in the context of what happens to small companies. A lot of them fail."[25]

BOOKS AND BEETHOVEN: THE VOYAGER COMPANY

At one of four Markle-financed conferences on electronic publishing arranged in 1987 by The Aspen Institute, the foundation invited leading computer software producers to take part in a little contest. Each was given $2,000 to come up with an educational software prototype that the foundation might help to develop. "That's where I met Bob Stein," recalled Edith Bjornson, who judged the competition.[26] Stein, a partner and the acknowledged house genius in the critically acclaimed but financially marginal Los Angeles videodisc firm Voyager Company, bowled over Bjornson with what she later called "the finesse of his ideas and the passion with which he approached publishing."[27] Stein produced two videodisc prototypes for Markle's competition. One featured works from the Art Institute of Chicago, and the second was a multimedia exploration of classical music using text, graphics, and actual music. During the next decade, the foundation staff would be as dazzled by Stein's talent as they would be frustrated by his back-of-the-envelope style of doing business.

Voyager began in 1985 as a joint venture of Janus Films and Voyager Press, an interactive publishing concern founded a year earlier by Stein and his wife at the time, Aleen. No one, including Stein, a self-described Maoist and former antiwar activist, held a corporate title.The Criterion Collection of 150 video laser discs of classic films from Janus's library made up its steadiest source of income through the 1980s. Owing largely to Stein's freewheeling presence, Voyager stood out as an unusually creative, risk-taking corporation even in a youthful industry supposedly full of such mavericks. By 1993, when the editors of the computer magazine *MacUser* listed their choices for the best fifty CD-ROMs on the market, seventeen were Voyager titles, including the one picked as best of all—a brisk-selling multimedia rendition of the Beatles' 1964 film, *A Hard Day's Night*."[28] That year, Voyager's revenues were $11 million, up from $8 million the previous year. Even with its successes, Voyager, along with other software firms, was considered too risky for traditional venture capitalists interested in quick profits.

Multimedia explorations of classical music became the company's area of most dazzling innovation. Stein's novel ideas for multimedia music and art CDs fit perfectly within the foundation's larger goal of stretching the educational benefits of electronic publishing and software development for home and school markets. On the strength of Stein's proposals, Markle provided Voyager a $272,000 PRI loan in June 1989 to develop and market products based on the prototypes that had so impressed Bjornson at Aspen.

That year, Voyager produced a new CD Companion Series that included interactive discs of Beethoven's *Ninth Symphony* and Stravinsky's *Rite of Spring*. Beethoven's *Ninth*, in particular, was hailed by critics as a model of what the multimedia industry could be doing.[29] Besides the music itself, the Beethoven CD allowed listeners a range of learning and listening experiences, including the ability to compare particular points in the music, view pictures of Beethoven and his world, read scholarly commentary on the screen, follow the score on a computer screen as it was being played, and invent games based on the musical score.

After classical music, the next frontier for Stein and Voyager was interactive text. With its strong interests in educationally based electronic publishing, the foundation provided a second PRI loan of $212,780 in 1991. As Stein imagined it, "curling up" with what he would call a "really modern library" offered an unprecedented reading experience combining pictures, text, graphics, and sound.

As with Voyager's music projects, Stein concentrated on classic texts. The first project was the new Cambridge edition of Shakespeare's *MacBeth*, including a lengthy glossary, a video performance of the play, interpretive readings, and other materials. The second project, which proved to be more ambitious and controversial, was a multimedia CD-ROM history text of the United

States, *Who Built America*, based on a two-volume published work by Steven Brier and Roy Rosenzweig that chronicled U.S. history from 1876 to 1914.

Who Built America received critical raves when it first appeared in August 1993. It contained hundreds of pages of text, but, with the click of a mouse, readers could also listen to recorded speeches of such orators as William Jennings Bryan or gain access to hundreds of film clips, photographs, and audio excerpts of great moments in U.S. history. The CD also offered readers instant access to original documents, not just interpretive text.

True to Stein's leftist leanings, the history also featured footage of race riots, sweatshops and the growth of labor unionism, homosexuality in the Old West, and the history of birth control. Still, most reviews, even those in the conservative *Wall Street Journal*, discounted its political slant and praised it as a "stimulating, thoughtful work."[30]

Sales of *Who Built America* were less than dazzling in its first year—under six thousand copies—but received a lift when Apple Computer Corporation offered to distribute it to elementary and secondary schools. When Apple received complaints from some schools about its contents, the controversy over the CD's political content suddenly went public. Under pressure, Apple announced that it was ending its distribution arrangement, and *The Wall Street Journal*, which had hailed the CD in 1993, ran a prominent article in February 1995 that quoted critics who blasted it as "a politically correct, left-wing version of American history."[31]

Markle's staff took pains to distance the foundation from the public furor over the disc. "To this day," Stein said several years later, "I don't know what Lloyd or Edee [Bjornson] thought about [*Who Built America*] politically."[32] Well before that firestorm, however, Bjornson had emphasized to Stein that Markle was funding only the innovative process that went into developing the CD, not its contents. As with *Channels* magazine, which occasionally upset television's bigwigs, the foundation wanted to preserve its neutrality concerning the political content of material that resulted from its funding. This, as Bjornson well knew, was no easy distinction to make to a public often suspicious of the political leanings of foundations. "I didn't want us to be seen as taking a position one way or the other," she said. "I just felt we already had a reputation for being too liberal. I was trying very hard to move us off that perception, and *Who Built America* would not have been helpful.''[33]

Stein, for his part, did not cave to the CD's critics or Apple. He refused to change the content of the CD and waged a public relations war with Apple over its decision to drop the CD from school distribution. Amazingly, he won. Apple reversed itself and agreed to distribute the CD again.

By the end of 1996, with the Internet casting a lengthening shadow over the CD-ROM market, Voyager's cash was running out. With Stein and his business partners divided over Voyager's future, he quit the company in November. In 1997, Markle provided him a $756,800 PRI loan to start a new commercial venture, Night Kitchen, Inc., a name that symbolized to Stein ''a creative place, where you stay up late brainstorming over coffee or wine.''

Night Kitchen's goal was to develop an ''authoring tool'' that allowed nonprogrammers to engage in easy, low-cost multimedia electronic publishing. The tool embodied Stein's and Markle's shared conviction that, just as computer word processing had largely replaced ordinary typewriting, high-capacity CD-ROMS and DVD-ROMs would, in time, prompt a similar shift from traditional print to electronic book publishing. Stein hoped to provide an important element in this looming publishing revolution—authoring software that would make it easy for anyone to create electronic publishing products.

''Obviously this is a risk,'' Morrisett and his staff wrote to the board as they recommended the Night Kitchen project in 1997. ''It is betting that the transition from print and paper to electronic publishing will start to take place during the next five years. . . . The staff believes that this kind of early risk is exactly suited for The Markle Foundation's program and a program-related investment.''[34]

On another level, Markle was once again gambling on a person whose genius lay more in product development than in business or marketing. ''Creative talent of that sort deserves support,'' Bjornson said. ''Is that easy to manage? It is proving to be very *un*-easy.''[35]

As 2000 approached, Stein said that his authoring tool was nearing commercial release.

RESURRECTING ERASMUS: INTERACTIVE STORYTELLING

Between September 1995 and March 1998, Markle provided $350,000 to Chris Crawford, an iconoclastic inventor of computer games, who dreamed of reconceiving the ancient art of storytelling by using the interactive power of computers.

Interactive storytelling was not an entirely new concept. Artists, authors, and playwrights had experimented with ways to involve their viewers, readers, and audiences as partners in creating stories as they unfolded. Crawford wanted to take the idea a step further by devising a computer tool to create a "story world" that could simulate the myriad options that fiction writers have in their minds as they invent their tales. Using his tool, storytellers might develop a vast array of characters, imbue them with dozens of possible personality traits ranging from gullibility to greed and lust, and place them in scores of different dramatic settings in the story world. The possibilities within this computerized fictional world were designed by Crawford to be, in theory at least, nearly as limitless and multilayered as the human imagination.

"Interactivity is fundamental to the architecture of the human mind," Crawford told the author. "We've created the vast majority of our communication technology which places people in passive roles. You read a book, you watch a play. The human mind is only working some small fraction of its energy level when it's not interacting, when we're simply expostulating."[36]

Crawford's inspiration for this postmodern view of storytelling was the sixteenth-century visionary, Erasmus—"a loner and misfit," as Crawford characterized him—who had used the new medium of print to create a mass image of himself and to impart a view of the world that differed defiantly from that of anyone else of his time. Five hundred years later, Crawford now proposed to offer fiction creators a similar opportunity to defy convention and achieve Erasmian immortality by helping to reinvent the ancient art of storytelling: "Here's a new medium, a tool for creating a new kind of fiction and storytelling, and I'm looking for someone to make him or herself a superstar by using it."[37]

The Markle staff was not necessarily as enamored as Crawford was with the prospect of reinventing storytelling nor as confident that the attempt would succeed. Still, they considered Crawford an exceptionally innovative software producer and therefore worth a gamble to see what he might produce. Specifically, they hoped that the knowledge Crawford developed might be of value to game software in general, an area of increasing interest at Markle.

"Here we were experimenting with games as a vehicle, and here is someone saying, here's another method I can help develop that can be really exciting," said Cathy Clark, Markle's program director, who worked closely with Crawford.[38]

In 1997, the Erasmatron Author, Crawford's story world software, went on sale at $199 per copy at his website, www.erasmatazz.com. By mid-1998, the project had reached a discouraging crossroads. Potential users and marketers simply did not grasp his ideas. The business plan submitted by Crawford and his wife to Markle for marketing Erasmatron Author had set a modest goal of a few hundred sales per year. As of 2000, five had been sold, and Crawford told the author that his personal finances were "getting grim."[39].

"The world has had ample opportunity to find out about this," Crawford admitted to the author. "The reaction is incomprehension leading to abandonment. I have been trying to sell it to artists of all different stripes, and failing in all my attempts. I gave a speech to a meeting of science-fiction writers, and I bombed completely. Their response was, how dare you criticize our muse?"[40]

Clark said, "We told Chris that he was overestimating the computer readiness of ordinary people. Now the marketplace was telling it to him. It's really such a typical programmer problem. You develop some incredibly intricate product and you fall in love with it, and you can't see that nobody else is in love with it. And in this case you have to go even further because you're trying to sell it to authors, not programmers."[41]

Whether Crawford's vision of himself and his product as enablers of a new kind of fiction writer was brilliant, too futuristic, even for science-fiction writers to grasp, or simply not a very good or needed idea is something that only time and the marketplace can judge. The intrepid Crawford told the author that he "refuses to give up hope," and was ready to carry on with the project for the rest of his career, if necessary, until the right author created something dazzling enough with Erasmatron to stop the fictional world in its tracks.[42]

No one at the foundation had second thoughts about its gamble on Crawford or the value of the knowledge about interactivity that his work and thinking were contributing. As Clark put it, "Some of our projects are goal-directed, and some are for the sake of underwriting an exciting mind, which is something that Lloyd was always very interested in doing."[43]

THE ELECTRIC LIBRARY

With the platform of electronic publishing shifting rapidly during the 1990s from discs to the Internet, the computer world was left wondering what types of services would survive and succeed on the Web. For Markle, the question was even tougher. Could it identify the kinds of Internet-based services that would not only prosper financially but also serve genuine educational and social ends?

Infonautics, a Wayne, Pennsylvania, firm founded in November 1992, seemed to fit that description. It was headed by Marvin Weinberger, a born salesman with a passionate commitment to education and to what he called "information democracy." By 1993, Weinberger was developing his ideals into an on-line information service called Homework Helper, which featured an extensive library of databases for use by school-age children and college students. His idea was to cut through the clutter of information on the Internet and create an easy-to-use, efficient home learning service that could replicate, and improve upon, the library research experience.

By that fall, Weinberger had raised nearly $1.7 million from venture capitalists and other private sources but was still well short of the $3 million that he believed was needed to launch the service. In 1994, Markle decided to provide a $750,000 PRI equity investment in the new company to help meet its start-up needs. As with Multimedia Corporation, a board seat for Morrisett was part of the deal.

Homework Helper seemed a good bet for several reasons. It was, first of all, more advanced, extensive, and user friendly than comparable services. Children did not have to learn complicated computer commands to ask questions. They could get homework help simply by typing in a question in plain English. Homework Helper then offered a manageable list of articles and writings from scores of media and reference databases to answer the question. The market for Homework Helper also looked promising. The possible universe of customers was 45 million students, not to mention institutional subscribers, such as school libraries. Students of the 1990s were quite comfortable with computers. In 1993, more than 12 million households with school-age children had personal computers, and 4.6 million homes were equipped with modems.[44] Also appealing from a philanthropic standpoint was Weinberger's plan to offer the service for a low monthly fee of $9.95 for unlimited usage.

The possibility of Markle's involvement in the venture was greeted warily at first by some other Infonautics investors. Several phoned Morrisett to mention their concern that a foundation leader might be more preoccupied with achieving social goals than with commercial success. "My reaction to that," Morrisett said, "was that unless the company was a financial success, it couldn't be an educational success."[45] In 1994, the PRI was approved, and Morrisett took his place on the Infonautics board.

In March 1995, Homework Helper was launched on the Internet service Prodigy. It offered students access to more than seven hundred reference works and a daily updated archive of hundreds of periodicals and newspapers. Students could get answers to almost every conceivable question: How did Jerry Garcia die? How large is the national debt? What do manatees eat? When did women first serve on juries?

The low-cost, user-friendly service attracted favorable media coverage, including a feature in *USA Today,* which hailed it as "an impressive industrial strength research tool that parents will want as much as their kids."[46] The next three years produced more accolades. The number of Homework Helper subscribers reached twenty thousand by the end of 1995. By 1998, it had grown to 50,000 individual subscribers and about 5,000 school and library subscribers. In 1996, the service became available to anyone on the Internet, as well as Prodigy, and the Internet version adopted the more congenial name, Electric Library. The Information Association named Weinberger "Entrepreneur of the Year" in 1996 and cited Electric Library as the association's "Best Educational Product."

Still, Infonautics was struggling to get in the black. It reported net losses of $7.4 million in 1995, $13.7 million in 1996, and $17.3 million in 1997. To raise more capital, the firm went public with a $30 million stock offering in 1996. On the positive side, sales momentum was improving. Revenues increased to $6.8 million in 1997, compared with $1.4 million the year before.

By 1997, internal differences were developing between Weinberger and the rest of the board, including Morrisett. Serving children directly was what had always driven Weinberger. In 1997, he pressed the board to invest in developing a new Internet search engine to be called Electric Schoolhouse, which he hoped would keep Infonautics close to his mission of serving children directly, rather than through libraries or other institutions. But the board, including Morrisett, was committed to conserving resources, not embarking on expensive new ideas.

The majority of Infonautics board members had also come to believe that institutional, rather than home, subscribers were where the biggest profits existed. The philosophic and strategic rift between Weinberger and the rest of the board grew as the majority—again, including Morrisett—sought to shift the firm's sales effort to the institutional market. "That departed from Marvin's vision," Morrisett said.

By 1998, according to Infonautics's chief executive, Van Morris, home subscribers could purchase the service for $9.95 per month or $59.95 per year. The fees charged to institutions ranged from $995 a year for schools to $500,000 for a service contract with a midwestern multistate consortium.

Weinberger resigned his chairmanship in February 1998 and formed a new company, Electric Schoolhouse, to pursue his goal of providing Internet access to education-related information directly to families. He remained Infonautics' major shareholder, and Infonautics held a 10 percent position in his new venture. Morrisett succeeded Weinberger as chairman of Infonautics.

In the summer of 1999, Infonautics entered a deal with Bell & Howell to create a new corporate entity. Bell & Howell contributed its kindergarten through grade 12 business, and Infonautics contributed its institutional Electric Library business, for which Bell & Howell paid $20 million cash. In addition, Bell & Howell bought Infonautics's custom publishing business for $2 million. Bell & Howell owns 73 percent of the new entity, and Infonautics owns 27 percent. Infonautics was thus left with $22 million cash, the consumer Electric Library business, and its Web-based Sleuth business. "The future is yet to be written. It depends on how Infonautics spends the money. But the Bell & Howell joint venture was a very healthy step up," Morrisett said.

E-MAIL FOR ALL

By the early 1990s, more than one in four American homes had at least one computer, and the numbers were climbing fast. Accompanying that growth, the popularity and scope of the Internet was increasing at an almost inconceivable rate. From mid-1993 to 1995, the number of Web sites grew from 130 to 23,500. By 1995, as Morrisett noted in his annual essay that year, some 6.6 million Internet host computers existed in 106 countries.[47] A 1998 survey conducted by Nielsen Media Research and CommerceNet indicated that more than 70 million American adults were using the Internet.

Meanwhile, the rise of the Internet was obliterating the market for educational videodiscs and CD-ROMS, on which Markle had previously bet heavily at Voyager Company and Multimedia Corporation. As Morrisett had prophesied a decade earlier, electronic mail was becoming a ubiquitous part of life. He was now convinced that universally available E-mail might address many of the social, educational, and political goals that he had been trying to promote throughout his presidency. As he noted in his 1995 annual essay, more than one billion E-mail messages had been sent that year, a nearly fourfold increase over just two years earlier.

With his regrets still fresh over not giving Television Audience Assessment enough time or money to succeed, Morrisett was determined, this time, to devote every ounce of effort to secure the success of his universal E-mail initiative. From the mid-1990s on, "E-Mail for All" became Markle's slogan for a $3 million research and publicity effort to shape a national debate on how best to make this computer application available to everyone, rich or poor. As usual, research formed the starting point of Markle's strategy. This time, however, the foundation also financed a $1 million public relations campaign aimed at ensuring that the press, the public, the business community, and the government and policy leaders would take due notice of the research findings.

Morrisett's prescience about E-mail's possibilities had its roots in his long-standing personal involvement with the RAND Corporation. RAND had been at the center of the Internet's early history. During the early 1960s, RAND scientist Paul Baran had done pioneering work that led to computer networking. At the same time, JOHNIAC, a computer at RAND, was among the first that enabled researchers to communicate electronically with each other. Computer historians date the true beginning of the Internet to 1969, when the U.S. Department of Defense funded ARPANET, an electronic network that connected scientists at a number of universities and defense contractors, including RAND. Over the next decade, ARPANET expanded to include many more universities and other research institutions across the country. In 1983, ARPANET provided the backbone for what became known as the Internet. As a trustee of RAND since 1973, Morrisett thus had a front row seat to witness the early development of electronic mail and the Internet. As a result, he was able to prophesy the eventual popularity of E-mail, as well as its potential social, economic, and political benefits, ahead of most foundation leaders.

With E-mail, Morrisett saw an opportunity to counteract what he called the "benevolent tyranny" created by the dominant communications media of the twentieth century—telephones, radio, television, and even books. Each of those, he argued, had its virtues, but each also fostered habits of mind that were passive, rather than active, and acted against deliberative thought and conversation.[48] "It is significant," Morrisett wrote, "that we are called the 'information society'—not the thinking society, not the deliberative society, not the society of reason and rationality."[49]

Morrisett believed that E-mail might help change that. Unlike telephones, for example, that demanded instant replies, E-mail offered people a communications medium that allowed for more considered responses, as with letter writing. Beyond the virtue of regaining the art of reflective conversation, Morrisett believed that E-mail also might be a tool to connect people more effectively to government agencies and services and open new, convenient avenues to encourage more political participation.[50]

In short, Morrisett believed that E-mail, if made universally available, might be an antidote to the mind-deadening influence of traditional mass media and become a "technology of freedom"—a communications tool that might help reinvigorate participatory democracy and help people rediscover the art of reflective, deliberative thought. His gravest concern, on the other hand, was that the goals of an "electronic democracy" and newly invigorated habits of mind would be buried by commercialism and profit, thus repeating the sad pattern of other great media developments of the century. E-mail, he argued, had to be broadly regarded as a "necessity for democracy." Otherwise, its potential might well be trivialized into just another consumer product.[51]

As Markle embarked on its "E-mail for All" initiative in 1993, it was clear that the many unanswered questions about the feasibility, costs, and social, economic, and technical implications of universal access demanded research. The public policy debate, as Markle saw it, needed to confront how access should be created, who should pay for the needed equipment and for educating people in its use, what were the responsibilities of business, and to what extent should government be involved in creating access.

Not surprisingly, Morrisett turned to RAND and awarded $932,000 to a team of its scientists led by Tora K. Bikson. The result, in 1995, was a groundbreaking, 267-page policy report, *Universal Access to E-Mail: Feasibility and Societal Implications*. By 1998, three printings, totaling 4,200 books, had been sold or distributed—a best-seller by the humble standards of policy studies.

The RAND report reached several telling conclusions. It argued that there were no insuperable technical barriers to expanded E-mail access. E-mail technology could be made as commonplace in American homes as telephones or televisions for about $1 billion per year over the next decade. At the same time, RAND asserted that universality and its societal benefits almost certainly would not be realized if left entirely to the free market. The poor, the undereducated, the elderly, and other disadvantaged groups faced a variety of barriers to access and likely would be further disadvantaged as E-mail became more important in modern life. The report estimated that half of the nation's households would lack access by the next century. Without government policies aimed at promoting universal access, RAND concluded, the gap between technological haves and have nots would only grow. The Rand researchers wrote:

> In spite of the growth of . . . e-mail systems, the majority of U.S. residents probably will continue to lack access to e-mail well into the next century without social intervention . . . and . . . some citizens, such as inner-city minorities and the rural poor, are relatively disenfranchised and constitute groups that will be the last to be reached by commercial e-mail systems that evolve in private markets.[52]

In short, the RAND study argued that the marketplace, left on its own, would carry E-mail's growth only so far. Universality would likely not be achieved without public policy to make it so. That conclusion formed the basis for the rest of Markle's research and public relations activity during the following three years. It also raised the thorny and unresolved question of how much and what kinds of government intervention might be needed to achieve such universal access. "It's too soon to say whether the findings were accepted," Bjornson told the author. "It's not too soon to say that attention was paid, and that the findings are part of the general discussions about E-mail."[53]

In 1996, Markle funded a $700,000, follow-up RAND project that sought to demonstrate how E-mail might speed and improve communication between government agencies and citizens and, in the process, realize potentially significant cost savings in staffing, postage, and elsewhere. To develop case studies, RAND worked with two government agencies, the federal Health Care Financing Agency, which manages Medicare, and the California State Employment Development Department.

The resulting two-hundred–page RAND report, *Sending Your Government a Message: E-Mail Communication between Citizens and Government*, published in October 1999, concluded that the U.S. government, as well as statehouses and city halls, lag far behind in using E-mail to citizens as an economical, quick, and easy way to communicate with government agencies. The report found that ". . . there is a strong case to be made for government agencies whose work generates significant volumes of personalized communication to immediately begin developing the means to use e-mail as a supplement to the more traditional postal or telephonic channels."[54]

The foundation also provided $427,000 to a team at Bellcore, a spin-off of AT&T Bell Laboratories and the research arm of the Bell Operating Companies, to study the likely economic and social impact of universal E-mail service and to perform a survey of real and perceived barriers to Internet use. On its possible social effects, the researchers concluded that, far from an alienating force, the Internet is "a medium for friendship creation." Indeed, the authors estimated that as many as two million new face-to-face meetings had taken place as a result of Internet encounters.[55]

Markle was especially eager for Bellcore to examine whether universal E-mail would have unintended economic consequences for universal telephone service because the telecommunications industry might well be the big loser if universal E-mail resulted in a loss of long-distance revenues. The fear was that if universal E-mail threatened the complex system of cross-subsidies underlying universal telephone service, the telecommunications industry might see E-mail's growth as a threat and eventually oppose it. Bellcore's researchers concluded that E-mail was unlikely to have such a negative impact on universal telephone service, at least in the short run, and that "any effect . . . is likely to be partially offset by the effect of on-line service subscribers ordering extra telephone lines. . . ."[56] Still, Bellcore's research never squarely addressed the essential question of whether Markle's mission of achieving universal access would cut into the revenues of the telecommunications industry in the long run.

Taken together, the research by RAND and Bellcore provided Markle the raw material for advancing its larger goal of creating a national dialogue and policy debate about universal E-mail. Beginning in mid-1996 and continuing under Morrisett's successor, Zoë Baird, the foundation campaigned vigorously for policies aimed at promoting that objective.

In 1998, Markle's E-mail campaign included a thirteen-member "E-Mail for All" board of advisers consisting of business, government, and media leaders.[57] Markle's E-mail campaign drew favorable notice from the media. A Sunday magazine column on May 5, 1996, by Max Frankel of *The New York Times* likened the urgency of the E-Mail for All campaign to the national mobilization, thirty-five years earlier, to reach the moon.[58] An op-ed article by Morrisett in the December 19, 1997, edition of *The Christian Science Monitor* urged the FCC to regard universal E-mail service "not merely as an economic benefit for those who can't afford it, but a fundamental requirement for equal participation in society."[59] Reed Hundt, former FCC chairman under President Clinton and a member of Markle's E-mail advisory board, followed in 1998 with an op-ed piece in *The Wall Street Journal* that called for schools and libraries to use federal funds to create closer ties among parents, students, teachers, and librarians via E-mail.[60]

It is far too soon to assess the impact of Markle's E-mail campaign at this writing. Will government, business, and the public embrace and find ways to finance truly universal E-mail? If so, will E-mail live up to Morrisett's fondest hopes for it—a reinvigoration of participatory democracy and of more active, reflective thinking? Certainly, the possibility raised by the 1995 RAND study and other studies about a widening technology gap between rich and poor and between white and minority families appeared to be playing out. A survey in 1996 by Vanderbilt University researchers found that 44.2 percent of white high school and college students had home computers, compared with 29 percent of black students in those age groups.

Morrisett, for his part, was guardedly upbeat about the E-mail initiative after his retirement in 1998: "I think things are going our way, but I don't see an inevitability that it will be universal in the way we hoped. That's still unclear. Talk to me again in ten years."[61]

NOTES

1. Lloyd N. Morrisett, "The Computers Are Coming" (President's Essay in "The John and Mary R. Markle Foundation, Annual Report, 1981–1982"), 15.

2. Lloyd N. Morrisett, "The Markle Foundation 1985" (President's Essay in "The John and Mary R. Markle Foundation, Annual Report, 1983–1984 and 1984–1985" (the foundation produced a single annual report for that period), 9.

3. Ibid., 15.

4. Ibid., 9.

5. Morrisett, "Computers Are Coming," 9–10.

6. Ibid., 12–13.

7. For example, see Todd Oppenheimer, "The Computer Delusion," *Atlantic Monthly*, July 1997, 45–62, which challenges the belief that computers improve teaching or learning.

8. Karen D. Byers, Chief Financial Officer, The Markle Foundation, explained to the author that a PRI must pass several legal tests to comply with Internal Revenue Service regulations and internal foundation policies. PRIs cannot be "jeopardizing" investments; that is, they cannot involve exceptionally speculative activities, such as commodities trading. The PRI must fit directly within the foundation's program areas and be designed to further its educational and social goals. The primary motivation of the foundation's investment cannot be profit—though profit is perfectly desirable and legal. Instead, the aim must be to provide risk capital to stimulate activity and development in a foundation's program area that traditional capital markets would not likely support. Finally, the organization to be supported with a PRI cannot be engaged in lobbying or legislative activities.

9. Loren Renz, Cynthia W. Massarsky, Richard R. Treiber, and Steven Laurence, *Program-Related Investments: A Guide to Funders and Trends* (New York: The Foundation Center, 1995), ix.

10. Morrisett, interview, 14 Jan. 1998.

11. Byers, interview, 3 Apr. 1998.

12. Renz, Massarsky, Treiber, and Laurence, *Program-Related Investments*, 57. The four foundations ranking ahead of Markle in the value of PRIs to arts, culture, and media organizations were Freedom Forum International, Metropolitan Life Foundation, Margaret L. Wendt Foun-

dation, and Robert R. McCormick Tribune Foundation. With the exception of the Wendt Foundation, the foundations whose rankings exceeded Markle had several times more assets than Markle.

13. Morrisett, interview, 6 Apr. 1998.

14. Craig S. Miller, Jill Fain Lehman, and Kenneth R. Koedinger, "Goals and Learning in Microworlds," *Cognitive Science* 23, no. 3 (1999), 305.

15. Lehman, interview, 20 Apr. 1998.

16. Dannenberg, interview, 17 Apr. 1998.

17. Dannenberg, interview, 2 Dec., 1999.

18. Lehman, interview, 20 Apr. 1998.

19. Armstrong, interview, 8 May 1998.

20. Morrisett had become a frequent flyer to London. Because of its size, Markle had few foreign involvements, but Morrisett had made a number of friendships and developed several projects with the British. Besides the BBC, Markle gave grants to the British Film Institute's Broadcasting Research Unit, the London Business School, the London School of Economics, and the London Graduate School of Business. As mentioned in chapter 6, Professor Hilde Himmelweit, a social psychologist at the London School of Economics, became a close adviser to Morrisett on many Markle projects.

21. Morrisett, interview, 27 Apr. 1998.

22. Armstrong, interview, 8 May 1998.

23. Ibid.

24. Ibid.

25. Morrisett, interview, 27 Apr. 1998.

26. Bjornson, interview, 16 Apr. 1998.

27. Ibid.

28. "The Top 50 CD-ROMs," *MacUser*, November 1993, 90–99.

29. Daniel Kumin, in "Roll Over Beethoven," *CD Review*, February 1990, called it "among the more innovative uses of CD-ROM yet seen." Alan Rich, in "Wonders of Brave New World," *Los Angeles Herald Examiner*, 16 July 1989, E8, called it "a voyage and a half."

30. Walter S. Mossberg, "*Who Built America* Reveals Real Potential of Electronic Learning," review, *The Wall Street Journal*, 2 Sept. 1993, B1.

31. Jeffrey A. Trachtenberg, "U.S. History on a CD-ROM Stirs Up a Storm," *The Wall Street Journal*, 10 Feb. 1995, B1.

32. Stein, interview, 15 Apr. 1998.

33. Bjornson, interview, 16 Apr. 1998.

34. The Markle Foundation, staff memorandum prepared for Markle Board of Directors meeting, March 1997, in support of $756,800 PRI loan for Night Kitchen, Inc., 52.

35. Bjornson, interview, 16 Apr. 1998.
36. Crawford, interview, 5 May 1998.
37. Ibid.
38. Clark, interview, 8 Apr. 1998.
39. Chris Crawford, E-mail correspondence to author. 3 Dec. 1999.
40. Crawford, interview, 5 May 1998.
41. Clark, interview, 8 Apr. 1998.
42. Crawford, interview, 5 May 1998.
43. Clark, interview, 8 Apr. 1998.
44. Infonautics Corporation, "Homework Helper Fact Sheet," 24 Aug. 1993, 3.
45. Morrisett, interview, 11 May 1998.
46. Michelle Healy, "Kids Can Tap into a Wealth of Learning," *USA Today*, 9 Feb. 1995, 2D.
47. Lloyd N. Morrisett, "Habits of Mind and a New Technology of Freedom" (President's Essay in "The John and Mary R. Markle Foundation, Annual Report, 1995"), 11.
48. Ibid., 8–9.
49. Ibid., 8.
50. Ibid., 15.
51. Ibid.
52. Anderson, Bikson, Law, Mitchell, Kedzie et al., *Universal Access to E-Mail*, 2–3.
53. Bjornson, interview, 20 May 1998.
54. Neu, Anderson, and Bikson, *Sending Your Government a Message*, xxiii.
55. James E. Katz and Philip Aspden, "A Nation of Strangers?" *Communications of the ACM* 40, no. 12 (1997): 85–86.
56. Jiong Gong, Veena Gupta, Richard Simmett, and Ansa Varghese, "A Report to the Markle foundation on the Potential Implications of Universal Email for Universal Telephone Service" (executive summary), 2.
57. The board included Charles Ardai, President, Juno Online Services; W. Bowman Cutter, Managing Director, E. M. Warburg, Pincus & Co.; Gene DeRose, Chairman and Chief Executive Officer, Jupiter Communications; Esther Dyson, Chairwoman, EDventure Holdings; David Ellington, Chief Executive Officer, NetNoir, Inc.; Jeff Greenfield, political commentator, CNN; Reed Hundt, former Chairman, Federal Communications Commission; Julia Johnson, Chairwoman, Florida Public Service Commission; Macdara MacCall, Director, Business Development, iVillage; Daniel Okrent, Editor, *New Media*, Time, Inc.; Jonathan Peizer, Chief Information Officer, Open

Society; Shabbir Safdar, principal, Mindshare Internet Strategies; and Christine Varney, partner, Hogan & Hartson.

58. Max Frankel, "The Moon, This Time Around," *The New York Times Magazine*, 5 May 1996, 40.

59. Lloyd N. Morrisett, "Applying 'Universal Service' to the Net—A U.S. Imperative," *The Christian Science Monitor*, 19 Dec. 1997, Opinions and Essays page.

60. Reed Hundt, "Better Education@Email.com," *The Wall Street Journal*, editorial section, commentary, 31 Mar. 1998.

61. Morrisett, interview, 26 May 1998.

8

Aging.org

IF THE NEW HOME COMPUTER ERA had all the trappings of a genuine communications revolution, it also threatened to be an exclusive one—of, by, and for the young. The brainy tycoons inventing consumer-oriented hardware and software in back rooms and garages were almost all tykes in their twenties. College dropout Steven Jobs was twenty-one years old when he cofounded Apple Computer in 1975 and joined Radio Shack and Commodore in the nascent home computer market. A year later, Bill Gates, also twenty-one years old, cofounded Microsoft. Steven Wozniak, another college dropout and a junior programmer at Hewlett-Packard, developed the innards of the Apple I microcomputer in his spare time.[1]

Not only were the generals leading this revolution youthful and youth-minded. Computers themselves were inherently more demanding of their users than any previous mass-market communications tool. Manufacturers could claim all they liked that "anyone" could easily learn to use one. Yet, one look at the inches-thick volumes of indecipherable directions that came with home computers was enough to convince most potential purchasers that there was far more involved in mastering these new tools than, say, flipping a television switch or dialing a telephone. Personal computers, particularly those of early vintage, demanded a high level of literacy, patience, typing skills, dexterous fingers, and healthy eyes. Add to that the considerable cost of hardware and software, and the admissions price to the computer age seemed as if it might stay beyond the reach of the poor, the underschooled, and another group: older people.

As Robert Harootyan, an official of the American Association of Retired Persons (AARP), said in 1987, "It's not a question of resistance, but rather what the technology is good for, what need it fulfills, and how much energy it takes to use. Today the personal computer asks most people to put in too much for what they get out."[2]

Morrisett, for his part, dismissed such concerns: "Human beings are very adaptable. Everyone uses a telephone now but at the dawn of the century 'telephone literacy' courses were offered commercially. Television spread fast and grew enormous. Electronic hand-held calculators advanced to everyday use in just a few years. When there's resistance, it's only temporary."[3]

"To be seventy years young," jurist Oliver Wendell Holmes, Jr., wrote, "is sometimes far more cheerful and hopeful than to be forty years old." As Morrisett saw it, Markle's goal was to help make that Holmesian view of active, engaged old age a more universal reality with the aid of the new computer technologies emerging during the 1980s and 1990s. To Morrisett, his staff, and Gertrude G. Michelson and other members of Markle's board, the risk that older persons would be left behind in this youth-oriented movement fully justified foundation action.

From 1984 through 1996, Markle devoted more than $7 million to a variety of explorations of technology and the aging population. Nearly half went toward basic research—to establish, first of all, how older individuals live their lives and, second, how communications technology might serve their needs. Much of the balance, some $4 million, went to support the work of an earnest, passionate, and sensitive educator, Mary Simpson Furlong. Her project, called SeniorNet, was an effort to create for the older population a first-of-its-kind nationwide online community supported by a network of learning centers to teach seniors how to use computers. This project also would become one of the most intense and bittersweet endeavors ever undertaken by the foundation.

Morrisett's sensibilities about old age stemmed from boyhood memories. Each summer during the late 1930s, he and his parents would make the long drive in the family's yellow Buick from their adopted home in Yonkers, New York, to Edmond and Hobart, Oklahoma, to visit cousins, uncles and aunts, and grandparents. During the Dust Bowl years, Hobart was a farming town of rutted roads and parched fields. As Morrisett's family drove into town, they invariably saw the older people rocking on their front porches. His Southern Baptist relatives permitted themselves few diversions. Card playing, radio, and movies were considered works of the devil. Mostly, they read the Bible. When Morrisett's family received news of older relatives, his father referred to their "miseries." For older people fifty years ago, the list of miseries was long—unattended health problems, poverty with little relief from the government, an inability to get around, failing vision or hearing. In Morrisett's preadolescent eyes, old age seemed to mean just passing time, little more.

Years later as a foundation leader, Morrisett's belief that computer-based technology might help older people lead more active, productive lives was simply one more expression of his consistent theme of using technology to serve neglected groups. In 1974, he had noticed a magazine article titled "Foundations Are Failing the Aged," by Jack Ossofsky, executive director of the National Council on the Aging, Inc. Noting that the older population was the fastest growing segment of Americans, Ossofsky said that the problems of aging were nonetheless being scandalously ignored by U.S. foundations and received less than 1 percent of their grants.[4] Helping older individuals, therefore, seemed to be wide open territory for any foundation willing to go after it—especially the idea of exploring how communications technology might address the special health, educational, recreational, and social needs of the aging population.[5]

By the 1980s, the United States was "graying" at an astonishing rate, even as myths and misconceptions abounded about what old age actually meant in the late twentieth century.[6] A 1988 paper prepared for The Markle Foundation indicated that, by the year 2000, fully one fourth of the U.S. population would be over sixty-five years old. Demographers were saying that as the twenty-first century approached, one baby boomer would be turning fifty years old every seven seconds. By the mid-1980s, 28.5 million Americans were age sixty-five or older, 22 million were age fifty-five to sixty-four, and, just behind them, another 23 million were age forty-five to fifty-four—a total of 75 million people preceding the baby-boom generation into old age.[7] By the year 2000, an estimated 34.7 million Americans were age 65 or older, up 35 percent from 25.7 million in that age group in 1980, according to U.S. Bureau of the Census statistics.[8]

The largely overlooked point, as Markle considered these issues during the 1980s, was that overwhelming majorities of older people were both willing and able to live actively and continue to contribute to their communities.

Although the older population was slowly coming into vogue within government and policy circles by the 1980s, the opposite seemed to be the case in the communications and technology industries. Youth continued to dominate the strategies of such firms as Apple Computer and much of the software industry. Such corporations were giving away millions of dollars worth of free or deeply discounted hardware and software to schools in order to gain dominance in that market. Yet, practically no foundations or corporations were paying heed to how the computer revolution might meet the needs of seniors. Apparently, the older population was considered either too decrepit or too technophobic to master computers. Aging in America, in most minds, still meant disability and dependence. Even those who recognized the flaws in that stereotype had no idea what computers might do for older people.

It was that gap in the nation's knowledge about the realities of aging that Morrisett hoped to fill as the computer revolution took firmer hold. What were the aspirations of the older population? How well were their needs and wishes being met by the government, the media, and the technology industries? What were the attitudes of older people toward the new high-tech tools? How could these technologies add usefulness or pleasure to their lives? Was it really true, as was commonly believed, that they resisted learning how to use computers? Could these new tools be made easier for them to master?

With the image of his grandfather rocking away his final years on a front porch in Oklahoma never far from his mind, Morrisett framed the essential challenge: Would the older population continue to be viewed as a burden, rather than as an untapped resource?[9]

RESEARCHING THE OLDER POPULATION

In December 1984, Markle took its first step toward calling the attention of the communications and information industries to the older population when it sponsored a conference titled "The Computer Comes of Age: Services for Older People" in Princeton, New Jersey. The gathering included geriatric specialists from academia; a senior employment specialist representing the AARP; and, most crucially, psychologists and other professionals from the Human Factors Division of Bell Laboratories.[10]

Morrisett opened the conference on a personal note. A relative, he said, had recently developed trouble finding papers or remembering when to take medication. He also did not like getting help from others. Could an electronic "older people's companion" be developed—a computer device that would act as a memory aid—to enable older people to work, shop, or bank at home, to communicate with each other, and, in general, to allow them to live more self-sufficiently?[11]

The day-long discussion continued in the same largely speculative vein. Dr. Stuart Schwartz, a medical professor from California, said that from his experience in senior citizen centers, he was concerned that older people would find operating computers too difficult. Others worried that such technologies as computers might reduce interpersonal contact, as bank teller machines already had done.[12] The need to modify existing computer terminals or keyboards to make them easier for older people to use was also discussed. Slower speeds, larger type, or repetition of instructions were among the possibilities.

In hindsight, the Princeton meeting was fascinating because it revealed both the prevalence of myths about aging, even among experts, and the needs that communications technology was thought most likely to address. The common view seemed to be that the computer would be a high-tech crutch—a memory aid, perhaps, or a device to surmount various sensory or motor problems. It was also assumed that older people would welcome computers, if at all, as a way to avoid the exertion of leaving home to shop, walk, or drive to the bank. On the other hand, there was concern that this presumably sedentary population would resist learning to use computers—or having done so, would use them as a tool to isolate their lives further.

Those early surmises would be proved largely wrong.

The first major research supported by Markle following the Princeton conference was directed at answering how computers could help people to plan for a more satisfying retirement. For many, retirement was a time of apprehension, opportunity, and loss. Could a computer network connecting people on the brink of retirement with actual retirees help them plan their time more effectively, maintain social contacts, ease their anxieties about retirement, and reduce the stress resulting from the loss of daily work routines? Might such electronic connections also make possible a more gradual kind of retirement where people could, through telecommuting or part-time work, continue to lead active lives even after formal employment ended?

The research was conducted at the RAND Corporation under the leadership of Tora Bikson. In 1986, Markle provided $464,000 for a two-year experiment to see how older people would use computers to interact with each other. Bikson worked with thirty-nine older employees and forty retirees—all men, most in their early sixties—from the Los Angeles County Department of Water and Power. The volunteers were divided into two "retirement task forces"—one used a computer network, and the other did not. Their job was to spend a year in planning various aspects of retirement. Each group was free to perform the task any way it wished—by meeting together, corresponding, forming committees or subgroups, or working alone.[13] Both groups then divided the larger task into six study groups, each charged with examining specific topics for preretirement planning: family and social interaction; self-esteem, community service, and educational opportunities; the planning process; financial issues; health issues; and time management.

The RAND researchers discovered that computers did not divide or isolate people. To the contrary, those in the computer group developed more positive attitudes about retirement than those in the noncomputer group. Most tellingly, those using computers kept in more frequent contact with each other and were likelier to know the names of other task force members. There was also far more collaboration among the six study groups than in the noncomputer group, where participants tended to limit themselves more rigidly to their assigned problem areas.[14]

In short, RAND's work demonstrated that computers do not breed social isolation but, instead, encourage cooperation and collaboration in achieving a common goal. And that is as true for the older population as it is for the young.

Markle's research agenda was moving on several other fronts. An early question confronted by the foundation concerned which group of older people it should concentrate on—the very old or infirm, or those still active and reasonably healthy. Regardless of its choice, the 1984 meeting in Princeton had pointed up the need for further research on how the complexities of computer hardware and software might be overcome for seniors.

At one of the many meetings on aging that Bjornson attended, she met Sara J. Czaja, a professor of mechanical engineering at the State University of New York in Buffalo and research director at the Stein Gerontological Institute in Miami, Florida. In 1987, Czaja proposed a two-year experiment to examine how older people relate to computer equipment and how such components as keyboards might be modified to make their use easier. Markle provided $305,000 for the project that Czaja conducted from 1988 to 1990 with Bellcore.

Czaja's study involved thirty-six Florida women age sixty to ninety-five. Computers were installed in their homes and the experiences and difficulties of the women monitored. Based on those experiences, the software, keyboards, and terminals were modified and reevaluated. Czaja learned, for example, that older people, especially those with poor vision, tended to confuse certain function keys, such as "send" and "cancel" that were similar in size and shape.

The project developed a computer system featuring highly simplified forms of E-mail and text editors, as well as health and weather information. Operating commands were reduced to a bare minimum. There were no lengthy log-on procedures, and E-mail messages came onto printers automatically. Extraneous keys on the keyboard were disabled or specially labeled. Czaja's research also gave further evidence of what older people actually wanted from computers. "What we found," she told the author, "was that all of our participants liked the system and found it valuable. But what they wanted were everyday, practical features that had utility, not games."[15] To Czaja's delight, the women also began to use the computer network to socialize with each other and to exchange recipes. They formed their own on-line social club and even named themselves the "Markle-ettes" in honor of their financial patron.

The product designs and modifications developed by Czaja were never picked up by any computer manufacturers. Still, years later, her experiment continued to be cited as seminal in scholarly work. It was further confirmation for Markle's staff that older people would use computers if their value were made clearer and the complications eased.

"The assumption was that the elderly couldn't learn," Bjornson said. "Sara found that there were resistances. But she was one of the first to come up with the notion that if you approach these people, aware of their anxieties and limitations in dexterity and processing ability, that they are as capable of learning as any other group."[16]

The most widely publicized research commissioned by Markle was a $330,000 survey by The Daniel Yankelovich Group, "Aging in America: Current Trends and Future Directions." The survey's findings received extensive press coverage, including the major wire services and The New York Times. Released in 1988, the survey of three thousand older Americans sought to produce data on how they lived, spent their time, and used technology. At the same time, Morrisett said, the study was intended to catch the attention of corporations in the technology field: "We might have been a little ahead of the game, but clearly older people were going to be an increasingly important segment of the population, and therefore increasingly desirable for corporations to address."[17]

The myth-exploding picture that emerged from the survey was of people growing older "quite successfully" and not inherently resistant to new consumer technologies, Morrisett wrote at the time.[18] Six out of ten rated their health good to excellent. Similarly, many older Americans were financially secure. More than half of those surveyed owned their homes, mortgage free, according to the data. Only 5 percent of people over age seventy owned computers at the time of the survey but not because they were technophobes. Instead, the survey suggested that older people were not about to buy any technology whose value did not clearly match their needs. Much of what was being marketed was designed for members of the younger generations who saw computers as a way to shop or bank at home. In fact, older people wanted to get out of the house to bank or shop. What they wanted from computers were tools that made daily activities simpler, easier, and more enjoyable and that created new activities.

As Morrisett wrote when the study was being publicized: "The older generation is more interested in filling time. Older Americans report that they enjoy doing business with tellers; they would rather go to the theater to see a movie than rent one for the VCR; they plan their schedules to be home for their favorite TV shows; they enjoy food shopping, and they enjoy shopping in general."[19]

The research by Czaja, RAND, and Yankelovich validated the basic premise of Markle's emerging program on technology and the aging. Older people were better off, busier, and less technophobic than was commonly assumed. Markle decided to concentrate on the "young-old," those whose energy, health, and financial means made them an appealing but overlooked demographic group for corporations shaping the computer revolution.

It would be another research project, SeniorNet, that would lead to Markle's most determined and expensive effort to translate those ideas into concrete results over the next eight years.

SENIORNET: CREATING AN ELECTRONIC COMMUNITY

All along, Morrisett understood that merely making computers available for home use would not ensure that older people would use them. That kind of mass acceptance required an investment in education, in time, and in leadership. The kind of charismatic standard-bearer, with a breakthrough idea, that Peggy Charren and Joan Cooney had been for children's television was needed for the cause of bringing older people into the computer age. The person who emerged in 1985 was a soft-spoken educator from Washington, D.C.: Mary Simpson Furlong.

As an assistant professor of education at Catholic University of America from 1979 to 1983, Furlong specialized in using computers as a teaching tool. At the time, she had a seventy-five–year-old babysitter taking care of her toddler son and she came to admire the zest for life and learning in older people. She wondered if seniors, as a group, could be interested in learning and communicating with computers. In the summer of 1983, she and a teaching colleague, Greg Kearsley, began to operate workshops on personal computing at hospitals, senior centers, and nursing homes in the Washington area. They found that older people were eager and willing to learn basic computing.

Anxious to extend the reach of their work and, like all junior faculty, needing to publish, Furlong and Kearsley co-wrote *Computers for Kids over Sixty*, a 1984 guide on computer basics for seniors. During the next two years, Furlong searched for research funds to explore ways to connect older people to computers but found little interest. "I must have knocked on seventy-five doors of foundations and corporations," she told the author. "This was the time when the thrust was all toward getting kids computer literate. No one got it. They either weren't interested, or weren't capable."[20]

In 1984, Furlong moved to the University of San Francisco's School of Education where she continued teaching computer classes for older people. The classes were novel enough to catch the attention of Knight-Ridder Newspapers, *USA Today*, and the computer magazine, *InfoWorld*.[21] Convinced that she was on to something big but still unable to find money to take the idea further, she took the advice of friends in the computer world and contacted The Markle Foundation. It proved to be the right moment. "Lloyd was looking for a grantee at the same time I was looking for a sponsor. It took us two years to find each other," she recalled.[22]

Furlong's proposal to Markle in April 1985 was modest: a six-month project to establish and study a prototype computer network that she dubbed SeniorNet. It would provide terminals to five senior centers and to twenty older people so that they could communicate with each other and tap into information sources, such as the AARP and the Congressional Select Committee on Aging.[23] She would then study how older people might be trained to use computer networks for E-mail, bulletin boards, and conferencing.

Morrisett sent his program officer, Christine Russell, to San Francisco to meet Furlong. Russell was impressed but convinced that it would take more than six months to do proper research.

In November, the Markle board approved a one-year, $62,790 grant.

SeniorNet officially started in March 1986. It opened five teaching sites at senior centers in Framingham, Massachusetts; Menlo Park, California; Falls Church, Virginia; Syracuse, New York; and Colorado Springs, Colorado. Each site was linked by General Videotex Corporation, a private computer network that offered varied services of interest to older users. Furlong persuaded Apple Computer Corporation to supply equipment and cable, thus freeing Markle funds for additional software and terminals. Questionnaires indicated that older users were enthusiastic and that many would join the classes if given the chance.

The first year was a stunning success as far as Markle was concerned. Furlong proposed expanding the project to ten sites serving 150 seniors, adding staff, and continuing to do research on how a computer network could serve the needs of seniors. In November 1986, Markle agreed to a second, $87,000 grant for fiscal 1987 and 1988 and later added $50,000 to fund development of a business plan.

The research phase of SeniorNet continued until 1990. In those early years, the project had five stated goals: to develop local sites (renamed "learning centers" in 1991), where seniors could be introduced to computers; to develop and operate an on-line network linking the centers and individual members; to produce materials, such as newsletters, videos, and software, to support individual members and centers; to sponsor an annual conference to exchange ideas; and to conduct research on ways to harness information technology to serve the needs of seniors.

For Furlong, the heart and soul of the project was the creation of a safe, wholesome, inclusive community for seniors. Her newsletters to members, the media, and potential funders were full of stories about how SeniorNet provided ways for older people to connect and to feel a sense of usefulness and belonging. There were more than a dozen marriages brought about by computer connections. An eighty-four–year-old Dallas woman, bedridden for two years and resigned to die, read about SeniorNet, got out of bed, bought new clothes, and went to class. "I wasn't sick," she said. "I was bored to death." Another older user wrote to Furlong: "If I am unable to sleep at night, all I have to do is go to my computer and there's always someone to talk to, to laugh with, exchange ideas. And because SeniorNet is in so many sites across the country, I feel like I belong to the nation."[24]

Such stories soon had the national media swooning over SeniorNet, and Furlong showed herself adept at gaining publicity. Bjornson worked her own journalistic contacts and got *USA Today* to run a prominent spread on SeniorNet in January 1987 with the headline, "Whiz Kids, Beware! Computers Entice Older Crowd." Other features followed on the Voice of America radio network and in *The Washington Post*. By mid-1988, more than one hundred articles about SeniorNet had appeared. The small answering machine in Furlong's university office could not keep up with the thousands of inquiries from prospective members from Florida to Hawaii.

In May 1988, Furlong further fanned the publicity flames by holding her organization's first annual SeniorNet Conference, jointly sponsored by Markle, Apple Computer, and Pacific Telesis Foundation, at the University of San Francisco's Lone Mountain campus. The meeting brought together more than 150 older users of her network; commercial vendors, including IBM, Bank of America, Delphi, Apple Computer, and Pacific Bell; and swarms of technology and feature reporters.

Morrisett had raised his own sights for SeniorNet. No longer just another research effort, it seemed to have the potential to become a pioneering national organization for older people in its own right. Furlong had shown herself to be charismatic and entrepreneurial. SeniorNet had undeniable social and educational impact, and it was pushing the window on how technology might be used to connect and inform people who were among society's neglected. At the learning centers, seniors were gaining word-processing skills, going on line, learning financial management through the use of spreadsheets, and practicing "electronic citizenship." As Morrisett told the Markle board in June 1988, "SeniorNet can realistically aim to become a national organization established on a firm financial base."

Furlong was also gaining corporate backers and increasing the number of SeniorNet teaching sites. By mid-1989, the number of sites had risen to twenty-five—from Vermont to Calgary to Honolulu. Each depended on local or corporate sponsorship, and regional Bells were among the most eager supporters. US West, Pacific Bell, NYNEX, and Bell Atlantic were especially active in supporting new sites. Each corporate sponsor paid SeniorNet an initial $6,000 plus a $3,000 annual fee. SeniorNet also became a pet cause of national organizations of eye doctors, including the Outpatient Ophthalmic Surgery Society, that provided several modest grants. Following speeches by Furlong and Richard Adler, SeniorNet's director of marketing and development, at the society's annual convention in 1989, individual ophthalmologists sponsored new SeniorNet teaching sites in Hawaii and Florida.

In short, SeniorNet was exceeding everyone's hopes during its first years. To Morrisett, it appeared to be one of those rare opportunities, like Children's Television Workshop, for a foundation to be at the leading edge of an overlooked idea with national, and perhaps commercial, possibilities. Furlong was beginning to imagine herself as a "Joan Ganz Cooney of the elderly," with Markle's help.[25]

What was less clear to Morrisett and his staff was whether Furlong, a teacher with little marketing or management experience, was the right person to lead SeniorNet through the next difficult steps of development. Furlong and her tiny part-time staff of four were becoming overwhelmed by the administrative demands of rapid growth. Callers found it difficult to sign up for classes at learning centers, many of which had long waiting lists. From its initial 20 members, SeniorNet had now taught more than 3,000 individuals to use computers either by taking classes at the sites or through the on-line network. Some 3,500 more wrote letters asking for information about how to learn to use computers or join the on-line network. The initial excitement over SeniorNet might be squandered, Morrisett and his staff feared, unless Furlong received some expert help to keep up with the demands of its surging growth.

Early in 1988, Furlong had hired Adler, an on-line marketing expert from Silicon Valley, whom Bjornson had met a year earlier at an Aspen meeting on electronic publishing. Adler became a critical partner in Furlong's management and fund-raising efforts during the next several years. Still, Bjornson and Morrisett felt with increasing urgency that Furlong needed staff with more marketing and on-line experience if SeniorNet were to realize its potential for national impact and eventual self-sufficiency. And this had to happen quickly before the giants in the field of aging, such as AARP, discovered for themselves the power and reach of computer networking and squeezed the pioneering but financially feeble SeniorNet out of the picture.

Morrisett decided to increase the foundation's support. Markle's next two grants between 1988 and 1990 totaled more than $600,000 to help Furlong's organization gain administrative strength and marketing expertise. In a further effort to help Furlong develop a business strategy, the foundation hosted a retreat in Monterey, California, in the summer of 1989, that brought together top legal, financial, and management consultants. In addition to Morrisett, Bjornson, Furlong, and Adler, the gathering included Donald Campbell, a California attorney; Ed Rover, Markle's legal counsel from the Manhattan firm of White & Case; Sandra Powers, a public relations specialist; James Collins, a business professor from Stanford University and also a management consultant; and Edward Hamilton, a management specialist and former New York City deputy mayor.

The two-day meeting resulted in several fateful conclusions. Everyone agreed that SeniorNet had outgrown its affiliation with the University of San Francisco and should move as quickly as possible to become an independent, nonprofit organization. Therefore, SeniorNet needed to build a larger administrative staff with expertise in marketing, business, and technology, along with a competent and credible board of directors. Most important, the group urged Furlong to concentrate far more on making SeniorNet a membership organization providing on-line products and services for which seniors would be willing to pay good money year after year. The modest levels of corporate support that Furlong had gathered were helpful, but they would never be enough to make SeniorNet self-sufficient.

The tough message to Furlong at Monterey, then, was that her strategy of building a loose confederation of teaching sites for seniors almost certainly would not secure SeniorNet's future. Common sense and demographics indicated that the supply of seniors who needed elementary computer instruction would gradually shrink, whereas the number of seniors searching for a useful, enjoyable on-line service would grow dramatically in the long run.

Morrisett and Bjornson, especially, worried that Furlong's concentration on opening more learning centers at the expense of establishing an appealing, money-generating on-line network, would lead SeniorNet to a financial dead end. "What Edee [Bjornson] and Lloyd helped me see," Furlong told the author, "was that there was this big demand, and that we should be a membership organization and charge fees."[26]

It was never entirely obvious to Morrisett or Bjornson, however, that Furlong was acting on that advice. "Mary told me she thought the Monterey meeting was very valuable," said Morrisett. "But neither Edith nor I felt that she followed up effectively on the suggestions that were made."[27] Nonetheless, February 1990 marked the formal end of the five-year research phase of SeniorNet. That month, it incorporated as an independent, nonprofit organization. Ten months later, it received tax-exempt status from the Internal Revenue Service and moved from its one-room campus office to more spacious quarters in San Francisco.

By this time, too, corporations and the public were beginning to awaken to the needs and the economic clout of the older population—thanks, at least in part, to the press attention that SeniorNet had received during its formative years. An estimated 9 percent of seniors between ages 60 and 69 were using computers at home in 1990—less than the national average among other adults of 24 percent but a sign that more older individuals were open to advanced technology when its uses were made clear.[28] Between November 1990 and April 1991, two dozen articles about SeniorNet appeared in such national media as *Business Week*, as well as in Bay Area newspapers—far more press coverage than any Markle-financed project had ever received. The market for the healthy older population and, right behind it, aging baby boomers, could no longer be ignored by computer hardware and software designers.

Whatever doubts Markle's staff harbored about Furlong's management abilities or her willingness to follow their counsel, the foundation was now ready to place a far bigger bet on SeniorNet. "With its initial success and its goals for expansion," Morrisett told Markle's board, "SeniorNet is central to our program of communications and an aging population. To realize its plans, this project must have adequate support for a long enough period to become financially independent and to implement a realistic and constructive business plan.''[29]

At Markle's June 1990 board meeting, the foundation approved Furlong's request for a two-year, $1.2 million grant—the first of three such exceptionally large sums that the foundation would appropriate through 1996.

SeniorNet's first years as an independent nonprofit brought continued good news, at least on the surface. By mid-1990, it claimed 3,510 members. Apple Computer Corporation, regional Bell companies, Microsoft, American Express Corporation, Manpower, Inc., and Chevron Corporation continued to provide modest grants for the SeniorNet annual conferences. Furlong's book, *Computers for Kids over Sixty*, was in its third printing and was being given to new members as a premium for joining. Her newsletter was getting better and more informative with every issue. The number of teaching sites had risen to thirty-two.[30] In April 1991, Microsoft agreed to a cooperative arrangement to develop teaching materials for Microsoft Works word processing, spreadsheet, database, and telecommunications software for SeniorNet members. Furlong called or wrote to Morrisett and Bjornson with these glad tidings—news of strategic alliances with corporations, continued press raves, new learning centers opening. Why, then, weren't they as unreservedly happy about SeniorNet's progress as she was?

Despite the outer trappings of success, Markle remained SeniorNet's lifeline. Roughly half of SeniorNet's $1.18 million budget for 1991–1992 came from the foundation. With all of the national publicity that SeniorNet had garnered, membership was still just slightly over four thousand by May 1991—out of 30 million seniors nationwide. Barely one out of three members signed up again after their first year.[31] By Furlong's own estimates, membership was producing just 13 percent of SeniorNet's revenues in fiscal 1992–1993.

By 1992, several of Markle's board members were openly questioning whether SeniorNet's growth rate would allow it to achieve self-sufficiency. When the final two-year funding cycle for SeniorNet was put up for board consideration in June 1994, key members, including board chair Michelson, were pressing

Morrisett to tell Furlong that this was SeniorNet's last chance to turn itself around. "The impression we got was that Mary Furlong was a wonderful conceptualizer, but maybe was not a great administrator who could turn the idea into a viable entity," Michelson said.[32]

The year 1994, the beginning of what was to be the final two-year, $1.2 million grant cycle, marked a new and increasingly strained period in SeniorNet's and Markle's relations. Morrisett had issued warnings to all Markle grantees, SeniorNet included, that his retirement was only a few years away. There was no assurance, he told them, that Markle would fund any Morrisett-generated projects beyond his planned departure as president at the end of 1997.

Beyond that general alert to all grantees, Morrisett and his staff decided to subject SeniorNet to heightened scrutiny. In February, Bjornson visited SeniorNet in San Francisco and laid it on the line—Markle's final grant money, she told Furlong, should be viewed as an endowment to support the growth of the online network. That was Markle's programmatic priority, and that alone was what it would support. Any activities, including annual meetings, that did not pay for themselves should be reduced or eliminated. SeniorNet, Bjornson said, had to get a clearer fix on how much it was costing to attract each new member, why it was getting only one paying member for every ten inquiries, and why only four in ten members were renewing their memberships. Surely, she told Furlong, this low rate of renewals suggested serious deficiencies in what SeniorNet was offering on-line members.[33]

In response, Furlong submitted a series of strategic business plans to the Markle staff during the months that followed. Each sought to assure Morrisett, Bjornson, and the Markle board that she understood the message about the need to enhance the on-line service. Membership, she pointed out in the second such draft business plan submitted to Markle in April 1994, had nearly doubled in a single year and now topped thirteen thousand. SeniorNet's on-line service, she pointed out, included such features as "Getting into Computers," "Health and Wellness," "Generation to Generation," and a general forum. Furlong laid out plans to connect SeniorNet to other information sources and services. In

March 1994, she met with AARP representatives to tout SeniorNet as an outlet for information to its members.

From the foundation's viewpoint, however, those efforts fell short. Even Morrisett, whose affection for Furlong and his aversion to conflict had led him to hold his fire, told Furlong in mid-1994 that "faced with the eventual loss of almost 50 percent of your current operating budget, both Edith and I believe that SeniorNet is likely to face a severe crisis."[34] Despite those heightened concerns, Morrisett had not lost hope that SeniorNet could become a trendsetting national on-line presence. In June 1994, the board approved a final two-year, $1.2 million grant. This time, however, the terms were more stringent. Payments would be at Morrisett's discretion and contingent on SeniorNet's staying on target for achieving its goals of self-sufficiency.

Having invested upward of $3 million, Morrisett dispatched his chief financial officer, Karen Byers, to San Francisco in July for an audit of SeniorNet's books and operations. Her findings quantified what everyone in Markle suspected. SeniorNet was actually losing $91,904 on its dues-paying members, when the costs of attracting and keeping them were taken into account.[35] Barely one in four members was renewing after the first year. Even the ostensible strong points of SeniorNet—the learning centers and the annual conferences—were netting less than a combined $87,000, according to Byers's report. The roster of corporate backers totaled twenty-three, but almost all of their contributions were small. There was nothing to suggest that the corporate sponsors would provide anywhere near the support needed to fill the gap that would result from Markle's eventual withdrawal.

"Overall," Byers reported, "the revenue generating departments are yielding a deficit of $5,273. Thus the management and fund-raising total expense of $465,657, plus the program services deficit, are being funded by Markle money. Obviously this is what has to change."[36]

SeniorNet seemed to be headed for extinction unless its actual spending, and not just its stated intentions, dramatically shifted toward propping up the on-line service. As Bjornson later recounted, "It seemed clear that there was no way that she could establish enough learning centers to train enough older people to sustain an on-line service for this population, either in terms of interest or in financial terms. By now she had managed to fund more centers. But that was happening because she had a tiny staff. That was happening at the expense of a really robust on-line service. And there was a disconnect between what was being taught at the centers and the capacity of those students to migrate into active use of the on-line SeniorNet."[37]

Morrisett and Bjornson suggested ways for SeniorNet to build revenue without sacrificing its cherished communitarian ideals. Morrisett observed, for example, that information about the older individuals who made up SeniorNet's membership might be a valuable commodity that could be compiled and marketed. Members of Furlong's own staff had suggested franchising SeniorNet's learning centers. Bjornson suggested that the on-line network might attract and keep many more paying members if it featured useful, revenue-generating services, such as sales of automobiles, insurance, travel, and investment products.

"Lloyd's argument to Mary was that you could have something that's highly commercial, and simultaneously something that retains that wonderful community sense that you're afraid you're going to lose. She apparently did not see it that way," Bjornson said.[38]

Meanwhile, Furlong and her board at SeniorNet began to explore other options for survival after Markle's withdrawal. For the next two years, Furlong looked to other foundations to develop and finance a larger on-line service but received no positive responses. She proposed unsuccessfully to the AARP that SeniorNet become the giant lobby's internet outlet. She asked her own corporate sponsors for bigger checks to advertise on SeniorNet and to help develop a more viable Web site. She approached Bell Atlantic and asked for $1 million to underwrite an "electronic citizenship" area within SeniorNet—a kind of virtual town hall for seniors to discuss and debate public policy issues.

"I thought if I could sell six of these different areas, I could sustain the organization that way," Furlong said. "I got in pretty high at Bell Atlantic but I couldn't sell it."[39]

Having failed with those strategies, Furlong decided in 1996 to talk with venture capitalists to finance a new, for-profit, commercially oriented on-line service. Under that scenario, the nonprofit SeniorNet would be given an equity stake in the new entity. If all went well, the money secured from the venture capitalists would replace the endowment that Markle provided and the nonprofit SeniorNet thus would be able to live on. Eventually, Furlong found a group of interested investors in the Bay Area who met her conditions for mutual trust, as well as her condition that SeniorNet had to be a beneficiary of any new for-profit venture. By June 1996, an agreement was near.

To Morrisett and Bjornson, however, the entire SeniorNet affair had taken a deeply troubling turn. Under the deal that SeniorNet's board seemed to be reaching with the venture capitalists, the on-line service and the name SeniorNet—its most prized asset—would be simply handed over to a new for-profit entity. The remnants of the nonprofit entity that Markle had been funding all these years would be left with a limited on-line service and a network of learning centers. The nonprofit entity would receive an as yet undetermined stake in the new, for-profit venture, but that stake would have value only when, or if, the new venture turned a profit. Furlong, meanwhile, would relinquish her leadership of the nonprofit organization to lead the for-profit venture, but she also wanted to keep her seat on the nonprofit's board—an arrangement that Morrisett and Bjornson saw as a clear conflict given her new commercial interests. Finally, Furlong wanted Markle to consider making the remaining payment of its grant—some $300,000—to the nonprofit SeniorNet to help it survive the transition.

To Morrisett's and Bjornson's chagrin, it now seemed that Markle was being asked to surrender the enterprise on which it had spent some $4 million, along with its most prized asset—its name—to others who might then profit from it. Equally unsettling was the fact that these arrangements had been negotiated without Markle's involvement or direct knowledge. In fact, Markle learned of them only through a late-night call to Bjornson from a management expert who had been dispatched to San Francisco by Markle to counsel Furlong. Had that call not been made, Morrisett and Bjornson would have faced the awkward prospect of learning about the deal as a fait accompli when they were scheduled to make an annual visit to SeniorNet in June.

The situation made for a tense meeting when Morrisett and

Bjornson arrived for that San Francisco visit on June 19, 1996. They wished Furlong and her new venture well but informed her that Markle was canceling the remaining $300,000 of its grant. In a follow-up letter to Furlong a week later, Morrisett stressed that he considered it vital that nonprofit SeniorNet be given a "satisfactory" stake in the for-profit venture. To Morrisett, that meant at least $900,000 up front in cash and equities. In reality, Markle had little left to bargain with, and the eventual settlement was not nearly so generous.

Furlong stepped down as president of SeniorNet in July 1996 to become chief executive of ThirdAge Media, Inc., the new, for-profit descendent of SeniorNet. Negotiations concerning the stake that SeniorNet would get from ThirdAge dragged on through the fall. SeniorNet's board grew so frustrated with the talks that it played its last remaining trump. It flatly refused to give up the SeniorNet name and threatened to kill the whole deal unless it was given a reasonable stake in the new venture. Thereafter, it was agreed that the nonprofit organization would retain the SeniorNet name and also receive a small cash settlement plus a 10 percent equity share of the for-profit company. Furlong kept at arms length from the discussions because of her divided loyalties. She told the author that she helped the nonprofit board to obtain good legal advice and strongly supported the decision to have it retain the SeniorNet name.

In January 1997, a group of private investors led by SOFTBANK Holdings, Inc. agreed to put up $3 million to sustain ThirdAge. In June, it went on line, at www.thirdage.com. The new for-profit venture decided to target "aging boomers," forty-five to sixty-five years old. In October, ThirdAge received a second, $10 million infusion from a group of investors led by US West Interactive Services Group, which gave it a 20 percent stake in the service. That fall, Furlong gave up her seat on the nonprofit SeniorNet's board at the board's request. The big break came in June 1999, when a group led by CBS Corporation and Merrill Lynch & Co., Inc. invested $89 million in ThirdAge. Along with a 30 percent stake in ThirdAge, CBS received advertising and promotional consideration on the Web site for seven years. Furlong stayed on as ThirdAge's board chair.

SeniorNet, for its part, was experiencing continued good press and a new burst of growth and prosperity in 1999, according to Ann Wrixon, Furlong's successor as president.[40] It has remained, by far, the most popular Web site for the older population with 1.5 million visits per month through its sites on America OnLine and the World Wide Web. By the end of 1999, the number of SeniorNet learning centers had reach 185 and more than 32,000 members were enrolled in classes. Membership renewal rates were about 35 percent, close to the levels achieved by Furlong. SeniorNet is safely in the black financially, Wrixon said. Membership fees covered slightly less than half of SeniorNet's $2.5 million annual budget, with much of the balance coming from on-line corporate sponsorship from such firms as Charles Schwab & Co., Inc., IBM, and Microsoft.[41]

Perhaps no project during the Morrisett years stirred stronger emotions or caused more mixed feelings in retrospect than SeniorNet. Before SeniorNet appeared in 1986, no one—not the old-age lobbyists, the computer industry, the news media, or the rest of the foundation world—had seriously thought about the role that technology might play in improving the lives of seniors. The foundation's lengthy commitment to SeniorNet, combined with Furlong's personal magnetism, helped to draw national attention to the cause. As a result, America's older citizens never again could be casually dismissed as technology troglodytes.

By 1997, the number of internet users age fifty or older was approaching 8 million. A 1998 survey by Media Metrix, Inc., which tracks computer usage in fourteen thousand homes, found that men and women age fifty-five or older who owned terminals passed more than 130 minutes per day on their computers, which surpassed the average 117 minutes for all groups. By the late 1990s, computer marketers fully understood that the fifty-plus net surfer was a commercial gold mine. Indeed, they had become the wealthiest on-line group, with average earnings of more than $60,000. Whereas SeniorNet had the field virtually to itself during its first years, more than a thousand Web sites were catering specifically to the needs of the older population by 1999. New online service centers for seniors included, for example, GrandmaBetty.com; GoldenAge.Net; The Resource Directory for Older People, which includes government and other agencies dealing with aging; and WWII—Keeping the Memory Alive archive and message board for World War II veterans and families.

Still, as much as any endeavor during Morrisett's presidency, SeniorNet demonstrated how improbable it is that the person who conceives a breakthrough idea will also possess the management and marketing skills to transform the vision into a viable, sustainable organization. Looking back, Morrisett, who maintained friendly relations with Furlong, said that he and his staff should have intervened in SeniorNet's management and basic direction earlier and more decisively, when the first inklings of problems arose at Monterey in 1989:

> We should have been more directive, either in trying to provide benchmarks and controls to ensure that those things happened, and/or changing the leadership in the organization. That was the time to do it.
>
> Ten years from now, we may look back and say it was all a great success. We don't know. And Mary is a different person. She went through two very hard years in raising money for Third Age and making the deals to keep it going. I suspect she's much more tough minded than she was four or five years ago.[42]

Regardless of its rocky history and limited reach, SeniorNet was a pioneering partnership by Markle and Mary Furlong that helped call the nation's attention to the gap between the computer age and the aged. It remained, however, one of Morrisett's more bittersweet experiences.

NOTES

1. Winston, *Misunderstanding Media*, 217.
2. Quoted in Michael Rice, "Toward Harnessing New Electronic Technologies to Meet the Needs of Elderly People" (report of the Aspen Institute Planning Meeting, Wye Woods Conference Center, Queenstown, Md., 24–25 Mar. 1987), 8.
3. Quoted in ibid.
4. Jack Ossofsky, "Foundations are Failing the Aged," *Foundation News*, July/August 1974, 30–39.
5. Ibid.
6. Lloyd N. Morrisett, "The Markle Foundation 1985" (President's

Essay in "The John and Mary R. Markle Foundation, Annual Report, 1983–1984 and 1984–1985"), 12.

7. The Daniel Yankelovich Group, "Aging in America: Current Trends and Future Directions," March 1988, 1, Markle Archive Collection.

8. "Profile of Older Americans: 1999," census statistics from the Web site of the Administration on Aging, U.S. Department of Health and Human Services (http://www.aoa.dhhs.gov/aoa/stats/profile/default.htm).

9. Lloyd N. Morrisett, "Aging In America: New Issues, New Opportunities" (President's Essay in "The John and Mary R. Markle Foundation, Annual Report, 1988"), 13.

10. "The Computer Comes of Age: Services for Older People" (report of conference held by The John and Mary R. Markle Foundation, Princeton, N.J., 14 Dec. 1984), 8–10.

11. Ibid., 3.

12. Ibid., 6.

13. Tora K. Bikson and Jacqueline D. Goodchilds, "Experiencing the Retirement Transition: Managerial and Professional Men Before and After," in Stuart Oskamp, ed., *The Social Psychology of Aging: The Clarement Symposium on Applied Social Psychology* (Thousand Oaks, Calif.: Sage Publications, Inc., 1989) (reprint of article, RAND Corporation), 85.

14. Ibid., 103–4.

15. Czaja, interview, 28 Jan. 1998.

16. Bjornson, interview, 2 Feb. 1998.

17. Morrisett, interview, 2 Mar. 1998.

18. Lloyd N. Morrisett, remarks in "Study Reveals Older Americans Need More Useful Technology" (press release accompanying The Daniel Group, "Aging in America").

19. Ibid.

20. Furlong, interview, 11 Feb. 1998.

21. *InfoWorld*, 7 May 1984, 25.

22. Furlong, interview, 11 Feb. 1998.

23. Mary Furlong and Greg Kearsley, "SENIORNET: A Computer Communications Network for Senior Citizens" (proposal submitted to The Markle Foundation, 1985), 6.

24. Anecdotes cited in Edith C. Bjornson, correspondence with Rick Ratliff, business writer, *Detroit Free Press*, 27 June 1988.

25. Furlong, interview, 12 Feb. 1998.

26. Ibid.

27. Morrisett, interview, 2 Mar. 1998.

28. Irene Recio, "The Password is Geezer: Golden Agers Log On," *Business Week*, 10 Sept. 1990, 74.

29. Lloyd N. Morrisett, untitled memorandum to Markle Board of Directors, November 1989, 42.

30. Mary Furlong, letter to Lloyd N. Morrisett, 3 Aug. 1990.

31. Mary Furlong, "SeniorNet Dec. '90–April '91: Report to the Markle Foundation," 31 May 1991, 1–2.

32. Michelson, interview, 4 Mar. 1998.

33. Bjornson, interview, 2 Feb. 1998.

34. Lloyd N. Morrisett, letter to Mary Furlong, 18 Apr. 1994.

35. Karen D. Byers, untitled report to Lloyd N. Morrisett and Edith C. Bjornson, 22 July 1994, regarding Byers's two-day visit to SeniorNet, 2–3.

36. Ibid.

37. Bjornson, interview, 2 Feb. 1998.

38. Ibid.

39. Furlong, interview, 12 Feb. 1998.

40. Wrixon, interview, 8 Dec. 1999.

41. Ibid.

42. Morrisett, interview, 2 Mar. 1998.

9

Communications and Democracy

TO AFICIONADOS of political horse races, the 1988 presidential campaign was one to savor. A colorful cast of seven Democrats and six Republicans vied first for their respective party's nomination in a series of surprise-packed primary contests. The races produced a stream of lively copy. Televangelist Pat Robertson placed second in the Iowa Republican contest, a convincing demonstration of Christian conservatism's growing political potency. The Reverend Jesse L. Jackson, the civil rights leader, became history's first serious African American contender for the presidency with a string of Democratic primary wins from Michigan to the Deep South.

The eventual main contest between Vice President George Bush and Democratic nominee Michael Dukakis was a seesaw affair with sound bites and imagery memorable enough in tawdriness, if not wisdom, to enter the permanent lexicon of American politics: Texas Treasurer Ann Richards's reference to Bush as being born with a "silver foot in his mouth"; vice presidential candidate Lloyd Bentsen's deft deflation of his Republican foe Dan Quayle with his "you're no Jack Kennedy" comment in their televised debate; Bush's less than eloquent "vision thing" comments and his more artful "kinder, gentler nation" speech at the Republican Convention.

Sound bites staged in flag factories overshadowed such issues as education and the environment in the campaign as Republican image makers questioned the depth of Dukakis's patriotism because he vetoed a Massachusetts state law that would have required teachers to lead their classes in the Pledge of Allegiance. Willie Horton, a black prisoner who raped a white woman while on furlough from a Massachusetts state prison, became a symbol of Dukakis's alleged softness on crime. The name Willie Horton also came to symbolize, for all time, the most negative forms of political advertising.

The occasional news columnist lamented the inattention to serious issues by politicians and the press. "For those who would like the 1988 campaign to be a broad debate between Michael S. Dukakis and George Bush about a wide range of tough issues . . . the encounter so far has been a dud," wrote *The New York Times* political correspondent E. J. Dionne, Jr. Letters-to-the-editor sections of newspapers around the country, Dionne noted, were crammed with voter complaints about the dearth of issues that really mattered to them.[1]

Such passing pangs of conscience aside, most in the media seemed content to swim with the prevailing tide of imagery over substance. U.S. News and World Report tallied the number of times that each candidate was the butt of jokes by television comedians (George Bush was the hands-down winner). A tongue-in-cheek op-ed column, titled "The Height Report," by political scientist Norman J. Ornstein advised the 5-foot, 6-inch Dukakis to pick a running mate who didn't make him seem even less physically imposing.[2] (Ignoring the advice, Dukakis chose Bentsen, a tall Texan). *The New York Times* TV critic John Corry solemnly intoned that Bush "looks best in full face. From the side he can appear cadaverous. His features slope toward his chin. On a bad day, he may come across as thin-lipped and squinty." Dukakis, Corry wrote, ". . . looks like a gnome; his head seems to be mounted on someone else's shoulders . . . Where Mr. Bush is open, he's closed off. Mr. Dukakis bites off sentences, and although he's smiling, he sometimes appears to have removed himself from our presence."[3]

The horse-race mentality of the media sometimes clashed with the integrity of the voting exercise itself. CBS and NBC decided to reduce coverage of the March 8 "Super Tuesday" primaries after determining that no clear-cut victor was likely to emerge.[4] On election night, the major networks used exit polling to declare Bush's victory over Dukakis hours before the polls closed in western states—which left millions of voters west of the Mississippi wondering why they should bother casting their ballots.

How did American voters respond in the end? Barely 50 percent (91,602,291) went to the polls on November 8, the lowest percentage since 1924 and the eighth consecutive presidential contest where turnout had declined.

Although some people found great sport in the 1988 race, to Morrisett it seemed more like professional wrestling—one of the dreariest displays yet of the phoniness and lack of thoughtful discourse in electoral politics. In his view, participatory democracy had two basic requirements—capability and competence. Capability meant the right to vote, and that battle had been largely fought and won during the 1960s Civil Rights era. Competence, on the other hand, required adequate access to reliable information to form judgments about candidates and issues. The great paradox of modern politics, Morrisett now argued, was that even as the right to vote had been largely settled in the 1960s, fewer and fewer people were exercising it.

As early as 1976, Morrisett had suggested that, "We are now at a point in history when the responsibility of the broadcaster could focus on providing the public with the information needed to make free and informed political choices. As a public trustee, is it not the responsibility of the broadcaster to educate the public about candidates, and to do so not simply on behalf of the candidates, but on behalf of the public?"[5]

By 1988, as research funded by the Markle Foundation would soon document, the unholy alliance between the press and politicians had deepened the cynicism and apathy among the voting public. "As the complexity of issues increases," Morrisett said, "the job of evaluating political candidates grows more difficult. Yet as the need for substantive information is becoming more critical, the quality of much of the information available to the public is declining. The 1988 election demonstrated with disturbing clarity the extent to which the information available to the public is inadequate. Too often, messages were superficial, doing less to enlighten than to manipulate and even to entertain."[6]

For the rest of Morrisett's presidency, Markle undertook a range of projects aimed at challenging the three key players in modern electoral democracy—the politicians, the press and the public—to rethink their respective civic responsibilities. As Bruce Buchanan, a nationally prominent University of Texas political scientist who conducted much of the foundation's research in political participation, later characterized it, the goal was to restore a balance in which "citizens are sovereigns, candidates are supplicants, and the media are servants."[7]

Drawing from his boyhood experiences, Morrisett imagined that the media, especially television, might play the role of a "New Main Street," a national meeting place on the TV dial where citizens could come together and learn collectively about critical policy issues and debate them. In his 1990 annual essay, he recalled childhood visits during the late 1930s to relatives in the small town of Jerseyville, Illinois. Back then, he wrote, Main Street, with its movies, bowling alleys, shops, and ice cream parlors, was a daily gathering place to discuss and debate important community and civic matters. Half a century later, Morrisett wrote, "Television has, in effect, become America's Main Street." Every year on Super Bowl Sunday, television gathers tens of millions of people to share and debate a national event. Why couldn't television do the same with politics and elections?

Television, Morrisett stated:

> . . . is capable of attracting people to the campaign and encouraging their involvement. It can present the candidates to the public in a variety of situations and circumstances, allowing an appraisal over time of their judgment, consistency, and stands on issues. It can reveal their past records and provide the perspective for a fair evaluation; it can also furnish the grounds for predicting their future effectiveness. . . . Television, however, has yet to function as "Main Street" for these significant events. . . . To the contrary, most political analysts contend that television has undermined rather than strengthened civic life.[8]

Morrisett's interests in the media as both the cause of and the possible cure for voter apathy had been building well before the 1988 campaign. During the 1970s, the foundation backed a research project by political scientist Sidney Kraus of Cleveland State University that examined television's effects on voting behavior. Markle supported a project by the New York-based Regional Plan Association that unsuccessfully sought coordinated local television coverage of town meetings where citizens could discuss critical issues affecting the New York region. More sizable investments were made for work during the 1970s by Duke University political scientist James David Barber and by Thomas E.

Patterson of Syracuse University. Their explorations focused on the media's effects on voters and the increasing role of media consultants in the interplay between candidates and the national press. As discussed in chapter 3, Washington advocate and future Markle Fellow Henry Geller had considerable success during the 1970s in making the legal case for institutionalizing televised presidential debates.

Not until the mid-1980s, however, did "politics and the media" become a central focus at Markle. The foundation's spending on such projects jumped from less than $1 million dollars through the 1970s to nearly $5.9 million during the 1980s. During Morrisett's final seven years as president, media-and-politics projects became Markle's largest single priority, with nearly $15 million appropriated for such ventures.[9]

As Markle's interests in the subject grew, so did the variety and ambitiousness of its projects. Many were still research oriented. The foundation granted $238,000 in 1985 to the Institute of Politics at Harvard's John F. Kennedy School of Government for studies of the implications of new media technologies on democratic values and press coverage of politics.[10] In 1987, Markle provided $324,000 to ECRI, (Emergency Care Research Institute), a nonprofit organization in Plymouth Meeting, Pennsylvania, to publish a guide to the electronic voting machines that were fast replacing mechanical machines.[11] During the mid-1990s, Markle funded several projects by UCLA political scientist Shanto Iyengar that demonstrated how negative political advertising breeds cynicism about politics and discourages voter participation.

In the wake of the 1988 contest, Markle provided $400,000 to produce "The Public Mind," a four-part PBS series starring Bill Moyers. The programs, which aired in November 1989, won a Peabody award and featured, among others, media analyst Ben Bagdikian, journalist Bill Kovach, and Ronald Reagan's media adviser Michael Deaver. Moyers, who had been a press adviser for President Johnson during the 1960s, examined the power of pollsters, how media deception and manipulation influence events and public opinion, and how TV imagery and sales techniques have overshadowed content in political coverage.

In 1991 and 1992, Markle granted $162,000 to the Center for National Independence in Politics, a nonprofit organization established in 1989 by former Presidents Gerald Ford and Jimmy Carter to provide unbiased information to the public on critical issues. Markle's funding enabled the Corvallis, Oregon–based organization to set up a toll-free telephone information service providing journalists on deadline access to trustworthy information on candidates and public issues. Known as Project Vote Smart, the organization fielded more than 200,000 such calls from reporters and other individuals during the 1992 campaign. Markle provided another $300,000 to the center for the 1994 congressional campaigns. The center remains active in 2000.

FROM OPINION TO JUDGMENT: THE PUBLIC AGENDA FOUNDATION

One of Markle's most sustained partnerships was with the Public Agenda Foundation, a nonprofit research organization founded in 1976 by polling expert Daniel Yankelovich and former Secretary of State Cyrus Vance. Starting in 1981, Markle supported a series of Public Agenda's experiments aimed at developing new methods for the media to educate the public on such policy issues as health, education, and foreign affairs.

According to Public Agenda, the scattershot quality of typical news coverage often left citizens befuddled rather than informed about policy options. Public Agenda's proposed new model, "Citizens Choice," involved persuading local broadcasters and newspapers to offer coordinated, sustained coverage of a single policy issue for a period of several weeks. Armed with a more sophisticated understanding of issues and options, citizens could then vote their policy preferences on ballots appearing in newspapers or elsewhere and mail the ballots to Public Agenda for tabulation. Area media would then give prominent play to the results.

This was a far cry from mere opinion polling. The intention of Public Agenda and Markle was to use the power of print and broadcast media to move the public dialogue about critical issues from "mass opinion" to "public judgment."[12] The success of the Citizens Choice model depended, as well, on the credibility and lack of bias of the information supplied by Public Agenda. Any appearance of shoddiness or political bias would dash any hope that the model would be taken seriously by the press, the public, or policymakers.

"I would say that this is the most fundamental organizing principle for Public Agenda," Deborah Wadsworth, the foundation's executive director, told the author. "When this organization started, the purpose was to create a kind of go-between, an entity that would help leaders better understand the public's mindset, and at the same time be capable of translating the leadership agenda for public consumption. A major conduit, obviously, is the media. The notion was that the world did not need another public interest group, that the moment we erred on the side of a particular point of view, we were out of business."[13]

Public Agenda's earliest Citizens Choice experiments were among the most successful. With health insurance rates rising nationwide from 15 to 30 percent per year, Public Agenda worked closely with the Des Moines Register, a newspaper noted nationally for its public-spiritedness, and other area papers, broadcasters and cable operators, during a three-month public education campaign called Health Vote '82.

The project began with a random poll in July 1982 to gauge the public's knowledge about health care and what its policy preferences were. Not surprisingly, Des Moines citizens indicated that they wanted to rein in costs, but most respondents also demonstrated a muddled understanding of the economics of health care. The wish list of policy options supported by the majority—more spending for research, expanded care for the elderly, annual checkups for all schoolchildren, and the requirement that employers offer dental coverage—flatly contradicted the goal of curbing costs. The results of that first poll made clear that typical media coverage had contributed to disjointed opinions about health policy.

During the information campaign that followed, Public Agenda distributed brochures describing Health Vote '82 to every Des Moines household, presented televised announcements by Iowa Governor Robert Ray, sponsored numerous lecture series and community meetings at churches, clubs, area businesses, and schools, and provided polling data and other raw materials to aid print and broadcast journalists in their coverage of the health care issue. The media's educational campaign had the desired effect. Using ballots printed in the Des Moines Register, more than thirty thousand citizens voted in December on thirteen proposals for dealing with health care costs.[14] Their responses demonstrated that the media had, through its sustained and coordinated coverage of a single issue, helped voters to move from glib and contradictory opinions to a deeper understanding of the gray areas of public policy. The December balloting found, for example, that, following the media information blitz, a majority of citizens considered many policy options, such as accepting more out-of-hospital care, consulting nurse-practitioners, and joining a health maintenance organization (HMO), to be "negotiable."[15] The preferences expressed by the voters were convincing enough that Iowa lawmakers used the findings to help craft trendsetting health care legislation in 1984.

The success of the Des Moines experiment led Public Agenda to repeat Health Vote in five other cities in 1985: Dayton, Ohio; Kansas City, Missouri; Minneapolis–Saint Paul, Minnesota; Peoria, Illinois; and Raleigh, North Carolina. That same year, Public Agenda worked with WCAU-TV, *The Philadelphia Inquirer*, and other media in the Philadelphia area on an eight-week project called School Vote, which called on voters to recommend education reform measures. WCAU devoted thirteen hours of programming, including a ninety-minute community forum, to the campaign. More than 104,000 Delaware Valley citizens expressed their views on ballots. By overwhelming percentages, voters told city and school officials they wanted more time spent on educational basics, stricter discipline in classrooms, an end to "social promotion," lower class sizes, and job training for non–college-bound students.

For all its apparent success in smaller cities with less intense media competition, the Citizens Choice model proved difficult to spread on a national scale. By its nature, the model was costly and labor intensive, involving large amounts of fact checking and gathering and painstaking missionary work by Public Agenda's staff from newsroom to newsroom. Interest in the model continued into the 1990s, according to Wadsworth. But, as Morrisett pointed out, collaborations among newspapers and broadcasters that were possible in Des Moines or Peoria were less likely in the largest, most competitive media markets, such as New York and Washington, where coordinated, sustained coverage of specific issues by rival television stations and newspapers was far more difficult to imagine.

CREATING AN ELECTION REPORT CARD: THE MARKLE COMMISSION

The 1988 election signaled to Morrisett, the incurable social scientist, a need for data that would begin to allow the nation to chart long-term trends on how well the press, politicians, and the public were performing in their respective civic roles. He also realized, for the research to make a difference in the political process, that it would need a powerful public relations send-off—a high-profile launching vehicle that would lend excitement, credibility, and importance to the findings. A classic way for foundations to accomplish the dual goal of credibility and public attention is to form a prestigious commission. Midway through the 1988 campaign, Morrisett established the Markle Commission on Media and the Electorate.[16]

Morrisett hoped that his new commission would devise a "national report card on the media and political education"—a durable model for electoral data gathering that could be repeated every four years to help the public track the health of the presidential selection process.[17] The model drew on his experiences twenty years earlier with a Carnegie Corporation commission whose work led to the National Assessment of Educational Progress (NAEP), standardized tests periodically measuring U.S. student performance in basic academic subjects. Over time, the so-called NAEP "report card" became the most trusted measure of the nation's academic health. Could Markle's new commission create a similar report card on the health of U.S. electoral politics?

In fact, Morrisett had always been a bit skeptical about foundation-backed commissions. Nearly all of them were expensive in money and staff time, which made them more suited to large, wealthy foundations. He also regarded their record as uneven at best. Some, such as the Carnegie Corporation's Commission on Educational Television in the 1960s, had been highly effective in mobilizing opinion and getting results. Others, such as the Alfred P. Sloan Commission on Cable Communications, published a report in 1970 but, in Morrisett's view, accomplished little else. In 1977, Morrisett had toyed briefly with setting up a commission to examine media behavior and "to assess what types of media events might best serve the democratic process."[18]

Coming so late in the 1988 election season, the decision to form a commission was doubly risky, but Morrisett did not want to wait for four years to begin the task of developing good data on electoral behavior. He also hoped that a Markle commission would help make his foundation a more visible player in media and political circles.

The Markle Commission on Media and the Electorate differed from most blue-ribbon panels in that its raison d'être was research, first and foremost. Markle was also able to hold the budget to a modest $650,000 by limiting the commission to an advisory, rather than a directive, role. To manage the effort, Morrisett hired Bruce Buchanan of the University of Texas.

The commission had an additional purpose beyond data gathering—to begin a national dialogue on appropriate campaign behavior by the press, politicians, and the public. As Buchanan told the author, the core mission was "to develop a consensus on what the difference was between good, fair, and poor presidential campaigns." By suggesting such standards, Buchanan said:

> [The commission might] . . . insure that the actors—candidates, media and citizens—felt greater need to balance self-interest against the larger public interest. As matters now stand, office seekers are not pressured to answer questions like, "what obligations do political candidates have during campaigns other than winning?" News organizations are rarely asked to justify the air time/column space accorded the political horse race in comparison to issues and candidate qualifications. And citizens encounter little or no serious criticism of their political ignorance and indifference.[19]

The commission's research agenda had three main parts. First, and most interesting, was "content analysis" of eighteen prominent print and broadcast news organizations—what they covered during the campaign and how they covered it.[20] Second, the panel hired Louis Harris and Associates to conduct random national telephone surveys of voters—one after Labor Day and the second shortly before Election Day—to determine what voters "learned" during the campaign and how they changed their minds about candidates or issues. Third, to disentangle how various influences, such as the media and campaign advertising, "educated" voters, the commission held voter focus groups during the campaign in Elmsford, New York; Sacramento, California; Chicago, Illinois; and Houston, Texas.[21]

In May 1990, the commission issued its dismal verdict on the 1988 campaign: "American voters today do not seem to understand their rightful place in the operation of American democracy. Public indifference, lack of knowledge and political apathy are at an all-time high."[22] Voters lacked the information to recognize the distortions being fed them by the media and the candidates. Most disturbingly, they were seemingly unconcerned about their own ignorance.

"The American public," Buchanan observed in a subsequent book on the campaign, "act as if they believe that presidential elections belong to somebody else; most notably, presidential candidates."[23]

As for the media's performance, the commission found that nearly 60 percent of campaign coverage dealt with the horse-race aspects and candidate conflicts, whereas less than one third addressed issues or candidate qualifications. Commercial TV topped the list of offenders, particularly CNN—66 percent of its stories had to do with campaign momentum and prognostication.[24] While blaming both major presidential candidates for taking "the low road of attack campaigning," the commission saved its harshest words for the Bush campaign, which "set a tone with advertising that voters found distasteful."[25]

Overall, the commission's data were greeted in research circles as a social science breakthrough. The findings were among the first to establish the extent to which voters do, in fact, "learn" and change their views during a campaign, although much of the "knowledge" acquired in 1988 was slanted information fed voters by candidates via the media and TV ads. The data revealed, for example, a sharp increase in the number of voters who "learned" from attack ads by the Bush campaign that Dukakis was a shameless liberal who was "weak on crime."[26]

As gloomy as those underlying messages were, the research won praise for its quality and speed. "It was remarkable how well they did, considering how quickly it was done," said Kathleen Hall Jamieson, dean of the Annenberg School at the University of Pennsylvania and a prominent campaign analyst.[27] As 1992 approached, Morrisett decided that the exercise was well worth repeating but with some important modifications. During the 1992 campaign, Markle limited the effort to data gathering and made no policy recommendations (primarily because no one outside the research community had paid serious attention to the commission's first set of recommendations).[28] Although continuing with the research, Morrisett dropped the commission itself in 1992 because he concluded that it had not proved effective enough at drawing media or public attention to justify the expense. Without a commission to finance, Markle cut its costs in half in 1992 to $327,000.

Buchanan's election report card on the 1992 campaign was more upbeat than for 1988. Voter interest and involvement were markedly higher, largely as a result of public concerns over the economy and because of the influence of Ross Perot's third-party candidacy in focusing the media, the public, and the other major politicians on important issues.[29] Nearly four out of ten voters, queried by Louis Harris for Markle, said that they were paying close attention to the 1992 campaign, compared with just 25 percent in 1988. The increase in voter involvement, in turn, pushed candidates and newspeople to improve their performances.[30]

The perception that 1992 was a healthier campaign did not carry over to the 1996 presidential campaign among President Clinton, Robert Dole, and Ross Perot, an uninspired contest that led to the lowest voter turnout since World War II. Markle's project, renamed the Markle Foundation Presidential Election Watch in 1996, cost another $450,000 and featured regular reports by Markle to the press about the media's performance in covering the campaign.[31] This time, the data indicated that broadcast journalists were hogging airtime from candidates. Collectively, journalists used 73 percent of the speaking time in election news—six times more than the total allotted to the candidates themselves.

Fifty three percent of election stories dealt with the "horse race," whereas 37 percent focused on policy matters.[32]

Among the most striking findings was the degree to which the media themselves sat out the 1996 campaign. From Labor Day through November, the combined election coverage on evening newscasts of the three major networks averaged 12.3 minutes per night, a drop of 50 percent from the 24.6-minute collective nightly average of the three networks during the 1992 campaign.[33] Equally interesting, the public blamed itself for failing to meet its civic responsibilities. Asked to grade citizen performance in the election, a majority of those surveyed by Election Watch rated the public an average C, and 22 percent gave substandard D or F grades.

As disturbing as such findings were, their effects on the attitudes of the press, politicians, and the public have been negligible. As Morrisett put it:

> I think the public cares very little about this so far, but might be brought to care with an appropriate educational campaign. The media has selective knowledge. [*The Washington Post* columnist] David Broder knows about it, people at CNN, a lot of people in the major media are interested in it. Most are not in a position to exert much change. They are not the publishers or station owners. They tend to be the political correspondents. I think that's useful, and it's a start.
>
> The campaign handlers? I see no reason to think that their motivation is not just to win. As long as money is as important in campaigns, it will be the very rare politician who takes real account of this.[34]

Although the research sponsored by Markle had little impact on the larger political picture, its report card on three consecutive national campaigns established a well-regarded social scientific measure for tracking the behavior of voters, politicians and their handlers, and the media. Had Morrisett been a foundation executive who gauged the worth of his undertakings strictly by counting headlines or by the number of recommendations heeded by policymakers, he probably would have dropped the project after 1988. Instead, the longitudinal information provided the press, the public, and serious students of politics a means of quantifying the squalid state of modern democracy. As Professor Jamieson of the Annenberg School put it, the Markle Commission's work was significant because of its emphasis on media content analysis, because it documented that voters do learn over the course of a campaign from wholesome and unwholesome influences, and because "Markle was smart enough to stay with it for three campaigns."[35]

THE VOTERS' CHANNEL

His pale eyes at their iciest, his left hand clenched beneath his chin, Lloyd Morrisett stared out of a picture beneath this headline in the October 28, 1991, issue of *The New York Observer:*

PBS Spurned, CNN Wins New $3.5 Million Grant

By then, the events detailed in that article were familiar in broadcast and foundation circles. Eighteen months earlier, The Markle Foundation had offered the Public Broadcasting System $5 million, virtually every dollar at its command in a single year, to help make PBS "The Voter's Channel." PBS, the foundation had hoped, would become the "network of record" for the 1992 presidential campaign, much as CNN had been during the 1991 Gulf War. Its programming would be of such high quality and immediacy that, as with CNN's war coverage, PBS would command the attention not only of the public but of the rest of the media. There would be free airtime for candidates (which had not been done since 1964), interactive programs allowing viewers to sound off to candidates and each other about critical issues, original documentaries profiling issues and candidates, and enriched offerings on The McNeil/Lehrer News Hour, Frontline, and other outlets for public affairs.

The Markle Commission had amply documented that the public was not well informed about election issues. Yet, there was no single, nationally accessible print or broadcast source where people could turn for comprehensive, fair information. "The next obvious step," Morrisett said, "was to say that the distribution system available to almost everyone is television, and what more appropriate place than PBS? That's how we got there."[36]

Some thirty years earlier, when his focus was on using the media to address the needs of children, Morrisett was among the first education experts to make peace with TV viewing as a fact of childhood. From there, he had made the leap that the medium might be creatively harnessed for educational enrichment. Now he was making a similar case for political coverage. Why not accept television's dominance at long last and find ways for it to improve the process rather than continually cheapen it?

"It is much as it was in the 1960s before Sesame Street," he told Markle's board of directors. "The critics deplored the mindlessness of children's television and the possible harmful effects of the many hours children spent watching. Sesame Street accepted the fact that children were watching television and tried to find ways to use that time for their benefit. Now the challenge is to accept that national campaigns are largely carried out on and through television and find ways to use television to help people be fully informed citizens and fulfill their democratic responsibilities."[37]

Morrisett's willingness to place such a heavy bet on public broadcasting was not without reservations. Weighing on its side, PBS had an educational and civic mission consistent with Markle's. It also had the potential availability of airtime and a distribution system that was, for the time being at least, more extensive than cable's. On the other hand, thirty years of dealings with public broadcasting had also convinced Morrisett that PBS was "a fundamentally flawed system. The flaws were, and the flaws are, that it is not a system, but an aggregation of idiosyncratic entities that have different agendas, different ownerships, some owned by states, some by communities. There's never agreement on how policy decisions are to be made, there is no ability to get system-wide concerted agreement or action on anything."[38]

Still, Morrisett had beaten the odds once before, with *Sesame Street*, in getting public broadcasters to overcome their foibles and rally around a product of demonstrated excellence. He now believed there was a fighting chance that those same warring fiefdoms within PBS might be brought around to his ideas for improved election coverage.

By June 1991, after more than eighteen months of planning and futile negotiations, the hoped-for collaboration between

Markle and PBS lay in ruins. For PBS, it was a public embarrassment. The postmortems in *The New York Times*, *The Washington Post*, *Columbia Journalism Review*, and elsewhere painted PBS as so chaotic and balkanized with its 341 disparate stations that some called it broadcast's equivalent of Yugoslavia. The consensus seemed to be that PBS and its leaders had dithered and dathered and driven an exasperated Morrisett and his millions into the more willing arms of CNN.

Lawrence Grossman, president of PBS from 1976 to 1984, called it "a sad commentary on where PBS's priorities were, and are."[39] Ward Chamberlin, the head of WETA in 1992 and later programming chief of New York's public television station WNET, told the author, "It was one of the stupidest things PBS ever did."[40] James Day, a past president of WNET, cited the debacle as Exhibit A of everything that was wrong with public broadcasting.[41] Still, the available evidence suggests that the spurning by PBS of Markle's $5 million gift horse was not just a case of public broadcasting's endemic shortcomings, but also a result of missteps and misunderstandings by both PBS and Markle.

In October 1989, Morrisett for the first time had shared his ideas with PBS's president, Bruce Christensen for making public broadcasting the place on the TV dial where voters could be educated about the issues and where campaigns could be played out. Both men came away encouraged. As Christensen told the author, "I was very positive. I thought the ideas made sense. They were compatible with what our objectives were, and we were interested in seeing how it would play out."[42]

It was, however, an especially ticklish moment for such ideas within PBS. Since the late 1980s, there had been a growing recognition within PBS that if it was ever to be a "system" in the truest sense, there had to be some semblance of centralization of programming authority. To manage that sensitive task, Christensen in 1989 named Jennifer Lawson, then a forty-four–year-old fund-raising executive from the Corporation for Public Broadcasting and former civil rights worker and film professor, to the newly created position of vice president in charge of national programming. Her mandate was to pay more attention to audience ratings, to cut through the system's infamous bureaucracy, and to begin centralizing at least some of the authority long reserved for local stations and producers.

By all accounts, Lawson was well liked by PBS's station managers. Still, her newness on the job and the political sensitivity of her task made her particularly circumspect in the dealings that lay ahead with Markle. Even with its $5 million sweetener, Markle was regarded within PBS as an outsider—which made Lawson's task of selling the foundation's election ideas to more than three hundred intensely individual stations all the trickier.

Encouraged nonetheless by his first contacts with Christensen, Morrisett began sounding out leaders of local PBS stations. William Koban, president of KCET–Los Angeles, reacted enthusiastically, as did Ward Chamberlin, then at WETA. "That's the most exciting project I've heard of in many years. Furthermore, it is doable," Chamberlin wrote to Morrisett in December 1989. Morrisett's plans were also hailed by prominent campaign operatives in both major parties, including Republicans Roger Ailes and Lee Atwater and Democrat Robert Squires. For them, such ideas as free airtime for their candidates were quite easy to support, even if the price would be having their candidates' pronouncements instantly dissected by PBS correspondents for their accuracy or lack thereof.

In December, Lawson met with Morrisett to discuss a feasibility study for the project to determine its features and budget. Like Christensen, she was encouraging but noncommittal. In fact, she declined Morrisett's request for a PBS contribution to the $150,000 cost of a feasibility study. Joint funding of the study, Morrisett had hoped, would go a long way toward dispelling concerns within PBS that this was just a "Markle project." Lawson, for her part, worried that funding the feasibility study at such an early stage, with no knowledge of its eventual findings, might land her in trouble with affiliates.

Lawson did send Morrisett a list of candidates to direct the study. By February, Morrisett had selected Alvin Perlmutter, an old acquaintance, who also happened to be on Lawson's list. A veteran independent public TV producer, Perlmutter's credits included *The Great American Dream Machine*, *Adam Smith's Money World*, and, most recently, the Markle-funded series *The Public*

Mind. Well known and respected by both PBS and Markle's staff, he seemed the perfect go-between.

Perlmutter understood the delicacy of his job. He was being paid by Markle, on the one hand, to come up with a project that met the foundation's broad aims for improving election coverage. At the same time, Perlmutter's recommendations would stand a chance at PBS only if they were seen as emanating from public broadcasting itself. Through the winter of 1990, Perlmutter and his staff interviewed more than one hundred PBS producers and program heads, in addition to such PBS stars as Roger Mudd and Judy Woodruff, for their suggestions. As Perlmutter told the author, no one at Markle ever had editorial input in his final report: "I saw our role as seeking out thoughts from public television people about how public television might better inform people during the election. All the ideas came at some point from someone in the system, not ourselves."[43]

Perlmutter's report in May 1990 proposed creation of The Voters' Channel. Its key features included free airtime for candidates up to fifteen minutes per block, profiles of candidates, "voice of the people" programming that allowed citizens an electronic forum to talk to each other and to the candidates about critical issues, instant analysis and critique of paid and free campaign pronouncements, and regular in-depth programs about policy options and critical issues, whether or not the candidates themselves raised them.

The report assumed commitments of $5 million from Markle and $3 million from PBS and the Corporation for Public Broadcasting. It also argued, however, that it would take at least $12 million to provide enough original programming and ensure big enough audiences through promotion and advertising to make PBS a genuine "network of record" in the political arena. Markle would have to raise an additional $4 million to $10 million from other foundation and corporate backers. For that, Morrisett would need the unequivocal public backing of PBS's leadership.

That backing never took place. Despite Perlmutter's efforts, Christensen and Lawson remained noncommittal. "Bruce was very specific that he was concerned that we might come up with something that might light a fire with the stations, and he didn't want to have to put it out," Perlmutter said.[44]

An important deadline now loomed. Morrisett had expected that the project would receive PBS's official blessings in June at the system's annual meeting in Dallas. With that gathering just weeks away and with no endorsement for the election plans from Christensen or Lawson, an increasingly concerned Edith Bjornson decided to send Perlmutter's report to a few interested newspaper columnists. *Washington Post* political analyst David Broder wrote a glowing piece on the PBS–Markle project on June 17, just as the five-day Dallas convention was getting started.

"My attitude," Bjornson said, "was that they [PBS] were unilaterally withholding from us the kind of support that they said they would offer. They were losing the opportunity to present this from the platform as something that PBS wanted their stations to do. And I had the notion that because this was a great idea, if you could get Broder to write about it, it might strengthen the courage of PBS to do what was clearly in their best interests."[45]

Far from blessing the Markle venture, the PBS annual meeting was a fiasco. To Morrisett's and Bjornson's chagrin, Lawson had not distributed Perlmutter's report to attendees in advance as Markle's staff had requested. As a result, many local station heads and PBS news producers who had not dealt directly with Perlmutter during the course of his research were in the dark about his election proposals. Morrisett was also dismayed that the project, certainly the biggest new idea on PBS's political horizon, was never mentioned at the meeting's general sessions. Instead, discussion of the proposal was consigned to two small afternoon "breakout sessions" conducted by Perlmutter, with Morrisett as a participating panelist.

For Perlmutter, Dallas was also a letdown. "The contacts I had had with the stations had been very positive," he said. "What I expected in Dallas was some flack, some reservations from people like the programmers at McNeil/Lehrer, Front Line, and anybody who had a regular program who might justifiably feel they could do the same thing we were going to do. But I, too, went there feeling that we had a terrific product, and one of the reasons I felt so good about it was that it had been so well-received in so many quarters, like the David Broder column."[46]

On PBS's side, the presence of Morrisett and Perlmutter on a panel at its annual meeting and the decision to release the feasibility study to the press in advance of a final agreement seemed presumptuous and, in Lawson's mind, "raised issues of editorial control." Even the proposed name for the project, "The Voter's Channel," sounded like an encroachment and set off further alarms. "Calling it 'The Voters Channel' implied a commitment of time that we couldn't make. I was not in a position to commit to that on behalf of our 340 stations," Lawson said.[47]

In short, it now seemed to Christensen and Lawson that Morrisett was behaving more like an executive producer than a prospective underwriter. Compounding the difficulties, there was also considerable jealousy of Perlmutter within PBS.[48] Regardless of how well known he was at PBS, he was still an "indie"—an outside producer telling PBS's own programmers how to use their airtime. What was happening in Dallas was the old PBS story, Chamberlin told the author years later. The project was "not invented here" and therefore not to be trusted.[49]

Markle spent the balance of 1990 repairing the damage done at Dallas. At a lunch in Washington with Lawson, Bjornson told her how "taken aback" she and Morrisett had been with their reception: "Nine months of work had led us to expect to come away from that meeting with a commitment from PBS," she said. Markle staff had contacted Christensen and Lawson no less than nineteen times to keep them abreast of the progress of the feasibility study. How, she demanded, could Markle and Perlmutter have been treated at Dallas "as if no one had ever heard of us and as if we were just another supplicant with a program idea, since that was so evidently not the case?"[50]

"Our reaction to the whole [Dallas] meeting," Morrisett told the author, "was that we had gotten no real support from PBS at a crucial point. We still thought it was workable. We certainly talked to Bruce and Jennifer about what was a lack of support, and Jennifer said that this was her first attempt to talk about new programming directions, and while this was a good idea, it was a special case and didn't fit in. But they still wanted to go ahead."[51]

In the wake of the Dallas convention, Markle also halted its fund-raising because any approaches to foundations would have been futile and potentially embarrassing without PBS's unequivocal backing. In a lengthy letter to Christensen in September, Morrisett vented his frustration that The Voters' Channel was still being viewed by some within PBS as a "Markle project." "From the beginning," he wrote, "we emphasized our belief in strong, independent creative control and did not suggest participation by us in a governing body. At every stage of our exploration and the feasibility study PBS and public broadcasting have been fully involved . . . as partners in a common cause." He pointedly reminded Christensen that he was not about to simply hand PBS $5 million to spend as it wished: ". . . the Foundation is vitally concerned about its objective of seeing television better used in our electoral process. We will not compromise that objective and will test any proposed plan against it. . . ."

Signs of a thaw began to appear later that month. Lawson assured Morrisett in a telephone conversation that the project was "at the top of her priority list," and that she and her staff remained enthusiastic about it. By December, the title of the venture had been changed from the troublesome "The Voters' Channel" to the more neutral, homegrown "PBS Election Project." More important, on December 5, PBS and the Corporation for Public Broadcasting (CPB) issued a press release announcing that Perlmutter had been appointed to direct the 1992 public television election project. "We want to present the 1992 elections in a way that encourages viewers to get involved," said Donald Marbury, director of the corporation's Television Program Fund, in the press announcement.

That was the closest PBS would ever come to the clear public support that Markle so badly wanted. With Perlmutter now in place as the project's leader, Morrisett resumed his fund-raising activities. PBS, for its part, finally went beyond mere pledges of financial support. During the next six months, PBS and CPB contributed $254,417 toward this second development phase.[52]

In the spring of 1991, with planning time running short before the start of the campaign season, the project suffered fresh setbacks. The first was the continued resistance by PBS to make firm commitments of airtime for special programming. At a meeting in Perlmutter's New York office in March, Lawson dropped the bombshell that no prime-time slots were available for such programming in September or October 1992. In effect, PBS's chief programmer was telling Perlmutter that he was wasting his time.

"I called up Lloyd, went over to Rockefeller Plaza and I said we ought to reconsider the whole thing, the $5 million."[53]

The second blow came when PBS abruptly dismissed its advertising agency, Young & Rubicam—ordinarily an in-house matter. In this case, however, the result was the dismantling of a crucial element of the promotion and audience-building plan that Morrisett had been piecing together. All along, it was clear to Morrisett, and to PBS as well, that any hopes of making public television the "network of record" for elections depended on boosting its viewership, which was a fraction of that at the commercial networks. Perlmutter's plan had calculated that at least $4 million, over and above the $8 million already pledged by Markle and PBS, would be needed for promotion and advertising. Any hope of raising the money depended on convincing prospective corporate and foundation donors that a credible promotion and advertising plan was in place. For that, Morrisett had been relying heavily on his friend Alex Kroll, chief executive of Young & Rubicam. Kroll had agreed to drum up pro bono support for the PBS election project among his Madison Avenue colleagues.

"Lo and behold," Morrisett said, "in the spring of 1991, we learned that PBS was putting their advertising agency [Young & Rubicam] up for review. I asked Bruce [Christensen], have you considered waiting to do this until we get the project together? Well, either the person who was in charge of advertising wasn't communicating with the program side, or I don't know what happened. But Alex [Kroll] told me that if something went wrong with his relationship with PBS, he obviously couldn't continue [with the election project]. The next thing I learn, they decide to go with another agency, and Alex has to pull out. They didn't talk to us at all about this. To say that I was horrified is putting it mildly. It was unbelievable."[54]

"What put the quietus on the project was when PBS fired Alex Kroll," Bjornson said. "That got through to Lloyd in ways that other behaviors had not."[55]

On May 7, Morrisett fired off a letter to Christensen and Lawson, in which he called the abrupt loss of Kroll a serious and potentially fatal blow to the project. "If we expect to raise funds from other foundations, I believe we must be able to justify our ability to mount an effective promotion and advertising campaign, and at the moment, without Alex Kroll's involvement, I do not see how to do so."[56]

Christensen and Lawson, in a written reply a week later, blamed the affair on poor communications on both sides. If Morrisett was unaware that Kroll was out, they pointed out, Morrisett had never directly told them that he had been dealing with Kroll on the election project. "Had we each been more aware of what the others were doing, we could have avoided this problem," they wrote.[57]

By now, positions were hardening again. Morrisett repeated that the project would become interesting and powerful only at $12 million or more. Either a way had to be found quickly to raise more money, or, Morrisett said, "I think we ought to agree to stop." Christensen replied that the total of $8 million in hand from Markle and PBS was already four times more than PBS had in the previous election—certainly enough, therefore, to justify continuing with the project: "If our coverage in 1992 can be four times better than in 1988, we will have made remarkable progress."

By early June, Morrisett's hopes for a collaboration that would advance his original aims had evaporated. Markle's fund-raising effort had reaped only one offer of $500,000 from the Carnegie Corporation, and Morrisett was told that even Carnegie was "dismayed about the delays and difficulties of working with PBS."[58] Perlmutter still had no support to develop a cohesive set of programs. There was still no commitment of airtime. The $8 million in hand was not enough to allow for the original programming before Labor Day, free airtime for candidates or voter feedback—the distinctive features on which Perlmutter thought everyone had agreed in principle.

Over lunch on June 20, Morrisett told Christensen that the project was over. Christensen recalled:

> Lloyd expressed his deep regret at not being able to get this project to happen. He expressed his displeasure at how we had handled it. He thought we hadn't done it justice, he made that clear, and he informed us that the money would not be available.
>
> Obviously we were sorry. It wasn't so much that PBS was reticent about the project as it was not being able to come to grips with the real parameters of the project. Markle wanted to have a

> separate identity for The Voters' Channel, and they had specific requirements where stations had to commit airtime, and we weren't in a position to make those kinds of things happen. So the further we got into it, the more I got the feeling from Lloyd that "you have to be on board, we have the answers, and this is the way it has to be." He had a particular vision and outcome hoped for, but the approach never really came together as the kind of thing public television could support.[59]

What PBS's leaders evidently saw, then, was a well-intentioned foundation that had overstepped the customary bounds of program underwriting. In the wake of its divorce with Markle, PBS announced scaled-back election plans with the $3 million that it had committed. It eventually teamed up with NBC News to cover the major party conventions in the summer of 1992.

Morrisett, for his part, felt that PBS had once again demonstrated its disorganization and intransigence. It had spurned a historic opportunity to become the "New Main Street" for political discourse and election coverage. The breakdown of the PBS–Markle project was the last serious effort at collaboration between the foundation and public broadcasting under Morrisett. Once again, the natural allure between PBS and Markle might have been powerful, but it was not enough to produce a satisfying or lasting union.

PARTNERSHIP ON THE REBOUND: MARKLE AND CNN

By June 1991, as late as that was in the election calendar, the story was not over for Morrisett. He had received too much support from politicians and friends in the broadcast world to allow his ideas on reforming election coverage to die. The failed partnership with PBS had cost Markle some $600,000. That still left as much as $4 million in foundation funds to improve television election coverage in 1992 if Markle could quickly find a suitable and willing new partner. On July 1, Morrisett mailed a five-page letter, with a blow-by-blow account of the PBS project's demise, to about one hundred leaders in the broadcast, foundation, and policy fields. The letter also made clear that he was very much in the market for a new partner—including in commercial or cable broadcasting.

One recipient of Morrisett's letter was former President Jimmy Carter. Carter was a longtime friend of Tom Johnson, president of Cable News Network (CNN), as was Markle's board chairman, Joel Fleishman. Both Carter and Fleishman urged Johnson to consider a rebound marriage between Markle and CNN.

In fact, tentative talks between CNN and Markle had quietly begun weeks before the final split with PBS. Shortly after PBS had fired Kroll, Bjornson had put out feelers to Tom Hannon, political director of CNN, to gauge his interest in a deal in the increasingly likely event that the PBS venture collapsed. As Bjornson wrote in a subsequent memorandum that June to Morrisett, CNN seemed to be the best potential partner among commercial broadcasters:

> CNN sees its role as going well beyond just "campaign coverage." They feel that issues, qualifications and so on are part of their responsibility . . . and they reject the "apparent anti-politics stance of other broadcasters. They are particularly interested in involving voters directly. CNN is also most often cited for its work in '88 and came closer to being a "voters' channel" than any other broadcaster in that period. They are also looking for a way to recapture the audiences they enjoyed during the Gulf War, so many of the arguments that seemed so right for PBS are applicable to a degree for them, too.

In July, Morrisett met Hannon at an out-of-the way Afghani restaurant in Washington that was so quiet it had an almost clandestine feel. Those first talks went so well that Hannon urged Johnson to fly to New York for a meeting at the foundation to see if an agreement could be reached. Both sides realized that either the deal was there or it was not. At this late date in the election cycle, there was no time for haggling.

At their meeting in Rockefeller Plaza on Labor Day, Johnson, Hannon, and CNN-News vice president Ed Turner found themselves agreeing with Markle's broad aims. As with the abortive PBS venture, Markle would help CNN become "The Election Channel"—the place on the TV dial where citizens might turn in unison to become educated about critical issues, watch the campaign unfold, and, to the extent technically possible, participate in the campaign itself. Markle would contribute $3.5 million to CNN's existing $13.5 million election budget.

Under the agreement, CNN would retain total editorial control of its programming but would use Markle's funds to offer shows on issues and candidates that went beyond usual journalism to serious political education. It also promised Markle that it would experiment with interactive programming by using survey research, live 800 call-in numbers, and other means to promote more direct audience participation.

Markle's role, meanwhile, would be primarily consultative. The foundation would hold forums for CNN producers to learn more about how interactive technologies might involve voters in election coverage. It would introduce CNN to organizations like Public Agenda Foundation and the Council on Foreign Relations to help network producers select the best issues and topics for election programming. Beyond that, Markle assured CNN that it would not intrude in editorial content.

"From the beginning," Hannon said, "one of the things that really was crucial in our coming together was Markle's reputation of leaving folks alone once they gave them their grants. That was their MO [modus operandi], as we understood it, and that was what they indicated they would do with us."[60]

On October 14, Markle and CNN issued a press release announcing the unusual public service collaboration between a commercial cable broadcaster and a nonprofit foundation. "It was like night and day working with CNN and working with PBS," Morrisett said. "They said they were interested, we spent about an hour and a half talking about the range of possibilities, and they said, let's go back and make a decision. Within six weeks we had agreed. There were essentially no issues that couldn't be resolved quickly. And these were people who could make decisions. That was the key."[61]

The alacrity of the agreement, however, was not just a product of superior leadership at CNN. The CNN-Markle deal was inherently far easier to make than the PBS deal had been, not only because CNN came to the table with certain built-in advantages over PBS but because Markle, if it wanted a deal at this late date, was in no position to take the tough line with CNN that it had taken with public broadcasting.

At PBS, Christensen and Lawson would have had to make yeoman efforts to override the concerns and jealousies of local station heads. CNN's Johnson had no such warring factions to worry about when he shook Morrisett's hand. With PBS, Morrisett had to raise additional millions for promotion to boost public TV's audience. CNN's audience for election coverage was already approaching that of the three commercial networks.

At PBS, Markle's proposed name, "Voter's Channel," had become an emotional issue. With CNN, Markle was content to allow the programming that it was funding to come under the network's existing blanket label for election coverage in 1992: "Democracy in America." At PBS, Markle felt justified in pressing hard for free airtime for candidates. With CNN, it conceded that such a request was unrealistic. As Bjornson explained: "Ted Turner always said, and it's hard to refute, 'Time is what I sell. I don't give it away.' PBS doesn't sell its airtime, so it was entirely appropriate, we felt, for one of their innovations to be, let the candidate speak in his own voice in free time. PBS owns its own time in a way that a commercial broadcaster doesn't."[62]

If the timing, circumstances, and personalities made for smoother sailing for Markle and CNN, there were still complications related to the decision by Markle, as a tax-exempt foundation, to provide funds to a commercial broadcaster. There was at least one precedent. Between 1951 and 1956, before public television offered more clear-cut outlets for foundation assistance, the Ford Foundation had provided $3 million for CBS's Sunday afternoon program *Omnibus* with Alistair Cooke.[63] With that exception, however, Markle's plans with CNN were breaking new and, to some critics, controversial philanthropic ground. Given the probability that the collaboration would attract not only the attention of the press but also that of other foundations and, quite possibly, the Internal Revenue Service, Markle needed legal and financial safeguards to ensure that it did not end up on the wrong side of either tax laws or public opinion.

Markle addressed those concerns by assuming "expenditure responsibility" for the venture. The foundation required CNN to set up a separate account for Markle's funds and provide frequent reports on how the money was being spent. Markle also received tapes of all programs aired under its banner so that if ever questioned, the foundation could establish their propriety under IRS guidelines. Markle's funds could not be used for partisan programming that advanced either a candidate or a cause. Even though the foundation's officers had vowed not to meddle in editorial matters, they still had to assure themselves—and the IRS, if necessary— that Markle's funds were being used only for programs that advanced its philanthropic mission. CNN, for its part, could enhance its programming with Markle's grant, but it could not realize a profit from it. In short, the project had to operate, in every sense, as a public service by CNN.

At least one unforeseen complication cropped up. To play it safe with the IRS, Markle had asked CNN to limit commercials to "adjacencies" appearing at the beginning or end of any foundation-supported programming, with no commercials in the interior. This angered CNN's advertising sales staff because, under that arrangement, they were forced to sacrifice prime-time advertising commissions during an election year in which commercial time could be expected to sell at a premium.

Despite the complications, both sides seemed pleased with the hastily arranged collaboration. Markle's funds helped CNN produce ten hours of specials on the issues and the candidates. They included a four-hour series on the economy called "Promises, Promises" and six consecutive weeks of hour-long Sunday specials in September and October with close-ups of the economy, campaign finance, race relations, and profiles of presidential candidates Clinton and Bush and the vice presidential candidates. CNN's feature on race won an Emmy, and the network's Special Assignments Unit, under Pamela Hill, received the Joan Shorenstein Barone prize for its election coverage. Markle's money also supported regular segments by correspondent Brooks Jackson called "Ad Police" that analyzed political advertising.

CNN also had been willing to experiment boldly with interactive television. A program called "The Voters' Voice" allowed several hundred viewers to use their push-button phones to react instantly to the remarks by candidates Bush, Clinton, and Perot during their final televised debate in October. The result, a half-hour special offered a few days later on October 20, gave fascinating graphic proof that voters respond most positively when candidates explain their positions on issues of public concern and most negatively when they attack each other.

Morrisett's three-year roller-coaster adventures with PBS and CNN thus ended on an unexpected note. A commercial network, rather than public television, had proved to be the most willing partner for Markle's experiments in election coverage. As a result, Morrisett had set an unexpected philanthropic precedent that few foundations were in any rush to imitate. One that did was the Robert Wood Johnson Foundation, which granted $3.5 million to underwrite a two-hour, prime-time program on health care reform that NBC aired on June 21, 1994. Nevertheless, the precedent of sending foundation money to commercial networks remained controversial in philanthropic and media circles. "I was not a big supporter of pumping money to CNN, which was a cash machine," Larry Grossman, a former executive with both PBS and NBC, told the author. Bill Kovach, another critic who was then curator of Harvard's Nieman Foundation, said that he was "astonished at the use of foundation money to cover a thing that CNN for its own economic well-being would have had to cover."[64]

To Morrisett, however, the rebound liaison with CNN represented a near-miraculous salvaging of his goals for improving TV election coverage that only weeks earlier had seemed doomed. As the Markle Commission's second election year research survey documented, nearly one third of voters queried (more than at any of the three established networks) said that they obtained most of their political news from CNN in 1992. Another analysis by the Washington-based Center for Media and Public Affairs rated 91 percent of CNN's Democracy in America programming as "substantive"—nearly three times better by that yardstick than ABC, NBC, or CBS. With Markle's support, CNN had come closer than anyone to Morrisett's ideal of an "election channel."

On November 6, 1992, three days after Clinton's victory over Bush, Morrisett sent his praises to CNN's president: "Grafting a special project of this type onto a 24-hour news organization had to be difficult. It is really amazing that so much of such high quality was accomplished."[65]

The 1992 collaboration influenced CNN's coverage during the 1996 campaign and continued to do so again in the year 2000.

"We continue to do the deconstructing of television ads," Hannon told the author. "We have committed to long-form looks at issues and the candidates, apart from what's said on the campaign trail, or the daily scandal or miscues. Those came directly from our project with Markle. Their hope was that they could plant a seed in the commercial world without their continued support. In important ways, that's what they did."[66]

"We did not meet our original goals," Morrisett said after his departure from Markle, "but we demonstrated an unexpected thing: that you can work successfully with a commercial organization in the broadcast industry and accomplish a great deal."[67]

For all of its immediate satisfactions, the Markle-CNN deal was a one-time fling. With PBS, Morrisett had hoped for more: He had wanted to institutionalize television's educational role in politics in a way that public broadcasting seemed uniquely suited for but that seemed almost impossible to sustain with a commercial broadcaster. "You could do interesting things with CNN and they were certainly easy to work with. I give them highest marks on that. But there was no way to see how it could be continually fundable," Morrisett said.[68]

The adventures with PBS and CNN between 1989 and 1992 had also stretched Markle's human and financial resources to the limit. Whatever they had accomplished, Markle's staff did not relish repeating the experience. Besides, by 1996, Markle was becoming fixed on a newer, far less expensive way of reaching and reengaging voters than television—the Internet.

PLAYING POLITICS: COMPUTER SIMULATION GAMES

Morrisett's concentration on television in 1992 had been based on the assumption that TV was, and would remain, the most important mass medium for political education and involvement. By the mid-1990s, TV's hegemony was facing a new high-tech challenger. With the emergence of the Internet and the burgeoning popularity of home computers, Morrisett decided during his final years as Markle's president that it was time to explore these new technologies. First and foremost, he wanted to determine if they might accomplish, at far less cost, some of the goals for political education and participation that he had hoped to achieve with television.

The challenge, as he saw it, harked back to the one that led him to co-found Children's Television Workshop thirty years earlier. Might these new information media be used to educate about politics in ways that were entertaining as well? Beginning in 1995, Markle provided funding to develop several computer simulation games that dealt with critical public policy issues. "Playing politics," Morrisett thought, might be a way to entice the public into thinking more seriously about such matters as the federal budget or health care. In key respects, the games might even prove to be superior to television in meeting his goals for political education.

"One of the most difficult things to do in television and radio is fully explain complex ideas, detailing the ways various factors interact with each other so that there are no simple solutions," Morrisett said at the time. "With computer simulation, you can do that very well. People can try things out and see circumstances and consequences they may not have thought of."

The electronic game market also experienced spectacular growth during the 1990s. By 1997, some 33 million U.S. households had video games, and retail sales reached $5.5 billion, a 51 percent gain over the previous year, according to industry estimates.[69] Computer games also surged in popularity; some 19 million units were sold during the first half of 1997, a 40 percent increase over the previous year.[70] The time seemed right for Markle to test whether that thriving market, flooded with fun but frivolous offerings such as "Diddy Kong Racing," "NFL Quarterback Club," and "Myst," also might have room for some of Morrisett's educational and civic goals.

In 1993, at the height of the congressional health care debates in Washington, Markle provided $350,000 to Maxis Business Simulations, a Monterey, California, computer game producer, to develop a simulation game challenging players to plan their own nationwide health care system. Maxis had already produced several policy simulation games, including the top-selling "SimCity" that invited players to pretend they were city mayors and balance policy and spending options with various consequences.

With "SimHealth," each player began by being hit by a car, recovering, and then running for political office with the goal of reforming health care based on his or her personal values and experiences. To win, players had to think about ways to balance the cost of health goals with other competing government priorities. Granting universal health insurance might, for example, lead to tax hikes, bloated deficits, or crumbling schools. Success in balancing those concerns would make the player's job rating go up.

Launched at a press conference on Capitol Hill in November 1993, "SimHealth" attracted coverage in *The Washington Post*, *USA Today*, *The New York Times*, and elsewhere. Reviewers praised the game's technical quality and thoroughness in exposing players to the intricacies of health care policy, but they also pointed out that it was hardly light entertainment. Retailing at $29.95, it sold only a few thousand copies. As Markle's Cathy Clark later put it, "SimHealth" impressively met the foundation's goal of building an educational and responsible policy simulation game, but it was too serious to permeate the consumer marketplace. "Basically," Clark said, "it was not entertaining enough to be on the game shelf."[71]

"SimHealth" had been a stand-alone, boxed CD game. Markle now turned its attention to on-line policy games, which blended Morrisett's objective of political education with his eagerness to explore the Internet as a possible platform for fulfilling social goals. Beginning in 1995, the foundation provided more than $1.5 million to Crossover Technologies, a successful designer of on-line games, to develop several multiplayer policy games.

The first, "Reinventing America," invited players to join a six-month on-line interactive forum from November 1995 to May 1996. The game involved information gathering and weekly debates on critical issues and federal programs. The object was to decide, collectively, how much money should be budgeted for those priorities. The on-line conversations in December included, for example, immigration, federal employee benefits, medical research, and the National Service Program. It also brought in big-name experts to join this cybertalk. Among them were New York Governor Mario Cuomo, political scientist Norman Ornstein, American Civil Liberties Union president Nadine Strossen, Voice of America director Geoffrey Cowan, Martha Phillips of the Concord Coalition, and Pete Peterson of the

Blackstone Group. Players also could consult computer links to information sources all over the World Wide Web to find out more about the issues as they debated them.

Judging from the voting at the end of the twenty-six–week game, the "netizens" who participated were a fairly radical group of budget slashers but with a strong libertarian streak. The majority voted to privatize Voice of America, slash the military, welfare, Medicaid, and other poverty programs, end farm subsidies, abolish the U.S. Information Agency, cut Peace Corps funding by a third and aid to Egypt and Israel by half, eliminate most spending on the arts and public broadcasting, and gradually replace Social Security with private retirement accounts. At the same time, the majority favored more spending on scientific research and the environment and also advocated legalizing all drugs.

In July 1996, the results were submitted to Congress as Senate Bill 776, dubbed the Reinventing America Act of 1996, and a repeat of the budget game was launched on the Web as "Reinventing America II." This time, the debates included a number of hot political and social topics not dealt with in the first game, such as campaign finance reform, abortion, and gun control.

That same month, Crossover Technologies offered net-gazers a chance to play political campaign manager with a new Markle-funded game, "President '96." Available on both the World Wide Web and America On Line, the game invited players to shape the policy positions of one of ten fictional candidates, each bearing striking resemblances to the real 1996 cast that included Clinton, Dole, Perot, Pat Buchanan, New Jersey Governor Christine Todd Whitman, and General Colin Powell. Each simulated candidate had a home page with audio and video displays of his or her speeches. Players could have live chats with the fictional candidates and participate in mock opinion polls. The point, however, was not simply to set up a mock horse race but to use the fictional candidates as vehicles for serious thinking and discussion about policy issues. More than twenty thousand people played part or all of the game.

In the end, a majority of players elected fictional Democrat Vice President "Ben Hamilton," whose positions were patterned after the real Al Gore, to the presidency in 1996.

Markle's explorations of simulation games as tools of mass political education during the mid-1990s were a final demonstration of Morrisett's adventurousness in his chosen field of communications. By his own reckoning, "SimHealth," "Reinventing America," and "President '96" left mostly unanswered questions. Could a balance really be struck in computer simulation games between entertainment and measurable educational goals, as had been accomplished so effectively with *Sesame Street*? Are there commercial software designers able and committed enough to achieve that balance in the realm of political education and participation? Or, perhaps, would a new organization resembling Children's Television Workshop have to be established to create the kind of educational, entertaining software that Morrisett had in mind?

Evan Schwartz, a veteran writer and observer of the software industry who followed the foundation's projects as they unfolded, told the author that the problems encountered by Markle with "President '96" and "Reinventing America" almost certainly ran deeper than solving technical flaws. Unlike *Sesame Street*, Markle's games involved not just "fun learning" but a level of selflessness and high-mindedness about the public good from its adult players that placed those games leagues apart from any others on the Internet. "It was very difficult to sell," Schwartz said. "People who are interested in using the Internet are usually doing it to espouse their own views. These games called on people to cooperate and compromise. It wasn't necessarily fun to collaborate on a new health plan or budget."[72]

Still, the political games funded by Markle had raised intriguing possibilities. Whether or not the Internet ever rivals television as a venue for political education, it eventually might be shown to foster deliberative thinking and group discourse about politics and policy issues in ways that TV, so far, has not. In 1995, Markle Fellow Bruce Murray of UCLA began to delve into how Internet "hyperforums" featuring activity hubs, message centers, and supporting libraries of information might be created to promote high-quality discussion about complex policy matters like the environment.

Regardless of the medium, the core challenge of Morrisett's explorations of politics and the media remained consistent throughout his presidency—to create safe spaces, new electronic Main Streets, where people can gather, spend time, argue, learn, and make wiser and more deliberative public policy choices together.

NOTES

1. E. J. Dionne, Jr., "Race Reflects Voter Concern with Image over Substance," *The New York Times*, 18 Sept. 1988, 1.

2. Norman J. Ornstein, "The Height Report," *The New York Times*, op-ed column, 15 May 1988, sec. IV, 29.

3. John Corry, "Campaigns, Cameras and Beauty Contests," *The New York Times*, 15 May 1988, sect. II, 41.

4. Peter J. Boyer, "2 Networks to Cut Election Coverage," *The New York Times*, 24 Feb. 1988, 18.

5. Lloyd N. Morrisett, "Broadcasting and Political Equity" (President's Essay in "The John and Mary R. Markle Foundation, Annual Report, 1977"), 18–19.

6. Lloyd N. Morrisett, "The Right to Know and the Right to Vote" (President's Essay in "The John and Mary R. Markle Foundation, Annual Report, 1989"), 7.

7. Buchanan, interview, 12 June 1988.

8. Lloyd N. Morrisett, "A New Main Street" (President's Essay in "The John and Mary R. Markle Foundation Annual Report, 1990"), 8.

9. The John and Mary R. Markle Foundation, "Strategic Assessment, Preliminary Foundation Review" (report prepared for the Board of Directors), 11 Mar. 1998, 9.

10. The resulting "Study Group on New Communications Technology, Public Policy, and Democratic Values" was a remarkable assemblage. Chaired by Joseph G. Nye, professor of government and policy at the Kennedy School, the panel included, among others, Daniel Bell, Harvard University; the Honorable Stephen G. Breyer, then a circuit court judge and future Supreme Court justice; Les Brown, *Channels* magazine; Archibald Cox, former Watergate prosecutor and professor of law, Harvard University; Henry Geller; and Roger Mudd, chief political correspondent for NBC.

11. The resulting publication was ECRI, *An Election Administrator's Guide to Computerized Voting Systems*, 2 vols., 1988.

12. Public Agenda Foundation, "Curbing Health Care Costs: The Public's Prescription" (interim report on public attitudes on health care

costs in Des Moines and surrounding Polk County, prepared as part of Health Vote '82), April 1983, 3.

13. Wadsworth, interview, 15 June 1998. Prior to joining Public Agenda, Wadsworth had been a program officer at Markle, 1980–1984.

14. Public Agenda Foundation, "Curbing Health Care Costs," 16.

15. Ibid., 30.

16. The commission, chaired by Robert M. O'Neil, former president, University of Virginia, included James David Barber, professor of political science, Duke University; John C. Culver, former Democratic senator from Iowa; Joan Konner, dean, Columbia School of Journalism; Charles McC. Mathias, former Republican senator from Maryland; Eugene Patterson, former publisher, *St. Petersburg* [Fla.] *Times*; and Eddie Williams, president, Joint Center for Political Studies.

17. Lloyd N. Morrisett, "The Media and Political Education" (concept paper prepared for the Markle board for its June 1988 meeting), 3.

18. Lloyd N. Morrisett, "Mass Communications and Presidential Campaigns: Planning for 1980" (internal planning paper), 31 Mar. 1977, 5.

19. Bruce Buchanan, "The 1988 Markle Commission on the Media & the Electorate: What We Did and Why We Did It" (background paper for Markle Foundation planning meeting), 31 Jan. 1991, 7.

20. Ibid., 4.

21."The Markle Commission on the Media and the Electorate: Status Report for Markle Foundation Board of Directors," 22 Mar. 1989, 1.

22. "The Markle Commission on the Media and the Electorate: Key Findings," May 1990, 8–9.

23. Buchanan, *Electing a President,* 5.

24. "The Markle Commission on the Media and the Electorate: Key Findings," May 1990, Table 4.2, 17.

25. Ibid., 21.

26. Buchanan, *Electing a President*, 95.

27. Jamieson, interview, 16 June 1998.

28. Among its recommendations after the 1988 campaign, the commission had suggested making an agreement to debate four times a condition for public campaign funding; making candidates "pledge to conduct clean campaigns"; instituting "simultaneous poll hours throughout the 50 states by establishing a 20-hour election day"; having Congress direct the FCC to "call upon the networks regularly to offer public service airtime . . . to educate the electorate on the democratic process"; and "establish an 'American Citizens Foundation'—a permanent, non-partisan organization devoted to improving democratic practice in American electoral politics."

29. Buchanan, *Renewing Presidential Politics*, 2.
30. Ibid.
31. In 1992 and 1996, the Center for Media and Public Affairs, Washington, D.C., conducted Markle's media content analysis. In 1996, Princeton Survey Research Associates, Princeton, N.J., conducted the opinion surveys.
32. Markle Foundation Presidential Election Watch, "Networks Yawned, Public Shrugged at Campaign '96" (fifth in a series of "campaign report cards," issued as press release), November 1996, 2.
33. Ibid.
34. Morrisett, interview, 17 June 1998.
35. Jamieson, interview, 16 June 1998.
36. Morrisett, interview, 29 June 1998.
37. Lloyd N. Morrisett, memorandum to Markle Board of Directors in support of funding for a feasibility study of The Voter's Channel, February 1990, 2.
38. Morrisett, interview, 29 June 1998.
39. Grossman, interview, 16 July 1997.
40. Chamberlin, interview, 7 July 1998.
41. Day, *Vanishing Vision*, 1–4.
42. Christensen, interview, 8 July 1998.
43. Perlmutter, interview, 29 June 1998.
44. Ibid.
45. Bjornson, interview, 13 July 1998.
46. Perlmutter, interview, 29 June 1998.
47. Lawson, interview, 2 July 1998.
48. Ibid.; Christensen, interview, 8 July 1998.
49. Chamberlin, interview, 7 July 1998.
50. Edith Bjornson, conversation with Jennifer Lawson, Washington, D.C., 28 Aug. 1990 (written record).
51. Morrisett, interview, 29 June 1998.
52. The author is indebted to Patricia Hunter, Vice President for Programming, Administration, and Public Communications, PBS, for compiling and confirming the PBS–CPB figure.
53. Perlmutter, interview, 29 June 1998.
54. Morrisett, interview, 29 June 1998.
55. Bjornson, interview, 13 July 1998.
56. Lloyd N. Morrisett, letter to Bruce Christensen and Jennifer Lawson, 7 May 1991.
57. Bruce Christensen and Jennifer Lawson, letter to Lloyd N. Morrisett, 13 May 1991.
58. Barbara Finberg, Executive Vice President, Carnegie Corpora-

tion, conversation with Lloyd N. Morrisett, 13 June 1991 (written record).

59. Christensen, interview, 8 July 1998.

60. Hannon, interview, 15 July 1998.

61. Morrisett, interview, 29 June 1998.

62. Bjornson, interview, 13 July 1998.

63. Brown, *New York Times Encyclopedia of Television*, 314.

64. Quoted in Timothy Noah, "CNN Is Positioned to Set the Agenda for the 1992 Presidential Campaign," *The Wall Street Journal*, 5 Feb. 1992.

65. Lloyd N. Morrisett, letter to Tom Johnson, President, Cable News Network, 6 Nov. 1992.

66. Hannon, interview, 15 July 1998.

67. Morrisett, interview, 29 June 1998.

68. Ibid.

69. Kristen Kenedy, "U.S. Video Game Sales Hit $515 Billion," *Computer Retail Week*, 23 Jan. 1998 (article appearing on World Wide Web at http://www.techweb.aol.com/investor/story/INV19980123S0008).

70. "Game Sales on the Rise," *GameSpot Magazine News*, 12 Sept. 1997 (article citing PC Data figures; posted on World Wide Web at http://headline.gamespot.com/9709/12toptwenty/).

71. Clark, interview, 1 July 1998.

72. Schwartz, interview, 22 July 1998.

Epilogue

"So What Do You Do, Give Away Money?"

On April 30, 1997, sixty-four floors above Rockefeller Plaza in the Pegasus Suite of the Rainbow Room, The Markle Foundation's board of directors and about one hundred invited guests dined sumptuously on red snapper and veal and listened to Lloyd Morrisett's final words to the foundation that he was preparing to leave after twenty-eight years. Morrisett had been uncharacteristically emotional as he rehearsed his talk hours earlier with Amy Brisebois, his assistant. That evening, as well, he found himself choking back tears during a half hour of reminiscences about friendships made and intellectual debts—from undergraduate days at his beloved Oberlin through his foundation years at Carnegie and Markle.

Accompanying the evening's sentimental mood, Morrisett raised questions that such valedictories inevitably invite. How did all those efforts add up? How much good did Markle do, and how might that be measured?

Viewed one way, the record suggests that Morrisett's experiences at Markle's helm were marked with more frustration and futility than outright success, particularly when measured against his spectacular early triumph with the Children's Television Workshop and *Sesame Street.* There were, of course, some notable accomplishments. Markle under Morrisett can take considerable credit for the survival of the *Columbia Journalism Review,* for launching Action for Children's Television as an effective and durable national advocate, and for nurturing centers of media and communications research at Harvard University, MIT, Duke University, and the Aspen Institute. SeniorNet, the cornerstone of the foundation's effort to bring the elderly into the computer age, seems on relatively sound footing after a rocky start as an independent nonprofit. Infonautics, Markle's entrepreneurial effort to create an information resource for children and other users on the Internet, faces a similarly optimistic future.

Beyond those endeavors, however, many of Markle's major initiatives to insinuate the values of access, equity, quality, and content into the communications revolution proved less successful. Television Audience Assessment, which was supposed to change the coinage of audience rating to include the quality and impact of programming, produced interesting research but little else. Morrisett's dream of creating new media-based Main Streets, in either television or the newer computer-based media, to engage citizens in more informed political dialogue proved largely futile, given the forces arrayed against its realization. The coming of cable has yet to produce the bonanza of high-quality educational, cultural, and interactive programming that Markle had tried to promote in numerous costly attempts. The foundation searched largely in vain for ways to bring radio into new glory days of excellence and quality. Its initiatives to make journalism more responsive and responsible—notably the National News Council and *Channels* magazine—were ignored or met with contempt by the news industry's powerhouses. And, with the possible exceptions of Infonautics and the as-yet-uncertain future of Markle's "E-mail for All" initiatives, the foundation's efforts to harness the Internet for social, political, and educational ends seem long shots, at best.

Still, such a summary of the Morrisett years seems unfairly reductive. It is hardly the whole story.

Under Morrisett, a respectable but staid foundation was transformed into one that ventured with uncommon courage into uncharted and often forbidding philanthropic waters—how the mass media and communication technologies might be used to revitalize cultural, educational, and civic life. During nearly three decades, Markle provided more than 1,011 grants. Its expenditure of more than $80 million yielded some 1,500 products that included books, periodical articles, audio and video products, TV and radio productions, CDs, and Internet Web sites.

Inevitably, those efforts created only small ripples in a world dominated by profit-driven media titans. Perhaps the very idea of a small foundation trying to be heard through the din of the new media revolution was naive or hubristic from the start. That, too, seems an unduly harsh assessment, ignoring as it does the very real impact that small institutions and even lone individuals have had in effectively raising momentous policy issues against seemingly impossible odds. Perhaps the most important point in considering this history is that the hundreds of projects that Markle undertook constituted a significant force in creating, for the first time, a more informed, morally based national conversation about what mass communications should deliver to the public—over and above the profits gained by its proprietors. Just as Ralph Nader and his "raiders" systematically marshaled irrefutable facts and legal arguments for making safety and air quality equal to speed and style in the automobile industry, The Markle Foundation and its many partners succeeded in introducing the principles of access, equity, quality, and content into national debates about children's television, telecommunications policy, the Internet, and electronic mail. The body of knowledge and experience produced by Markle since 1969 has made it far more difficult for anyone to skirt entirely the questions of education and civic purpose in setting the future course of the Information Age.

Beyond their contributions to the recent history of mass communications, Markle and Morrisett enriched the world of philanthropy itself. The twin challenges of impact and accountability that Markle confronted are both ancient and interlocking. Traditionally, foundations have regarded themselves mainly as purveyors of socially beneficial ideas. Few have habitually accepted the more arduous task of helping grantees to develop the management capacity necessary to ensure the staying power of those ideas. A 1997 *Harvard Business Review* article, "Virtuous Capital: What Foundations Can Learn from Venture Capitalists," noted: "Many social programs begin with high hopes and great promise, only to end up with limited impact and uncertain prospects."[1]

During Morrisett's presidency, the activism and heightened accountability implied by the phrase *social venture capital* became a Markle trademark. It meant investing, rather than just giving grants. Investing, by its nature, demanded a more sustained, energetic, and direct involvement by Markle's staff, not only in conceiving projects but in helping to create durable new institutions capable of sustaining social and educational goals over the long haul—much as a traditional venture capitalist would do to protect his or her investment.

Morrisett's entrepreneurship stands in baffling contrast, however, to his reticence to make his own voice more publicly heard. He stood out in the nonprofit world with his eagerness to subject his social goals to the crucible of the commercial marketplace. He grasped more thoroughly than many in philanthropy that true victory for social and educational ideas lay not so much in acceptance by academia, or even by Washington, but by the world of commerce. And, in common with many foundation leaders, Morrisett saw his task as "shaping debates." Nonetheless, his unwillingness or inability to use the bully pulpit of a foundation presidency more often or more effectively to capture the attention of the public seems curious for a small foundation attempting to be a player in an arena dominated by the most amplified corporate voices in America. It is tragic, in a way, that much of the brilliance of Morrisett's thinking about the communication age is tucked away in essays in Markle's annual reports.

Still, in the end, Markle's thirty-year quest for excellence, equity, and education in mass communications ought not to be reduced to a litany of hits and misses. It is especially difficult for foundations, particularly those with limited staffs and money, to be fully successful in developing innovative social ideas as well as creating from scratch durable, well-managed organizations to keep those ideas alive. The brief existences of *Channels* magazine, Television Audience Assessment, and Multimedia Corporation attest to those challenges. More significant than short-term results was Markle's willingness to cultivate a more demanding form of philanthropy that combined social ideals with sound management. The long-term triumph of the Children's Television Workshop demonstrated, that one magical time, that "social venture capitalism" can produce spectacular results despite the long odds.

In his final presidential essay, "Philanthropy and Venture Capital," published in the 1997 annual report, Morrisett offered his own thoughts on how to assess the social value of Markle's endeavors:

> In September of 1969, when I became President of the Markle Foundation, I began to hear questions from friends and acquain-

> tances such as: "Okay, so you are a foundation president. What do you do, give away money?" Since I did not really believe that "giving away money" was what we were about, I struggled with my annoyance at the questions and even more at not having a ready answer. . . .
>
> The nagging question, "so what do you do . . . ," led to many frustrating conversations and blank looks until I hit upon a useful metaphor that silenced most questions. I said that we were most like a venture capital company, but that instead of financial profit we measured ourselves by "social benefit."[2]

"The years since 1969," Morrisett wrote, "have been a voyage of discovery to see if the metaphor, 'venture capital for social benefit' really is the best description of what the Markle Foundation has been trying to do."[3]

In June 1997, the board selected Zoë Baird to succeed Morrisett as Markle's president. A forty-four-year-old corporate lawyer who had held senior posts at General Electric Company and Aetna, Inc., Baird had a brief brush with national prominence in 1993 when President Clinton unsuccessfully nominated her for U.S. Attorney General. Her prior career included legal work involving the media and entertainment fields. As a member of the President's Foreign Intelligence Advisory Board, she became an expert in the globalization of crime in the technology age. Unlike Markle's wholesale shift from medicine to media under Morrisett, there would be no overnight switches in mission under Baird. The board decided at a retreat in 1994 that communications would remain the foundation's focus.

Still, by July 1999, just a year into her presidency, Baird was demonstrating that she might be every bit the risk taker that Morrisett had been. She was also demonstrating none of the publicity shyness of her predecessor. In a ten-page public letter, "Markle Foundation: Improving Life in the Information Age," Baird wrote, and *The New York Times* prominently reported, that Markle was about to spend $100 million—a sum equivalent to more than half its $187 million endowment, and more than twice the $10 million a year it had been spending during the late 1990s—in just three to five years in a gamble to make a real impact in the Internet-driven media revolution. Henceforth, the priorities for foundation spending, Baird wrote, would be public engagement, children, health care, and communications policy.[4]

What will come of that spending spree is difficult to predict. With luck, it may produce enough tangible successes to create heightened awareness of Markle as a force for the public good in this era of new media. If the stock market remains exceptionally kind, the foundation's endowment may also hold steady despite the stepped-up spending.

As for Morrisett, he moved north a dozen city blocks in the winter of 1998 to more spartan quarters at the Children's Television Workshop where he continues, as he has since 1970, as board chairman. The social venture capitalist had settled under the roof of his first and most successful foundation offspring.

NOTES

1. Christine W. Letts, William Ryan, and Allen Grossman, "Virtuous Capital: What Foundations Can Learn from Venture Capitalists," *Harvard Business Review*, March–April 1997 (reprint 97207), 2.
2. Lloyd N. Morrisett, "Philanthropy and Venture Capital" (President's Essay in "The John and Mary R. Markle Foundation, Annual Report, 1996–1997"), 5.
3. Ibid.
4. Zoë Baird, "Markle Foundation: Improving Life in the Information Age," July 1999, 6.

BIBLIOGRAPHY

BOOKS AND DOCUMENTS

Except as noted, all correspondence, memoranda, internal documents and reports of the Markle Foundation and personal memorabilia of Lloyd N. Morrisett cited in this history are from The Markle Foundation Archive Collection at Rockefeller Archive Center, Sleepy Hollow, New York (cited in Notes as Markle Archive Collection). The Markle archives are not open to the public without permission from the foundation. The author is grateful to Morrisett for allowing him unlimited access to these files throughout his research.

Anderson, Robert H., Tora K. Bikson, Sally Ann Law, Bridger M. Mitchell, Christopher Kedzie et al. *Universal Access to E-Mail: Feasibility and Societal Implications*. Santa Monica: RAND Corporation, 1995.

Bagdikian, Ben H. *The Media Monopoly*. 5th ed. Boston: Beacon Press, 1997.

Baker, William F., and George Dessart. *Down the Tube: An Inside Account of the Failure of American Television*. New York: Basic Books, 1998.

Barwise, Patrick, and Andrew Ehrenberg. *Television and Its Audience*. London: Sage Publications, 1988.

Brogan, Patrick, *Spiked: The Short Life and Death of the National News Council* (Twentieth Century Fund Paper). New York: Priority Press Publications, 1985.

Brown, Les. *The New York Times Encyclopedia of Television*. New York: Times Books, 1977.

Browne, Donald R., Charles M. Firestone, and Ellen Mickiewicz. *Television/Radio News & Minorities*. Queenstown, Md.: Aspen Institute, in association with Carter Center of Emory University, 1994.

Buchanan, Bruce. *Electing a President: The Markle Commission Research on Campaign '88*. Austin: University of Texas Press, 1991.

Buchanan, Bruce. *Renewing Presidential Politics: Campaigns, Media, and the Public Interest*. Lanham, Md.: Rowman & Littlefield Publishers, Inc., 1996.

Carnegie Commission on Educational Television. *Public Television: A Program for Action*. New York: Bantam Books, 1967.

Carnegie Corporation Project. Transcript, New York: Oral History Research Office, Columbia University, 1967.

Castle, Alfred L. *Evaluation Essentials for Small Private Foundations*. Washington, D.C.: Council on Foundations, 1991.

Cook, Timothy E. *Governing with the News: The News Media as a Political Institution*. Chicago: University of Chicago Press, 1997.

Davidson, Robert, ed. "Children's Television Workshop: The Early Years." Oral history privately published by Children's Television Workshop to mark its 25th anniversary, 1993.

Day, James. *The Vanishing Vision: The Inside Story of Public Television*. Berkeley: University of California Press, 1995.

Dennis, Everette E., Donald M. Gillmor, and Theodore L. Glasser. *Media Freedom and Accountability*. Westport, Conn.: Greenwood Press, 1989.

Diamond, Edwin. *Behind The Times: Inside the New New York Times*. Chicago: University of Chicago Press, 1995.

Dominick, Joseph R., Barry L. Sherman, and Gary Copeland. *Broadcasting Cable and Beyond: An Introduction to Modern Electronic Media*, 2nd ed. New York: McGraw-Hill, 1993.

Foundations, Private Giving and Public Policy: Report and Recommendations of the Commission on Foundations and Private Philanthropy. Chicago: University of Chicago Press, 1970.

Gillespie, Gilbert. *Public Access Cable Television in the United States and Canada*. New York: Praeger Publishers, 1975.

Grant, William. *Cable Television*. Reston, Va.: Reston Publishing Company, 1983.

Gray, Sandra Trice, ed. *A Vision of Evaluation: A Report of Learnings from Independent Sector's Work on Evaluation*. Washington, D.C.: Independent Sector, 1993.

Horowitz, David, and Lawrence Jarvik, eds. *Public Broadcasting & the Public Trust*. Los Angeles: Center for the Study of Popular Culture, Second Thoughts Books, 1995.

Hyman, Sidney. *The Aspen Idea.* Norman: University of Oklahoma Press, 1975.

Johnstone, John W. C., Edward J. Slawski, and William W. Bowman. *The News People: A Sociological Portrait of American Journalists and Their Work.* Champaign: University of Illinois Press, 1976.

Kisseloff, Jeff. *The Box: An Oral History of Television, 1920–1961.* New York: Viking Press, 1995.

Lagemann, Ellen C. *The Politics of Knowledge: The Carnegie Corporation, Philanthropy, and Public Policy.* Chicago: University of Chicago Press, 1989.

Lesser, Gerald S. *Children and Television: Lessons from Sesame Street.* New York: Vintage Books, 1974.

Mickiewicz, Ellen, and Charles Firestone. *Television & Elections.* Queenstown, Md.: Aspen Institute, in association with Carter Center of Emory University, 1992.

Morrisett, Lloyd N. *Collected Essays, 1969–1997.* Reprint, New York: The John and Mary R. Markle Foundation, 1999.

Neu, C. Richard, Robert H. Anderson, and Tora K. Bikson. *Sending Your Government a Message: E-mail Communication between Citizens and Government.* Santa Monica, Calif.: RAND Publications, 1999.

Noll, Roger G., and Monroe E. Price. "Communications Policy: Convergences, Choice, and the Markle Foundation." In *A Communications Cornucopia: Markle Foundation Essays on Information Policy,* edited by Roger G. Noll and Roger E. Price. Washington, D.C.: Brookings Institution Press, 1998.

Park, Rolla Edward. *The Role of Analysis in Regulatory Decisionmaking.* Lexington, Mass.: Lexington Books, 1973.

Renz, Loren, Cynthia W. Massarsky, Rikard R. Treiber, and Steven Lawrence. *Program-Related Investments: A Guide to Funders and Trends.* New York: The Foundation Center, 1995.

Shipan, Charles R., "Keeping Competitors Out: Broadcast Regulation from 1927 to 1996. In *A Communications Cornucopia: Markle Foundation Essays on Information Policy,* edited by Roger G. Noll and Monroe E. Price. Washington, D.C.: Brookings Institution Press, 1998.

Sloan Commission on Cable Communications. *On the Cable: Television of Abundance.* New York: McGraw-Hill, 1971.

Spence, Robert J., ed. *John Markle: Representative American*. New York: Leonard Scott Publishing Co., 1929.

Strickland, Tamara G., and Stephen P. Strickland. *The Markle Scholars: A Brief History*. New York: Prodist, 1976.

Walton, Richard J. *Swarthmore College: An Informal History*. Swarthmore, Pa.: Swarthmore College, 1986.

Winston, Brian. *Misunderstanding Media*. Cambridge, Mass.: Harvard University Press, 1986.

PERSONAL SOURCES

The author interviewed the following individuals:

Allina, Franz, attorney with New York Capital Defender Office

Arbeiter, Larry, Director of Communications, University of Chicago

Armstrong, Peter, Codirector, OneWorld Online; former Chairman, Multimedia Corporation

Balk, Alfred W., former Editor, *Columbia Journalism Review*; founding Editor, *World Press Review*

Bartlett, Hannah H., former Assistant to the President, The Markle Foundation; consultant to the Cleveland Foundation

Bjornson, Edith C., former Vice President, The Markle Foundation

Boccardi, Louis D., President, The Associated Press

Boylan, James, former Editor, *Columbia Journalism Review*

Brown, Les, Director, The Television Pantheon; former Editor, *Channels of Communications*

Buchanan, Bruce, Professor of Government, University of Texas

Burns, Red, Chair, Interactive Telecommunications Program, New York University

Byers, Karen D., Chief Financial Officer, The Markle Foundation

Chadwick, Lynn, President and Chief Executive, National Federation of Community Broadcasters

Chamberlin, Ward, Programming Chief, WNET

Charren, Peggy, former President, Action for Children's Television

Chijioke, Mary Ellen, Curator, Friends Historical Library, Swarthmore College

Chisman, Forrest P., Director, Southport Institute for Policy Analysis

Christensen, Bruce, Dean, College of Fine Arts and Communications, Brigham Young University; former President, Public Broadcasting System

Cooney, Joan Ganz, Chair, Executive committee, Children's Television Workshop

Crawford, Chris, creator, Erasmatron

Czaja, Dr. Sara J., Professor of Psychiatry, University of Miami Medical School

Daniel, D. Ronald, Director, McKinsey & Co., Inc.; board member, The Markle Foundation

Dannenberg, Roger, research computer scientist; Professor, Carnegie-Mellon University

Dillehay, George, Publisher, *The New York Law Journal;* former Publisher, *Channels of Communications*

Ekman, Paul, Professor, Human Interaction Laboratory, University of California–San Francisco

Estey, Peter, Head, Dalton School; former President, SeniorNet

Firestone, Charles M., Director, Program on Communications and Society, Aspen Institute

Firstenberg, Jean, Director and Chief Executive Officer, American Film Institute

Fleishman, Joel L., President, Philanthropic Service Co., Inc.; board member, The Markle Foundation

Freundlich, Lillian, retired piano instructor, Peabody Conservatory of Music

Furlong, Mary Simpson, chairman, ThirdAge Media; founder, SeniorNet

Gardner, John W., former President, Carnegie Corporation; Consulting Professor, Stanford University

Geller, Henry, former Director, Washington Center for Public Policy Research; Markle Fellow

Giza, Dennis F., Associate Publisher, *Columbia Journalism Review*

Goldberg, Eric, President, Crossover Technologies

Grossman, Lawrence, President, PBS Horizons Cable Network;

former President, NBC News; former President, Public Broadcasting System

Hannon, Tom, Political Director, Cable News Network

Hertz, David B., lawyer; management consultant; retired former Director, McKinsey & Co.; former trustee, Columbia University

Horn, Harold, President, CTIC Associates, Inc.

Husni, Samier, Professor of Journalism, University of Mississippi

Iselin, John Jay, President, The Cooper Union for the Advancement of Science and Art

Jamieson, Kathleen Hall, Professor and Dean, Annenberg School of Communications, University of Pennsylvania

Johnson, Leland L., consultant to RAND Corporation

Konner, Joan, former Publisher, *Columbia Journalism Review*

Kotlowitz, Robert, Senior Vice President, WNET

Lagemann, Ellen Condliffe, Professor of History and Education, New York University; board member, The Markle Foundation

Lawson, Jennifer, Vice President of National Programming, Public Broadcasting System

Lehman, Jill Fain, research computer scientist; Professor, Carnegie-Mellon University

Lesser, Gerald, Bigelow Professor of Education and Developmental Psychology, Harvard University

Lotito, Margaret, President, Fund for Investigative Journalism

Michelson, Gertrude G., retired Senior Vice President, R. H. Macy & Co., Inc.; former board member, The Markle Foundation

Mickiewicz, Ellen, James R. Shepley Professor of Public Policy Studies, Duke University

Miller, Dolores E., former Corporate Secretary, The Markle Foundation

Milton, Mary C., former Program Officer, The Markle Foundation; founder, M2 Interactive Corporation

Minow, Newton N., Sidley & Austin, Chicago; former chairman, Federal Communications Commission

Morris, Van, Chief Executive Officer, Infonautics, Inc.

Morrisett, Lloyd N., former President, The Markle Foundation; Chairman, Children's Television Workshop

Nielsen, Waldemar, philanthropic historian and consultant

Oakes, John B., retired Editorial Page Editor, *The New York Times*
O'Donnell, Kendra Stearns, Principal Emerita, Phillips Exeter Academy
Oettinger, Anthony G., Gordon McKay Professor of Applied Mathematics, Harvard University
Perkins, James, the late Chairman and Chief Executive, International Council for Educational Development
Perlmutter, Alvin, independent television producer
Pifer, Alan, former President, Carnegie Corporation
Pitney, James G., attorney; former board member, The Markle Foundation
Price, Monroe E., Professor of Law, Benjamin N. Cardozo School of Law, Yeshiva University; Markle Fellow
Rees, William M., retired Chairman, The Chubb Corporation; former board member, The Markle Foundation
Rosenthal, A. M., former columnist, *The New York Times*; columnist, *New York Daily News*
Rover, Ed, legal counsel, The Markle Foundation; partner, White and Case
Schwartz, Evan, freelance technology correspondent, *Wired Magazine*, *Business Week*, and other publications
Stein, Robert, founder, Night Kitchen Productions
Swenson, Emily, former Executive Vice President and Chief Operating Officer, Children's Television Workshop
Toms, Michael, founder, New Dimensions Radio, Yukiah, Calif.
Wadsworth, Deborah, Executive Director, Public Agenda Foundation; former Program Officer, The Markle Foundation
Wallace, Dr. Andrew, Dean, Dartmouth Medical School
Weinberger, Marvin, former Chairman and Chief Executive, Infonautics
Winfrey, Carey, Assistant Managing Editor, *People Magazine*
Wrixon, Ann, President, SeniorNet
Zemmol, Jonathan I., principal, International Advisory Group

INDEX

ABOUT THE AUTHOR

LEE MITGANG has been a journalist, author, foundation consultant, and researcher for nearly thirty years. His coverage of education, politics, business, and urban affairs for Associated Press and United Press International has won more than a dozen awards. From 1992 to 1997, Mitgang was a senior fellow of the Carnegie Foundation for the Advancement of Teaching, where he wrote and researched national studies of school choice and the professional education of architects. Formerly assistant director of the Hechinger Institute on Education and the Media at Teachers College, Columbia University, he is currently Director of Communications for Wallace–Readers Digest Funds and is a contributing editor of *Architectural Record*.